FIVE GENTLEMEN OF JAPAN

the portrait of

FIVE GENTLEMEN OF JAPAN

a nation's character

FRANK GIBNEY

CHARLES E. TUTTLE COMPANY
Rutland, Vermont & Tokyo, Japan

Representatives

For Continental Europe:
BOXERBOOKS, INC., *Zurich*

For the British Isles:
PRENTICE-HALL INTERNATIONAL, INC., *London*

For Australasia:
BOOK WISE (AUSTRALIA) PTY. LTD.
104-108 Sussex Street, Sydney 2000

*Published by the Charles E. Tuttle Company, Inc.
of Rutland, Vermont & Tokyo, Japan
with editorial offices at
Suido 1-chome, 2-6, Bunkyo-ku, Tokyo, Japan*

Copyright in Japan, 1973, by Frank Gibney

All rights reserved

Library of Congress Catalog Card No. 74-781480

International Standard Book No. 0-8048-1108-3

*First edition, 1953 by Farrar, Straus and Young, New York
First Tuttle edition, 1954
First Tut Book edition, 1973
Fourth printing, 1984*

PRINTED IN JAPAN

to H. H. G.

CONTENTS

INTRODUCTION TO THE NEW EDITION *ix*
ACKNOWLEDGMENT *xi*
NOTE *xiii*
PROLOGUE *3*

1. THE WEB *7*
2. BORROWERS AND BUILDERS *34*
3. THE NATIONAL FACE LIFTING *61*
4. THE PARALYZED DEMOCRACY *94*
5. THE WILL TO WAR *124*
6. THE DEFEAT OF GLORY *152*
7. THE EMPTY SHRINE *179*
8. ADVANCING GARRISON ARMY *201*
9. THE COMMUNIST ATTACK *237*
10. RICE, MOUNTAINS AND MACHINES *267*
11. FIVE KINDS OF HOPE *301*
12. THE PROSPECT OF JAPAN *333*

EPILOGUE *371*

INTRODUCTION TO THE NEW EDITION

It is almost exactly twenty years since I put the cover on my typewriter and finished the last chapter of *Five Gentlemen of Japan*. At the time I thought that the book would have at least a limited audience, which I hoped would increase over the years. For it represented not only my best efforts at attempting to analyze and explain the national character of the Japanese people, people with whom I had lived and worked for some years, but was also the effort of an American journalist to bring some appreciation of a great, formidable, and interesting, if exasperatingly special national society, to his own people at home. I have been happy that the book has received some acceptance over the intervening twenty years, and I have a sense of satisfaction in seeing this new edition.

To attempt to set down a nation's "character" inside two covers is a presumptuous exercise. It is even more so when one writes merely as a journalist, unbuttressed by the theology of anthropologists or sociologists, who normally set themselves such tasks. I wrote much of the book while I was on the line as a correspondent for *Time*, a weekly news magazine for which I had to observe daily and weekly deadlines. I also had the advantage of living in Japan and professional concentration on Japanese matters, an experience that began with an apprenticeship at the Navy Japanese Language School during World War II, continued with many contacts with Japanese as an intelligence officer in the Pacific War, and culminated both in my service as an officer in the U.S. Occupation and in two years working as a journalist in Japan.

In 1966, I returned to Japan, after many years' absence, not as a journalist, but as a publisher, involved in doing business with the Japanese in a Japanese company, and I have remained in this function for the last six years. Observing a society is one thing. To live in the middle of a society, obeying its laws, responding of necessity to its trends and attitudes, saluting its bankers, and negotiating with its union organizers, is quite another experience. It deepened the sense of observation I had first developed among the Japanese and gave me a more poignant appreciation of their moods and concerns than I felt I had enjoyed before. Yet, as I review the book I wrote in 1951 and 1952, I find that my later experiences have changed my basic thoughts about the Japanese and their development as a modern national society very little. If some of the immediate judgments in this book show clearly the perspective of 1952—for example, the fact that Japan's greatest trading future would seem to lie with Southeast Asia rather than the United States—the thrust of my predictions about their energy and capacities seems to have been generally confirmed by events.

Japan has risen to be a power greater in an economic sense than anything I, or anyone else at that time, could have imagined. Japan has maintained its own peculiar democratic identity, threaded through as it is with the give-and-take of consensus politics and feelings for unanimous judgments or personal compromises that are exasperating to the Westerner, if indeed he understands them at all. Japan has remained a peaceful power and seems likely to continue in this direction, despite the alarms one hears about a new resurgence of militarism.

Given the pushes and pulls of fortune in Japan over the last twenty years, it is remarkable that the Japanese have continued to keep their national identity so strong and singular, the while adapting, molding, and fitting a variety of international discoveries, pressures, malevolences, and benevolences to their own designs.

Yet at the same time, the achievements of postwar Japan should not mask the problems that lie ahead of it. Certain sea changes, at least, are in the making. In the decade of the '70s the Japanese people must translate their achievements as an economic power into a wider social and political context. Japan also approaches the time of the changing of the guard, when the last of the prewar and wartime generation must give up the seats of power to one new generation, which has known the war briefly but has a strong connection with the past before it, and yet another, the very young, which knows the war and what people call the "old Japan" little, if at all.

The five gentlemen noted in the book were, incidentally, real people. One of them, a friend of mine, still works in Tokyo. I remain most grateful for the cooperation I received in writing this story.

Of course, in making my observations about the Japanese, I went far beyond the individual existences of these five people. The book embodied my reflections on the Japanese as I saw them and knew them—and it continues to represent the thoughts of one foreigner on the Japanese, as they live and work today.

Tokyo

ACKNOWLEDGMENT

In writing this book, I have drawn on my own experience as a correspondent in Japan, as well as my contacts with Japanese both before and after this period. I have read many books and picked many brains. It would be impossible to acknowledge, singly, each author and each acquaintance from whom I have learned. I am especially grateful for the work of two fine scholars, Sir George Sansom, at present head of the East Asian Institute of Columbia University, and Mr. Herbert Norman, of the Canadian Department of External Affairs, for their studies on the Meiji period.

I am indebted most of all to two members of the Time and Life bureau in Tokyo, Mr. Kay Tateishi and Mr. Frank T. Iwama. They are responsible for a great deal of the research done in preparation for this book, and their counsel and wide knowledge of Japanese history and customs were of continual help to me. Without their assistance, this book would have been impossible.

The editors of Life suggested, in the first instance, that I write a long article on Japan for them. This article, which appeared in September, 1951, contained the germ of the present book. I am grateful for their suggestion, and for the encouragement given me in putting it into actuality. I thank my publishers, also, for the cooperation they showed while the book was in the writing. Before coming to their offices, I had not thought that a man writing a book could expect such generous and intelligent treatment.

NOTE

In Japanese usage, a man's last name is written first, the first name last. This fact has always caused some confusion among Westerners, particularly when they are writing books about the Japanese. In this book, I have followed a rule of thumb which is practical, if not consistent. Names of historical figures have been written with the surname first, e.g., Itagaki Taisuke, since they are most commonly written this way elsewhere. But the names of prominent Japanese in this and the last generation have been better known to American newspaper readers in their inverted form, e.g., Hideki Tojo; therefore the principals of current history, as well as the five gentlemen of Japan, I have called according to the Western order of their names.

Since 1941, at least, a similar rule of thumb has been necessary when giving the foreign monetary equivalents of the Japanese yen. Until the outbreak of World War II, the yen was worth slightly under 25 cents. The ryo, the standard unit of currency in Tokugawa times, was worth roughly 10 yen at this rate. After 1945, as inflation gripped the country, the yen started a long series of dives in its value. The occupation fixed the exchange rate at 15 yen to the dollar in 1945. This was revised upward to a rate of 50 to one in 1946. By 1948, the official rate was hiked to 270 to one. Meanwhile, on the black market, the yen was off to the races. In March, 1950, it was quoted in the shadier circles of Tokyo finance at 620 to one. At present, however, it is stabilized at the new official rate of 360 to one, and the black market price is only slightly above this. Because of these frequent changes, I have despaired of giving dollar equivalents each time the yen figure is mentioned in the course of the book.

FIVE GENTLEMEN OF JAPAN

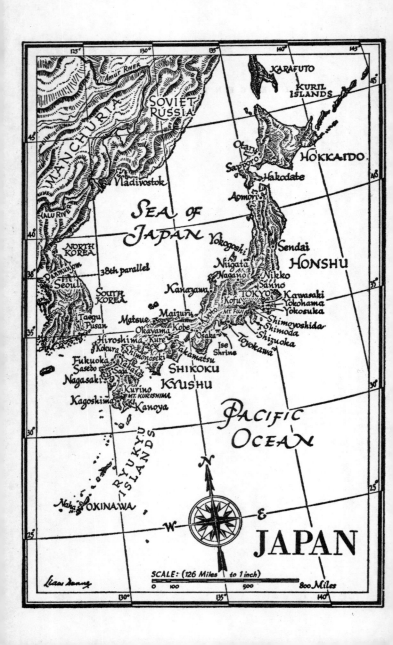

PROLOGUE

Like a bow too tautly strung, the Japanese islands stretch athwart the northeast of Asia. They are steep with mountains, thick with forests and thin of soil, divided by swift-running rivers and covered by a fretting of overworked fields. They are not the kind of land that produces philosophers or individualists. This is a turbulent country with taut, dynamic people—excessively kind and excessively cruel, makers of delicate poetry and revolting wars, born as artists, living as bondsmen, dying as gods.

Switzerland and Belgium are in the true sense of the word countries. Britain is a tradition. Russia is a mood. America is a way of life. Japan is a spirit, insular and protesting. It is a spirit that hurls itself in the face of physical facts—a troublesome spirit, unsure of its place, but jealous of its station. Wherever Japanese are, this spirit shows itself. It is not quietly stubborn like the Chinese spirit, which, even beneath its layer of Communism, is ever the repository of a culture. The Japanese is oddly young. He is childlike in his refusal to admit defeat. He is childlike also in his plastic ability to assimilate new ideas and adjust to sudden changes in his situation.

The Japanese look towards their continent—and towards the world—with the great injured innocence of island nations. They are at once a reluctant part of the continent and an insistent part of it. The mainlander can never understand the mixture of condescension and persuasion in their talk. "*Shimaguni*—the island country" is what they call their nation. It is spoken as one word, as if each term needed the other to attain its fullness.

Secure in their island stronghold, the Japanese taught themselves easily what to others came only by migrations or by the sword. The arts and religions that burned their way across the mainland of Asia came to them by peaceful invitation. Without interruption they molded what came to fit their own patterns. While they learned, the mainland forgot them.

But the dynamism of the islanders and the lessons of the mainland—and the whole world outside—were explosives that could act as catalysts upon each other. When they mixed too suddenly, or fermented after long imprisonment together, the results were dread: 200,000 *samurai* storming through Korea in the sixteenth century, the Battle of the Yalu in the nineteenth, Port Arthur, the Marco Polo Bridge and Pearl Harbor in the twentieth. In their last battles, the Japanese fought with a concentrated fury which the rest of the world had either forgotten or never experienced. All that was left to them was the spirit, warped and brutalized as it was, still the strongest national faith of the twentieth century.

In defeat, the falseness of the spirit withered. The early enthusiasm, also, was gone. The essence of the country almost seemed to have perished with its sad externals.

This was not true. The conquerors walked through the wasted area of their bombing and gaped at the reflexive efforts of thousands to set up their houses again, as soon as the bombers went away. Somehow the sum of these hopeless efforts, working with the instinct of cooperation, produced a result far out of proportion to the wretchedness of its parts. The conquerors helped mightily, and the islanders responded to their help. The conquerors brought forward an ideal new in the world's history—a sincere effort to recast an old enemy after one's own image, in the hope that this would make him a partner and a co-protector of peace, rather than its destroyer.

The spirit of the islanders was touched and quickened. Perhaps it was altered. But the conquerors found their objectives change before their eyes, with the rise of new warmakers. At the beginning of what some hoped would be the millennium of peace, the islanders are now once more moving to arms, puzzled by developments they have not influenced, pondering the fates that once more threaten to pivot the destiny of a continent on their decisions.

In essence, the spirit of these people, so plastic to the observer, could be neither clothed nor fed from the outside. *Yamato damashi*—the soul of Japan—has the toughness of swordmaker's steel. It has also the delicacy that makes the gauze beauty of a Japanese garden. On its surface it is a paradox: how does the brute cruelty of Nanking or Bataan fit into the slight shadings of an Utamaro print, or the omniscient hospitality of a wayside inn on the Tokaido?

This book is an attempt at explaining the paradox. It is a description not of Japan but of the Japanese, written in the form of a historical essay. It proposes to analyze the character of the Japanese people neither from the viewpoint of an academic historian nor a clinical anthropologist. It is a character study of a people, considered in the totality of their social, political and economic existence.

To do this the more concretely, the lives of five Japanese are considered in this context—the five gentlemen of Japan. Their occupations and social origins are diverse. Hirohito is the 124th Emperor of Japan. Sakaji Sanada is a farmer, sprung from generations of farmers. Fumio

Shimizu is an engineer, a former vice-admiral in the Japanese Navy. Tadao Yamazaki is a newspaperman. Hideya Kisei is a foreman in a steel mill.

None of the five gentlemen of Japan has ever met any of the others. Yet their experiences, the story of their lives and the lives of their ancestors, are surprisingly similar and complementary. This is because they belong to a peculiarly close-knit island civilization. Although the depths of meaning beneath Japan's story are very great, the focus can at least be narrowed. There are in fact, no strangers among this people. They are united—united in their greatness, their defects, their hopes, their eccentricities.

It is the author's hope that this book may introduce the five gentlemen of Japan, and their 85 million countrymen, to his readers in the West. In his personal experience, he has found them a great and, in some ways, a truly tragic people. He has also found them, in terms of simple human experience, a very appealing people, perceptive, friendly and possessed of a rich sense of humor. If some of the trials of their history and immediate experience, as here related, seem discouraging, it would be apt to remember what Lord Bryce, in writing *The American Commonwealth*, said of another great nation's history. "A hundred times . . . have I been disheartened by the facts I was stating: a hundred times has the recollection of the abounding strength and vitality of the nation chased away these tremors."

1
THE WEB

"These are the best people so far discovered, and it seems to me that among the unbelievers no people can be found to excel them."
St. Francis Xavier's Report on Japan

"The gentlemen of Japan were most polite and courteous, conducting themselves with refined and polished urbanity."
*Captain of H.M.S. Samarang, 1845**

Up the road from Yokohama to Tokyo, past the burned-out husks of Kawasaki's bombed factories and the rising furnaces of new ones, through the depressing ramshackle of Japanese souvenir shops and an American drive-in, speeds a severe gray Cadillac with a modest police escort. Pedestrians along the route notice the car as it sweeps over a road temporarily cleared of other traffic. Some bow deeply. Others smile or even wave. The man inside the car, a slightly stooped, mustached gentleman of middle age, wearing a crushed brown hat, nods jerkily in acknowledgment. He is His Imperial Majesty Hirohito, 124th Emperor of Japan.

The new Cadillac with the imperial crest—or the older Mercedes which the Royal Family also uses—are no longer rare sights on Japanese roads. For the moment, at least, the car is a better symbol of Hirohito's role than his moated palace in Tokyo, with the clumps of wisteria and

* As quoted by Sir George Sansom in *The Western World and Japan*.

cherry blossoms sparkling over its curved stone walls. He is a king who visits his people, still a semi-sacred object to most of them, but no longer the felt but unseen presence he once was. A kind and gentle man, the purpose of the change has appealed to him, but he is too shy to enjoy it. He has learned discipline as few men have, but poise he has never acquired.

He is a scientist by inclination, happiest when he is cataloguing specimens of marine biological life in his small laboratory inside the palace grounds. It is exhilarating to narrow the scope of his concentration so in private, a retreat from a public life where the parchment of an imperial rescript or the shading of an imperial gesture may have far-reaching and possibly uncontrollable effects on some 85 million people.

His wife, the Empress Nagako, is an affectionate, rather talkative woman with far more natural ease of manner than he. She has helped him. With their five children, they can sometimes enjoy a home life that gives at least a tiny compensation for the wearing job of being an earnest, intelligent cynosure. But even family life is hopelessly circumscribed by court chamberlains and an attendant bureaucracy, part of the swarm of faceless officials who have historically run the machinery of the Japanese state. It is probably only in the laboratory that Hirohito can be an unaffected identity, in the quiet, decently cluttered room dominated by the busts of Darwin, Lincoln and Napoleon —Darwin chosen for his science, Lincoln for his humanity and Napoleon simply because many years ago a crown prince of Japan, on a visit to Europe, spent a few hours of solitary shopping in Paris. The bust, found in an antique shop, is almost the only purchase he ever made by himself.

* * * * *

Tadao Yamazaki is approaching downtown Tokyo from another direction. A tall young man with a thick shock of hair and a thin, pale artist's face, he is jammed in one of the bulging cars on a commuter's train of the Tokyo Kyuko Kabushiki Kaisha—the municipal railway line. On the outside of the cars the initials of the company are painted in large yellow Roman letters—T.K.K. Tokyo people like Yamazaki, who have to imprison themselves in the T.K.K.'s run-down rolling stock for upwards of an hour and a half each day, have their own slogan for the initials —"*Totemo Konde Kuru*—Always crowded, always coming."

At the Tsukiji Station Yamazaki gets off and walks a few blocks to the rotund eight-story building that houses the Tokyo staff of *Asahi*, Japan's largest newspaper. Six days a week he goes up the scuffed stairs to his desk in the third-floor editorial rooms. There he works as a rewrite man on the city edition, a position of some responsibility in a newspaper with a 3,600,000 circulation. Barring the excessive crowding and signs written in unfamiliar characters, the atmosphere around him is one that an American reporter might feel at home in—asthmatic typewriters, littered papers, too many people for too few desks. Only the teacups on editorial desks and the odd clickety-clack of the abacuses in the accounting department provide a touch of Japanese background.

Yamazaki has a wife, Matsui, who was herself a reporter before her marriage, and a small, fourteen-month son, whom they have named Akito. In his home and in his work he is a happy man. He has already worked for *Asahi* for five years, and done very well as a reporter. He is outspoken without being impolite, a good student who has not let his scholarship get in the way of his reporter's nose for news. Still, other Japanese would call him an "interi" —an intellectual. He is less interested in day-to-day newsbreaks than in probing the respective verities of Marx, Jefferson, Keynes and Sidney Webb. The future of the Japanese, he and his friends speculate, depends on how well they can absorb and adapt all of these men's teachings.

* * * * *

There is not much time for speculation in Yahata, Kyushu. Hideya Kisei, a small, round-faced man of thirty-three, is a gang foreman at the Number 2 Furnace of the Kukioka Plant, Yahata Steel Works. He got his first job in the mill at fifteen. Since then, except for two periods of military service, he has spent almost every day of his life in the sooty atmosphere of Yahata, a gray and brown industrial city at the northern tip of the island of Kyushu, whose massed smokestacks pour their film over the green and yellow of the surrounding farm country.

Kisei is a quiet, stubborn man with wide interests and some strong convictions. After the war he helped organize the Kukioka branch of the All Japan Steel Workers Union. For a while he served as its chairman. He is a Socialist, earnestly interested in world peace and international cooperation, and disturbed by the drawn battle lines of the democracies and the Communist countries. He reads what he can to try to explain things to himself, but the exhausting job he has is too taxing for much intellectual study after work. Lately he has complained that he can no longer remember things easily. He is afraid that the years spent near the 1,300-degree heat of the furnace have permanently weakened his powers of concentration.

If Kisei has his way, his children will get the education that he missed. He and his wife Kiyoko, who also works at Yahata as a clerk in the company store, manage to put away a few hundred yen each month out of their combined salaries—not much, but a start. At that, they are far more comfortable than they were during the recent war —a sweated nightmare of air-raid sirens and grinding 16-hour days. They live, with Kiyoko's mother and their three children—Teruo, five; Minoru, three; and Reiko, one—in a tiny company house, run-down but spotlessly ordered inside. They have only three rooms. Outside, a small, square garden quietly challenges the furnace soot in the air.

* * * * *

To the dusty town of Toyokawa, set among the rice fields near Japan's Watling Street, the Tokaido, a soft-spoken man with clear eyes and high Mongol cheekbones has returned for a visit. Fumio Shimizu was once a vice admiral in the Japanese Navy, in command of the Toyokawa Naval Arsenal, 6,000 acres of factory and stockpiles, which once supplied machine guns, cannons, range finders and precision instruments to Japan's war machine. All that is left now is a tangle of bent girders and bare concrete floors, survivals of a B-29 bombing. Shimizu has come to Toyokawa to visit some relatives. He does not visit his old arsenal for sentimental reasons.

The Admiral, as many people still call him, is by trade and inclination an engineer. He is gently courteous, almost courtly in his manners, a man respectful to tradition. He is sixty-seven years old and has three grandchildren. Both his daughters Kazuko, thirty-two, and Yoshiko, twenty-two, are married—one to a young businessman, the other to an engineer. His son Toyotaro, twenty-five, is an engineer like his father. The Shimizu have always been a happy family, educated with discipline, but not with strictness.

This kindly gentleman has spent his lifetime manufacturing guns. He was not a "militarist." Like many other honest technicians, he tended not to connect guns with killing. When the B-29s smashed his arsenal, he was surprised and hurt that so many "innocent people" were killed. Now, in Tokyo, he is an advisor for the Japan Steel Company, which does work for the U. S. Army in Japan, repairing guns and tanks for the use of the U. N. command in Korea. He is a busy man at the office, constantly consulted about the problems of repairing new weapons on existing facilities, or supervising the research work of the company's technicians, some of whom once worked for him in the Japanese Navy. He is pleased that "an apparently discarded, useless human being" like himself can be of service.

* * * * *

North of Toyokawa, the sweep of its snowy cone brushing past plains and terraced fields from its beginning on the ocean floor, rises Fuji, the sacred mountain. At its base, in the town of Shimoyoshida, in Yamanashi Prefecture, Sakaji Sanada, a hollow-cheeked man of sixty-two, stands in the soft mud of his paddyfield, harvesting the autumn rice crop. Sanada is as tough and wiry as a piece of steel coil. At sixty-two, he had once hoped to live with his wife in *inkyo*—the retirement that is traditional for old people in Japan. But the pinch of hard times, he says, keeps him out in the fields, doing a long laborer's job each day on his shrunken six-acre farm, or supervising the work on one of his four precious hand looms.

For all his complaints, Sanada is a prosperous countryman. He has a large house with five rooms, spacious by Japanese standards. One of them, called a ten-mat room because of the number of *tatami*—the standard straw mats needed for its flooring, measures 15 feet by 12, rather large for Japan. In the town, he is looked up to as a leader, respected and upright. But he is a trifle too firm in his views to be universally liked. His wife complains that he has always played in village life the *nikumare-yaku*—the role of the despised, ungracious martinet.

The disapprobation of some of his fellow-citizens has never set too heavily on Sanada's shoulders. He is confident, cheerful and outspoken, ready with a jest or a homely proverb to sum up his misfortunes as well as his joys. He is the patriarch of a good-sized family. Besides his wife, Hie, there is his eldest son, Satoshi, thirty-seven, his wife and their four children. The Sanadas have a daughter, twenty-two years old, Kazuko.

The one missing member of the family is Sanada's great sorrow. His second son, Mitsu, a strong, clever boy, was killed fighting in the Japanese Army's last-ditch stand on Luzon, on the 15th of June, 1945. Mitsu was Sanada's hope. Since Satoshi was always rather sickly, it was Mitsu whom the old man wanted to inherit his farm, his responsibilities and his place in Shimoyoshida. He has never got over Mitsu's death. The house he built for him, in 1943, just a hundred yards from his own, is kept scrupulously clean and ordered. But it is not used.

* * * * *

Hirohito, Yamazaki, Kisei, Shimizu and Sanada—these are five gentlemen of the new Japan. In one sense they have very little in common. Each has his peculiar tastes and talents. Sanada the farmer likes to gather with his neighbors at local shrine festivals or, more regularly, enjoys listening at his radio to the reedy singing of *Naniwabushi*—the old folk songs that do the work of soap operas for the Japanese radio audience. The journalist, Yamazaki, is a subtle and appreciative observer of French films. Louis Jouvet is his favorite actor—a far cry, he feels, from the brassy, shallow types of Hollywood players.

When Hideya Kisei can get away from his duties at home and in the steel mill, he likes to go off by himself on short fishing trips. Admiral Shimizu, who was once quite a tennis player, now prefers golf. He is a long-time member of the Sagami Country Club, which is now improving its 18-hole course some 30 miles south of Tokyo. The Emperor is an adept swimmer. Legend insists that he can hold an umbrella with his toes, while doing a brisk backstroke. In more serious moments he likes to wade for hours in the rock-girt backwaters near his summer palace on Sagami Bay, gathering new specimens for his marine biology collection.

Knowing these men, one has difficulty fitting them into the usual visual images of the Japanese, put together by foreigners. Only Hirohito is "myopic" and uses glasses constantly; the others have excellent eyesight. Only Sanada and Kisei are short of stature; Shimizu is a six-footer, Yamazaki almost as tall, the Emperor of medium height. None of them has "buck teeth." None of them is continually "grinning," although they have a marked tendency to laugh when they are worried or embarrassed.

It is hard to pour them into the rigid casts of "Japanese character" which foreigners at different times have constructed. It is almost impossible to imagine them as part of a "maddened horde of banzaiing fanatics" charging up a hill in Burma, or bayoneting women and children in the streets of Nanking or Manila. If they are "shifty, treacherous and deceitful, just waiting for their chance to knife you in the back," as some modern American folklore suggests, the deception, which they and 85 million other ostensibly peace-loving Japanese must practice 24 hours every day, is nothing short of supernatural.

It is also hard to fit them into the land of Madame Butterfly and never-ending cherry-blossom festivals, faithfully and gullibly described by generations of Western tourists. Even Henry Adams, normally a perceptive spectator of foreign custom, could spend four months traveling in Japan—at a critical period of Japanese history—and then write to his friends in the United States: "This is a child's country. Men, women and children are taken out of the fairy books. The whole show is out of the nursery. Nothing is serious. All of it toy. . . ."

In its impartial way, history has often supported both these caricatures. On the record, the Japanese have established themselves as a struggling, living conflict of extremes. Their history seems to have more jarring blacks and whites and less comfortable shadings than that of any great nation. Judged from the outside, Japan has acted almost like a puzzling case in a mental hospital, alternating periods of long and moody solitude with violent, destructive energy. The Japanese guide in Kyoto who distributed polite tourist folders to visiting Americans in the thirties was quite possibly the same man who helped burn down Chinese villages during his compulsory military service just a year before. In 1941, Shimizu, Sanada, Kisei, Yamazaki and the Emperor, in varying ways, were all part of a savage total war effort, scarred with its own atrocities. In 1945, in the space of a few hours, the fury seemed to vanish with the defeat. The Japanese opened their souvenir shops again and stood docilely by to await the pleasure of their conquerors, at the start of the least resisted military occupation in history.

* * * * *

It is unfair to write of these Japanese in terms of caricature. It is, however, superficial to think of them hopefully as the Westerners of Asia, separated from contemporary Americans, Englishmen or Frenchmen—and the traditions they hold in common—only by the accidents of geography and a particularly difficult language barrier. For all their disarming individuality, each of the five gentlemen of Japan has had a share in his country's odd behavior. He is also a product of it. For all their familiarity with golf, radios and French film stars, the five are active representatives of the most unified, the most stubborn, the most eccentric national culture of the twentieth century.

There are certain obvious national characteristics which all of them possess. In the normal sense of the term, all of them are hard workers, earnest in their approach to a problem, not too eager to seize new responsibilities, but almost incredibly faithful to those they have. They have a strong feeling for discipline, and a deep sense of family and community loyalty. They are not overly religious, but they pay their debts. They have a good sense of humor, more broad than subtle.

A translation of the Japanese character into English-language virtues and failings is no more productive of a real understanding of the Japanese than the system of Latin parsing is capable of making order out of their primitive, but supple language. The Japanese can be called cruel, they can be called brave, or industrious, or practical-minded, but no amount of categorizing can well describe them, if we do not first examine the premises of their society—the ethos that makes it different from all others.

To get at the basis of Japanese society, one might, like Christian philosophers seeking to describe God, first posit what it is not. The foreigner must imagine a system where the traditional absolute values of Western civilization—the inheritance of Platonism and Christianity—are absent. However calmly Americans and Europeans rationalize their old religious philosophy, it remains true that their cultural heritage, their political and social institutions have been shaped by a belief in absolute values. This the Japanese conspicuously have never had. There are no root words for "good" and "evil" in their language. Well-educated Japanese like Shimizu or Yamazaki have learned in school and at the university that systems of absolute values exist. They are quite conversant with them. But the influence of those systems has played little part in forming their tradition.

When Sakaji Sanada was raising his son Mitsu, talking to him as he led his horse and wagon down the frozen ruts between his house and his farm, he carefully outlined a moral code for his guidance. The basis of this code was not godliness, or abstract honesty, or abstract purity, but something which Sanada and his fellow Japanese call *"shinyo."* *Shinyo* means trust, confidence, reliability. It is the goal of a social morality. To have *shinyo* is to be a man of honor, who fulfills commitments at whatever cost and whose trust in his neighbors is reciprocated by their confidence in him.

The idea of *shinyo* has been important in a society where virtue is more of a horizontal quality than a vertical one. In Japanese society—a strong clan system reinforced by Confucianism and the national religion of Shinto—the goodness of an act depends on the relationship of the doer and the recipient. It is purely circumstantial. Japanese ethics are founded on the social contract, not the abstract value. The highest virtue is loyalty to one's commitments—the hallmark of someone who has *shinyo*. The basest evil is to fail in it.

This system of contracts and commitments threads its way like a giant steel web through every segment of Japanese society. The web binds the individual in all directions—upwards to parents, ancestors, superior officers, downwards to children, employees and servants. Classically, it has only been by achieving equilibrium inside this web that the Japanese finds peace. Like the sinner in the old Buddhist fable, he reaches out from the depths to clutch the fine, but binding strands of the web of Heaven. Holding on to them, he is safe. Once he slips from the web, or loses his place in it, he falls back, doomed, into the void of *Jigoku*, the Buddhist hell. There is no more chance for redemption.

Historically, in the web society of Japan, the individual has had no real existence outside of his group. He has not, like men born in the Christian West, been a soul in his own right, with at least a tradition of God-given natural rights and duties, accountable only to just authority. He has lived only as a member of his family, his community, his nation. Even the gods of his national religion are family spirits, not necessarily good or bad in themselves, but honored because they represent a deep sense of community. Few Japanese have ever escaped the group demands made upon them. If a favor was given to an individual, it was automatically done to his group. One man's misstep, conversely, has generally brought a Confucian shame to fifty or a hundred others.

Fifty years ago Lafcadio Hearn described the stresses of this society: "Today . . . legally, a man can go where he pleases. But as a matter of fact, he can nowhere do as he pleases; for individual liberty is still largely restricted by the survival of community sentiment and old-fashioned custom. In any country community it would be unwise to proclaim such a doctrine as that a man has the right to employ his leisure and his means as he may think proper. No man's time or money or effort can be considered exclusively his own—nor even the body that his ghost inhabits. His right to live in the community rests solely on his willingness to serve the community; and whoever may need his help or sympathy has the privilege of demanding it. That a man's house is his castle cannot be asserted in Japan—except in the case of some high potentate. No ordinary person can shut his door to lock out the rest of the world. Everybody's house must be open to visitors: to close its gates by day would be regarded as an insult to the community—sickness affording no excuse. . . . And to displease the community in which one lives—especially if the community be a rural one—is a serious matter. When a community is displeased, it acts as an individual. It may consist of five hundred, a thousand, or several thousand persons: but the thinking of all is the thinking of one."

How obsolete is Hearn's judgment? On the surface the five gentlemen of Japan do not themselves seem to be throttled by this rigid society of their ancestors. Their world is in fact far looser in its demands upon them than it once was. Industrialization and the influence of the West have progressively softened the texture of the web. Defeat in war badly strained it. A military occupation, committed to producing a democratic Japan, pulled and tore at it. But it has not disappeared. It is still the invisible adhesive that seals the nationhood of the Japanese. Shimizu, Sanada, Yamazaki, Kisei and Hirohito were all born within its bonds. Despite their individual work, surroundings and opinions, they have lived most of their lives as cogs geared into a group society. Literally as well as figuratively speaking, none of them has a lock on his house door. In 1948, long after Hearn had gone to his grave, a Japanese sociologist, Takegi Kawashima, could write with much justice about the behavior of his contemporaries:

"The family system is not a moral quality of fidelity at all. It is merely a one-sided duty of a superior to an inferior, or vice versa. . . . In a social relationship like this the outstanding point of human relationship and the point of greatest importance to us at present is the impossibility for individual responsibility to exist, for within a system like this the follower cannot be aware of himself as having any individual worth. His actions will always be determined by another. Therefore there would never be any occasion for him to judge for himself or act by himself; nor would he have the ability to do so. He will ever be the child of a family, who is not yet an individual, and who will always need protection by the paternal feeling of one with power."

These are hard words. The system they described has been weakened to the breaking point. Perhaps it will not endure much longer. But Dr. Kawashima is a good sociologist, who has backed up his statements with long, detailed observations. If his conclusions are wrong, they are wrong only in degree. The web society may be doomed. But it still presses most Japanese in its bonds. None in Japan is totally free from it. In the story of its hold on the Japanese, and the efforts which they and others have made to modify or break it, lies the crisis and the fascination of modern Japan.

* * * * *

Of the five Japanese in this story, Sanada, the farmer, is most securely caught by the web—and most comfortable in its bondage. The town he lives in, Shimoyoshida, is a place of 15,000 population, the market center of a poor but sizeable farming community and the trading center of a fairly prosperous silk textile business. It has a hospital and three banks, a modern fire department, advertising offices of five Tokyo newspapers, thirty-odd *pachinko*, or pinball parlors, representing a new Americanized diversion, 2,993 radios, and a large floating population of sight-seeing American G.I.s. But the indigenous life of Shimoyoshida has not changed radically through the centuries. Neighbors cooperate. Marriages are arranged. Impoliteness is a taboo and to neglect repaying a favor, sinful.

Sanada lives in a district, called a *buraku,* named Shinya. There are about 100 households in the *buraku,* with a total of 500 people. There is a good deal of civic loyalty in Shimoyoshida, which finds its most obvious outlet in the annual Shinto festivals, like the display held each September to honor *Ko-no-Hana-Saku-ga Hime*—Princess-who-makes-the-flowers-of-the-trees-to-bloom—the goddess of Mt. Fuji. But Sanada's primary loyalty is to the *buraku.* He and his fellow-farmers help each other each June with the rice planting—and go out into each others' fields—men, women and children—when October comes, to harvest the crop. When a bridge is damaged, Sanada and his neighbors go out to repair it. If a neighbor's house is blown down, Sanada has a rigid obligation to help set it up again.

The measure of this community cooperation is the measure of a man's standing in the village—and his morality. A Shimoyoshida neighbor would not call Sanada an "upright man" in an intransitive sense. He would say that he is upright in discharging this or that obligation, that he is upright because he helps his neighbors and performs his duties to the community. There is no possibility of being considered "good" outside the community framework. Sanada's own hopes and aspirations betray this. His ideal is not an abstract "peace and prosperity." It is *"kyo-son kyoei*—work together and prosper together."

Hideya Kisei, the steel worker, lives in an industrial society. The sooty air of Yahata is a world away from the clear country breezes that sweep down past Mt. Fuji. The stale smell of cinders and furnace smoke hangs over the city, not, as in Shimoyoshida, the faint odor of burning charcoal cleaned by the mountain air. But Kisei and his wife, Kiyoko, are as deep in the web as Sanada is. Their sense of responsibility is as great. So are the demands made upon it.

The Kisei family lives in a company house, fifteen minutes by streetcar from the mill. There are several hundred other houses like it in their district, all of them the residences of Yahata steel workers like Kisei. But living in the heart of an industrial society has not prevented the householders from strait-jacketing their lives with the rigid sense of community they learned in their home villages. Kisei and his entire family belong to the *tonarigumi*—the neighborhood association of his area. They have fixed duties to be done for the association—improving the streets, organizing festivals, somewhat the same sort of thing that Sanada does for his *buraku*.

The power of the *tonarigumi*, in fact, was responsible for Kisei's marriage. When the shifts at the mill speeded up near the beginning of World War II, Hideya found that he was unable to keep up with his neighborhood obligations. He was home for barely eight hours each day—and then only to fall into a drugged sleep. The neighbors kindly but firmly suggested that he get married. He would then have a wife to hold up his household's end of its community responsibility.

Kisei agreed. The neighbors scouted around for a suitable bride. When they found one, acting as go-betweens they introduced Kisei to his present wife, Kiyoko, the daughter of another steel worker. In April, 1941, after a traditional Japanese introduction and courtship, they were married. They have lived happily.

The pattern of the Japanese web society that guides *tonarigumi* and *buraku* has also stamped itself on the life of Kisei's mill. He is a *gocho*, or foreman—the lowest supervisory rank at Yahata (and the same word, incidentally, as "corporal" in the Army). Kisei, like all Japanese, takes his rank and responsibilities seriously. They do not stop outside the plant. As a *gocho* he has a strong feeling of responsibility not only for helping the ten men in his crew with their work problems, but with any crises in their domestic lives. Regularly. twice a month, he takes them out on a drinking party. He feels that this is a good way of airing any problems they may have, with a minimum of tension. He accepts the strain on his budget for the beer and *sake* involved, as one of the corollaries of his job.

In the same way, Kisei is taken out by the two officials above him in the chain of command at Yahata. In keeping with their higher station, the *kumicho* (supervisor) and the *kakaricho* (section chief) throw in a dinner invitation, when they ask Kisei and the other foremen out for drinks.

A degree of social-business relationships exists in every country. On its face, Kisei's relations with his men might have been drawn out of the unwritten rules for employee relations in some New York corporations. But nowhere are these relationships so binding, so relentless, so much an inbred part of the business world, as in the web society of Japan.

Shimizu and Yamazaki, living in the more sophisticated milieux of Tokyo, are less visibly affected by the demands of the web than the residents of Shimoyoshida *buraku* or the *tonarigumi* in Yahata. But they have not escaped. Shimizu, as a career naval officer, lived most of his life in a military society where the rules of loyalty and *shinyo* that pervade civilian life were cruelly codified. As a technician, who seldom had direct duties of command, he was not the complete captive of the code, as others were. He observed whatever obligations he had to, however, and lived with his society as he found it. He is no social reformer.

Like Kisei, Sanada and Hirohito, his marriage was arranged for him.* His father-in-law, a wealthy farmer in Tochigi Prefecture, was a good friend of his father's. His wife has been a good and faithful companion. Like the

---

* This is not altogether just to Hirohito. Although the area of his choices was rigidly limited, he did insist on marrying a princess of the southern Satsuma clan, against the wishes of his most powerful advisor. Prince Yamagata.

wives of the others, she stays in the background, exerting her influence by indirection, dedicating her life to her husband and her children.

The bonds of the web only once made Shimizu wince with pain. When his arsenal at Toyokawa was bombed, he was shocked by the loss of life among the 60,000 civilian workers and their families, all living within a narrow perimeter of wood and paper houses near the factory buildings. His reaction was as painful and as personal as Hideya Kisei's feelings might have been, if one member of his ten-man crew were scalded at the furnace. There was no reason for him to feel blameful. Toyokawa had been defended as well as the desperate condition of the Japanese forces in 1945 permitted. The bombing was an enemy act, in which he had no conceivable part. But this in no way helped to cast off the responsibility.

The families of the workers, for their part, were bitter and disillusioned. They attacked Shimizu for his "negligence" after the raid, largely because he, as a high-ranking military man, was a handy scapegoat for their defeat and despair. He did not protest the injustice of their accusations. In his neat, five-room house in the Kakinokizaka district of Tokyo, a quiet residential area favored by bankers and comfortably fixed executives, he keeps a list of the dead and the injured. Every morning he prays for them. His conscience hurts him deeply, because he has not enough money to look after their families. In a sense, by the Japanese canons of morality, he has failed in a duty.

Tadao Yamazaki, the newspaper man, is the nearest approach in the web society to a home-grown iconoclast. His father, a high-school teacher, himself broke away from the traditional Japanese values as he saw them. There were never any Shinto ancestor tablets in the Yamazaki household and his father today does not expect his son to support him in his old age. Yamazaki met his wife Matsui, a college graduate like himself, when he was covering a story for *Asahi*. She was a reporter for *Josei Shimbun,* a women's paper published by the Tokyo YWCA. They fell in love and married, in the Western tradition. There were no go-betweens, nothing was arranged. "Our marriage was from a small romance," Yamazaki describes it.

His views and outlook are more understandable to an American than are those of any of the others. It would hardly be inaccurate to call him a "liberal" in the older American sense, as it was used before many alleged "liberals" became more totalitarian than the totalitarians they attacked. He is open-minded, curious to learn and conscious always that Japan is in a time of dangerous but exciting ferment.

He would not affirm that the web society exists around him. But its evidences are possibly too subtly wound into his life to be noticed. He unconsciously tries to harmonize his traditions with his critical outlook. "As a citizen of Japan I want to abide by the rules that stand," he has said, "simultaneously I want to see our politics from a rational, critical point of view."

Every morning, in the elevator of the *Asahi* building, Yamazaki cannot escape an obligatory round of hieratic bows and salutations as he recognizes his bosses or fellow-employees. In his relations on the newspaper, and with business acquaintances, he exercises a circumspection and a consciousness of rank and position that no American or European of his views and status would think of. He would like Japan to have a real system of social equality, without these shadings of position that dominate every Japanese social circle. But he has an insular resistance to sudden, violent change. The web hangs loosely around him, giving him, with the grace of elbow room, a special kind of perspective. He has the soul of a social reformer. But the presence of the web has kept him from becoming a revolutionary.

At the center of the web society stands the Emperor. He is no casual figurehead, installed to add a symbol value to a system that might work perfectly well without him. His presence and what it stands for make the great differ ence between the Japanese web system and the "family system" regularized by Confucius in China and found, with local variations, almost everywhere in East Asia. The Chinese family system is an institution. The Japanese family system is both an institution and an instrument. The Chinese family system is a social structure that may be exploited for political purposes, but need not be. The Japanese family system is curiously and confusingly bound up with the Japanese state. Throughout history, the two have challenged separation.

Presiding in a cutaway at the Convocation of the Diet, Hirohito is the national constitutional monarch. Bowing to his ancestors at the Ise Shrine, in the severe black and white of Shinto vestments, he is the national pontiff. Deeper in the hearts of most Japanese, he is the symbol and the purpose of their nationhood, in whom all web commitments begin and end.

No civilized, intelligent society can base its rules of conduct wholly on a system of horizontal contracts. The Japanese is no exception. The Emperor is the institution which gives a moral sanction to the contracts and stamps the web society with a seal of permanence. Japanese have never believed that he was a "God" in the Western sense. What they did believe before 1945—and what quite a few still believe—is that he is a god without a capital "G."

This does not imply obvious superhuman powers. It bases itself on a faith that the Emperor, descending in an unbroken line from the founders of Japan, who were gods, expresses the principle that Japan is a divinely inspired nation with a divine mission. It insists that the Emperor, as a result, can do no wrong. It is only his advisors who must take responsibility to the nation for their blunders. The Emperor is the one living man in the web who has no necessary obligations to his people. He does have an obligation to his divine ancestors, whom he still invokes regularly at the Grand Shrine of Ise, telling them of new developments in the nation and asking their guidance. It is an odd position for a marine biologist to find himself in.

Hirohito himself would like to be a normal constitutional monarch, as would increasingly large numbers of his subjects. But he can only become so if the web society is destroyed. It is dependent on him for its life and perpetuation. His position was bluntly set forth in *Kokutai no Hongi—The Basis of the National Polity*—a book published by the Ministry of Education in 1937 for the edification of teachers and other public officials: "The Emperor is not merely a so-called sovereign, monarch, ruler or administrator, such as is seen among foreign nations, but reigns over this country as a deity incarnate in keeping with the great principle that has come down to us since the founding of the Empire." If Yamazaki is the nearest thing the web society has to an iconoclast, Hirohito is the nearest it comes to having an absolute value.

* * * * *

The existence of this imperially centered web is the central fact of modern Japanese history. It has enabled the Japanese to move as one in the greatest national transformation of modern times; it has also betrayed them into the hands of leaders who were clever enough to find the levers which controlled the dynamics of this national society and use them for their own ends. The repressed individualism of men like Yamazaki and Kisei cries out against it; Shimizu coolly dissects it; Sanada occasionally puzzles over it, without realizing what his worry is about. But, in one way or another, the web still surrounds them, and distinguishes them as a people. Where foreigners have not understood this fact, they have resorted to caricature to express their frustration. To do the caricaturists justice, the earnestness, the cloying politeness, the brutality of modern Japan are by-products of this kind of a society.

"The most austere order in the church has no novitiate so severe as the apprenticeship to good breeding which must be served in Japan," wrote Fr. Alexander Valignano, S.J., the Provincial of the sixteenth-century Jesuit missionaries there, in a letter to the superior general of his society. This judgment would hold true today in many walks of life in Japan. Certainly, granted the loosening effect of war and occupation on a tightly bound social code, the Japanese, in 1953, still impress foreigners as the world's politest people. "Politeness" is the most obvious symbol of a society where a man's life depends completely on how he handles his relationships with others. Being a gentleman in Japan is as exacting a discipline as being a saint or a yogi somewhere else.

Caught in their web of crisscrossing loyalties and commitments, the Japanese have worked out an elaborate system of manners to express a man's exact position in society, without injuring either his own self-respect or that of others. No Japanese is free to ignore these social conventions, except the very young and the very old. The way in which Japanese formally excuse children and old men from following the codes of the web society is an odd proof of their recognition that it is a hard and demanding one. Japanese children, until the age of about ten, are the most indulged and undisciplined moppets in the world. The aged, at the other end of the scale, make a fetish of going into formal retirement, as soon as their descendants are judged ready to carry on their responsibilities. A man living in retirement may carry on his life exactly as before, down to participating in his business; the difference is that he is no longer held "responsible" for keeping up his station in society.

Many of the terms and situations of Japanese manners have their counterparts elsewhere. The Japanese wife, or more usually the Japanese husband speaking for his wife, bows to the guest and says *"Nani mo gozaimasen ga. . . .* —This is nothing at all, but. . . ."; then introduces the first course of a sumptuous dinner. This kind of deprecating is certainly not unique. It is redolent of the American hostess's coy comment, "Oh, it's just something I whipped up from what we had around the house," in answer to her dinner guests' protesting that she "shouldn't have gone to so much trouble for us." The difference is that what for Americans or Europeans is a polite comedy of manners is for the Japanese a tragically serious ritual, which must at all costs be observed.

The Japanese language is awkward and primitive in some ways. But for expressing grades of social distinction, it is as supple and delicate a tool as French is for delineating moods and feelings. There are at least ten different words for "I" in Japanese. The Emperor alone has had the right to use *"Chin"*—a super-regal "we." In ordinary conversation with acquaintances or superiors, a Japanese uses *"watakushi."* If talking to a servant or a very close friend, he will use *"boku,"* or possibly even the vulgar *"ore."* Another man's wife is called an *"okusan."* One's own wife is referred to as *"kanae,"* literally "inside the house." A level, ordinary way of saying "I am going home" is *"Uchi e ikimasu."* Polite language, used to a superior, will say *"Uchi e maerimasu."* Vulgar language, to an inferior or a good friend, will have it *"Uchi e yuku."* The average Japanese is a man who goes around wearing several linguistic overcoats, shedding them one after another as his familiarity with people increases, putting them on again as formality returns.

The uniformity of language and custom in the web society runs very deep. Thanks to a well-organized national school system, all Japanese go through at least six years of education. Yamazaki and Shimizu attended the university. The Emperor was tutored by the finest scholars in the country. But Kisei and Sanada, although they incline towards speaking with a slight local dialect, speak and understand a standard language with the others.

It is similarly true with the externals of living. Neither farmer Sanada nor Kisei, the steel worker, would shine as a porch or locker-room conversationalist, if Admiral Shimizu took them to the Sagami golf club. But there is not a great difference in their basic manners. In their social habits, they are astonishingly alike.* This the web society has done for them. Visiting Sanada's farm house, at the roots of Fuji, all of the five men would find their common starting point. They would all enter by the sliding door, respectfully remove their shoes—pretending not to see their host until he was ready to receive them. Squatting on the clean, bare mats they would accept tea with the right amount of polite protesting. Hie Sanada would serve them almost wordlessly—at best with a muttered word of polite greeting. They would acknowledge her presence— barely, and thank her husband for his hospitality. Then they would admire the austerely arranged flowers in the alcove. Here, at Shimoyoshida, is the old Japanese life, the culture of the web society: graceful to watch, but dangerous to pursue.

Within its toils, the Japanese is a model citizen. His bonds are taut enough to give him a sense of security and keep him in a state of precarious equilibrium. To all the objects of his duties—parent, child, employer, the visitor who must be entertained, the Japanese is thoughtfully, sometimes appallingly polite. He is the sort of citizen who would not think of disobeying a "Keep Off the Grass" sign in his own home district. In return for his own duties, he is helped and buoyed up by the reciprocating obligations of his fellow-citizens.

But the strain is great. "*Sekinin*—responsibility" is a fearful word to the Japanese. His life is surrounded by responsibility, which he cannot dodge without bringing disgrace on others as well as himself. If *sekinin* is fastened on him, he will discharge it faithfully and without question. But he will try to avoid adding to its burdens. Foreigners in Japan are recurrently puzzled by the lack of Good Samaritans. If a man has an accident on a crowded

---

* The writer once went to the cabinet meeting room in the Diet Building in Tokyo at lunchtime. He discovered the entire Japanese Cabinet sitting around the room eating their *bento* (box lunches)— the same kind of cold lunch, packed in the same way, that was being eaten by laborers pausing from their work in the Tokyo streets.

street, very few of his fellow-citizens will rush to help him. Their diffidence is not cruelty or callousness. It represents an honest horror of adding another complicated relationship of *sekinin* to their already burdened lives. For a Japanese Good Samaritan cannot simply bind up the injured man's wounds and go away. He automatically assumes a moral responsibility—and sometimes a legal one —and a relationship of favor and counter-favor with the victim, which may last for years.

Consciously or not, the Japanese will go to any lengths to free himself—even for a few hours—from this crushing bond. In its most innocent form, this takes the form of drunkenness. The Japanese are not so much poor drinkers, but more than any other race (even including northern Europeans and Anglo-Saxons) they are people who pounce on liquor as a release from their everyday responsibilities. Sake can dissolve the web for a short while. A few drops of it will transform a group of dignified Japanese businessmen into a brawling, noisy mob. Few people ever "want to get drunk" so desperately.

As the Japanese gets farther away from his home community, he relaxes his self-discipline. "*Tabi no haji wo kakizute*—A man away from home need feel no shame" is a famous proverb. In the tight island society of Japan, however, there are few places where a man can honestly call himself "away from home." * The temples are the same, the policemen are the same, there is the ubiquity of

---

* Public parks in large cities, especially during holiday times, and the crowded conveyances of city commuters are outstanding exceptions. The same citizen who will scrupulously observe a "Keep Off the Grass" sign in his own locality cheerfully litters the grounds of a civic monument like Ueno Park in Tokyo, where the ties of civic responsibility are too widely extended to give a sense of obligation to the individual. It is the same with streetcars and subway cars during the Tokyo rush hours. A man can push his neighbor with something like impunity, since the chances that he will know him are very slight. In this oblique way, the metropolis has done its bit to break down some classic Japanese conventions.

the national dailies like *Asahi* and *Mainichi* and the national radio, run from Tokyo. If there are no local ties of responsibility, there is always, at the least, the basic sense of responsibility to the Emperor and the divinely appointed nation. Wherever the web holds him captive, the Japanese is a cautious and ruthlessly self-disciplined man.

Occasionally, however, the Japanese finds himself temporarily in situations not covered by the set contracts of the web society, or with people to whom these contracts need not apply. Since his contract code of morality is a national one, he is only bound to foreigners as a result of commitments made by the Japanese nation. Where these commitments have not been made, or are relaxed, the Japanese can be brutal and dangerous—how dangerous the Japanese Army demonstrated between 1931 and 1945. With no absolute moral codes to restrain him, released by his superiors from his bonds, the thousand lifetime frustrations of the repressed little soldier boil over. In Nanking he rapes and pillages on the streets. At Bataan and in Manila he kills Filipino babies and bayonets helpless American captives. This is what happens when a Japanese is suddenly taken "out of context."

Without the web to hold him, he reacts against his long confinement. He does not, like the Germans, belong to a race capable of designing gas chambers and scientific medical tortures. His was the kind of atrocity that sprang from fear, sudden anger, and the brutalizing weight of a life hedged by the constant demands of group responsibilities.

The U. S. Army and Navy Joint Report on World War II Japanese atrocities in the Philippines, describes the Bataan death march. A section of it, taken at random, reads:

"Throughout the twelfth we were introduced to a form of torture which came to be known as the sun treatment. We were made to sit all day in the boiling sun without cover. We had very little water; our thirst was intense.

Many of us went crazy and several died. The Japanese dragged out the sick and delirious. Three Filipino and three American soldiers were buried while still alive.

"On the thirteenth each of those who survived was given a mess kit of rice. We were given another full day of the sun treatment. At nightfall we were forced to resume our march. We marched without water until dawn of April 14, with one two-hour interval when we were permitted to sit beside the roadside.

"The very pace of our march itself was a torture. Sometimes we had to go very fast, with the Japanese pacing us on bicycles. At other times we were forced to shuffle along very slowly. The muscles of my legs began to draw and each step was an agony.

"Filipino civilians tried to help both Filipino and American soldiers by tossing us food and cigarettes from windows or from behind houses. Those who were caught were beaten. The Japanese had food stored along the roadside. A United States Army colonel pointed to some of the cans of salmon and asked for food for his men. A Japanese officer picked up a can and hit the colonel in the face with it, cutting his cheek wide open. Another colonel and a brave Filipino picked up three American soldiers who had collapsed before the Japs could get to them. They placed them on a cart and started down the road toward San Fernando. The Japanese seized them as well as the soldiers, who were in a coma, and horsewhipped them fiercely.

"Along the road in the province of Pampanga there are many wells. Half-crazed with thirst, six Filipino soldiers made a dash for one of the wells. All six were killed. As we passed Lubao we marched by a Filipino soldier gutted and hanging over a barbed-wire fence. . . ."

The veneer of many centuries had done little to change the nature of Japanese cruelty, as combustible in 1942 as it was in the fourteenth century, when Japanese pirates ravaged the coasts of China and committed atrocities beyond speaking on the men, women and children whom they found in their path. It has so often been Japan's tragedy that cruelty and atrocities have formed the one escape valve for the freer human feelings which a ruthlessly tight society did its unconscious best to inhibit or suppress.

Back at home, with his web of tense respectability wound tightly around his kimono, the Japanese dimly tries to recall why these awful things happened. *"Moshiwake ga arimasen*—There is no way to apologize," he stammers. Seen from inside the web, Bataan and Nanking are unreal. The effort to synthesize is too great. *"Moshiwake ga arimasen,"* he repeats, and earnestly asks his visitor if he would like another cup of tea.

2
BORROWERS AND BUILDERS

"We must not forget that a phoenix rises only from its own ashes, and that it is not a bird of passage, neither does it fly on pinions borrowed from other birds."

Inazo Nitobe in "Bushido"

The origins of the Japanese people have never been settled. Some probably crossed to the islands from northern Asia; others, possibly, from south China or the Malay islands. Today, at least twenty centuries after the races of Japan merged themselves into one people, there are striking evidences of at least a dual origin. Fumio Shimizu, a spare-featured man, looks like an ancient Tartar. He once had a Navy captain serving under him who could have passed for a Filipino or a Malay—dark, squat, almost brown-skinned. "He is the Malay," the Admiral would say jokingly, "and I am the Mongol."

No one who has visited Japan escapes noticing this mixed ancestry. One can sit drinking tea with some aristocratic Buddhist monks in Kyoto, who look like the classic northern Asiatics, their features worked out as sparingly as the design of a Chinese painting. Off the coast of Shikoku, in the waters of the Inland Sea, a group of short, stocky fishermen heave together on their nets, shouting an undecipherable cry to the quickening beat of a drum. The image of China fades, and a spectator feels sure that here is a southern people; there is something Polynesian about the swaying bodies and the snapping chant.

It would be difficult, however, to generalize that the Mongol types in Japan come from the north, and the Malays—or Oceanic types—from the far south. No one knows exactly how much of what races came to Japan, or how they got there. The races have blended, but in the process each seems to have kept its Mendelian autonomy.

In the first century of the Christian era, the invaders, wherever they came from, were well settled in southern and central Japan. Until the ninth century the aboriginal Caucasian race called Ainu, a primitive hunting people, hung onto vast territories north of Tokyo. These noble white men, however, were slowly pushed back. They and, earlier, some southern aborigines, the Kumaso, were successively used as pawns in the struggles for power between the invading chieftains, in the way some British Celts were exploited by the Saxons. Finally, centuries afterward, the survivors of the Ainu fled across the northern straits to Hokkaido, which is still, racially speaking, the Wales or Brittany of Japan.

By the second century A.D. a strong monarchy was ruling a good part of Japan from the district of Yamato, not far from the present city of Kyoto. The race of Yamato, as the Japanese later called themselves, had already made several raiding expeditions against the coasts of Korea. But the raiders were a very primitive people. Their society was not much more than an amalgamation of clans, although the central clan chief, the progenitor of the current emperors, had already begun to levy taxes and collect national military expeditions.

The warlike islanders contrasted with the civilized China of the Han dynasty as sharply as the Teutons of the Saxon forests with the patricians of Imperial Rome. A Chinese report dryly records, "The men all tattoo their faces and adorn their bodies with designs. Differences of rank are indicated by the position and size of the patterns."

Like most peoples, the first men of Yamato explained the origins of time and the world in terms of their own surroundings and their own fancy. The first emperor of Japan, Jimmu (whose existence, to say nothing of his pinpointed coronation date—660 B.C., is legendary) was the great-grandson of the Sun-Goddess Amaterasu, who placed Japan under her protection. The accounts of Japan's earliest history found in *Kojiki* and *Nihongi*, the two great seventh-century chronicles, are well-padded with highflown court language, and influenced by older Chinese works. However, they were certainly based on a crude belief that Japan was a God-favored country, and the Japanese a race superior to the mainlanders of Asia.

At the beginning of time, the *Nihongi* says, shortly after heaven and earth were separated out of chaos, the god Izanagi and the goddess Izanami stood on the bridge of heaven and peered below them. " 'Is there not a country beneath?' they said. They thrust down the jeweled spear of heaven and with it found the ocean. The brine which dripped from the point of the spear became solid and grew into an island. They came down to dwell on the island and produced offspring."

Their very first children were the eight islands which formed the Great-Eight-Island Country—one of the classical names for Japan. After producing them, the book continues, "the August Izanagi and the August Izanami consulted together, saying, 'We have now produced the Great-Eight-Island Country, with mountains, rivers, herbs and trees. Why should we not produce someone who shall be Lord of the Universe?' They then together begat the Sun-Goddess, who was called Amaterasu O-Mikami."

Other gods arose besides Amaterasu. Some of them descended to earth and lived upon the new lands there. But it was Amaterasu who, after several Olympian encounters with her evil brother, Susa-no-wo, cleared the way for her descendants to inherit the original Great-Eight-Island Country of her parents. She sent her grandson down from the Plain of Heaven (*Takama-ga-Hara*) with a holy command:

"This reed-plain Land of Fifteen Thousand Autumns of Fair Rice-Ears is the country over which my descendants shall be lords. Do thou, my august grandchild, proceed there and rule over it. Go! And may prosperity attend thy dynasty, and it shall, like heaven and earth, endure forever."

The Goddess gave her grandson three tokens of his divine rule—a divine sword, jewels from the mountain steps of heaven and the mirror into which she herself had gazed. Going down, he alighted on a mountain, and began his rule over the country of Japan. The line of Japanese emperors traditionally descends from one of his sons.

The islanders, cut off by themselves, developed this theory of a divinely founded nation far more consistently than most other peoples. By 607 A.D., when Chinese records describe the visit of an ambassador from Japan to the Sui emperor's court, it was well established. When the ambitious and sophisticated Emperor Yang Ti asked the envoy to describe his master in Japan (then known as the country of Wa) the envoy piously replied, "The Wa Prince considers Heaven his elder and the Sun his younger brother." "This is most outrageous talk," Yang Ti commented.

Early in the Christian Era, the first peaceful contacts had been made with the neighboring peninsula of Korea. It was here that the Japanese began their long history of adopting and adapting the institutions of others. The art of writing in Chinese characters was imported from the Korean kingdom of Pakche, as tradition has it, in 285 A.D. In the next three hundred years, as a result of intermittent contacts with Korea, the Japanese got a good glimpse of the formidable culture of the mainland that centered itself south of the Korean peninsula. It was detailed enough to convince the rising emperors of Japan that the kingdoms of Korea were valuable only as cultural middlemen. It could be only by direct dealings with China, the source of Eastern culture, that this culture could be grasped.

The embassy to the Emperor Yang Ti was the first formal attempt to open up Chinese contacts. Others were more successful. A year later, in 608, two priests and two noblemen sailed across the China Sea, sent by Prince Shotoku, the Japanese regent, to study the civilization of China and report on how well the Japanese could adapt it for themselves. After thirty years these envoys were all back in Japan. They had brought with them a painstaking description of the laws and government of China, illustrating their observations with the writings of Chinese scholars. By the time they returned, Shotoku, who had sent them, was dead. Meanwhile other embassies had been exchanged. In the process, Shotoku's successors were wise enough to realize how superior the Chinese institutions were to their own. Their application to Japan could mean the difference between a strong central government and an uneasy rule over many warring clans.

Led by the minister Fujiwara Kamatari, the throne sent down a series of decrees that revolutionized the kingdom. The institutions of T'ang China, a great and worldly-wise empire, were transferred bodily to govern the rude clans of Japan. The population was registered, a new tax system was evolved, land was redistributed. From the new capitals of Nara and Kyoto, the first permanent capitals in Japanese history, a bureaucracy was organized, on the Chinese pattern, to rule the islands. Provincial governors were appointed. A standing army, based on conscription, was, in theory at least, created.

645 A.D., the year these changes were initiated, is listed in Japanese histories as the year of the *Taika* Reform. *Taika* means simply the "Great Change." It was a fair description for the beginning of a national transformation without parallel in any European history. Like engineers working from a blueprint, the Japanese rulers had their

priest-ambassadors, who returned from China, read them the edicts of the T'ang emperors and the works of the Chinese sages. Almost as soon as a Chinese document was digested by the Japanese rulers, it was put to use in the form of new laws laid down for the Japanese people.

The political rumblings of the Great Change dramatized the most spectacular Chinese imports. A century before, however, the Japanese had begun to bring two more intangible articles of foreign make into their islands—Buddhism and Confucianism. The writings of Confucius were taken from China, along with more workaday manuscripts dealing with administration and military strategy. By the eighth century the Treatise on Filial Piety was already a standard part of the Japanese scholar's education. The influence of Buddhism made itself felt at the same time. But while the fluid precepts of Confucius easily dissolved into the Japanese tradition, Buddhism, with its systems of theology and philosophy, needed sponsors and formal adoption proceedings before it became part of the ethos.

The regent Prince Shotoku is called by some historians the "Constantine of Japanese Buddhism." A scholar of the imperial line, he ruled Japan from 592 to 622. Although the Buddhist *sutras* had been chanted at the imperial court before Shotoku's time, it was he who legalized the religion and spread it throughout the country.

Sixth-century Japan was as ripe for Buddhism as the fourth-century Roman Empire was ripe for Christianity. The primitive Shinto cults of the Yamato people—the race of Amaterasu—were unsatisfying to generations who grew steadily more sophisticated. Aside from a real belief in the divinity of the emperor, and theories about the special position of the Japanese race, early Shinto was no more than a rude animism, using clumsy sacrifices and lustral rites to appease a spectrum of shadowy gods lurking over the rainbow.

The Buddhist monks, who came first from Korea, later from China, brought with them a new religious experience. They introduced the ideas of a life after death, paradise and hell, and a religious distinction between the virtues that brought reward and the vices that condemned to punishment. The air of mystery about the ponderous Buddhist rituals left a deep imprint on the minds of the average Japanese. For the scholars, a great and difficult philosophy yawned invitingly behind the saffron robes and the repetitious chanting.

As early as 684 an imperial ordinance ordered all provincial governors to erect Buddhist temples in their capitals. A century later the Buddhist monk had become a permanent part of the Japanese scene. Sects arose, divided and multiplied, as the cult of the Buddha attracted a widening allegiance. Unlike the Christianity of Constantine, however, the new religion never completely drove out the early Shinto worship. This was partly due to the vagueness of both faiths, which could easily be made complementary, rather than contradictory. It was partly due to the tradition, ill-defined but always present in Japan, of the divine emperor and the God-blessed land. The Great Buddha of Nara was cast in 749 and set, where it stands today, beneath the huge wooden roof of Todaiji, the St. Peter's of Japanese Buddhism. But, while the Emperor Shomu's builders worked on Todaiji, the black- and white-robed Shinto priests still prayed to the Sun-Goddess in the ancient shrines of the Ise Peninsula (as they do today). And pious Japanese managed to invoke the new Buddha without losing touch with the old gods of their nationhood.

To become a really popular faith, Buddhism had to make some severe compromises with native Japanese beliefs. In the eighth century the Buddhist sage Gyogi first suggested that the classic Shinto gods were simply reincarnations of the Buddha. This happy solution snipped away the most pressing differences between the old religion and the new. Buddhism rapidly became the chief cult of Japan.

In the space of one hundred years, between 645 and 745, the Japanese thus adapted for themselves a new religion, a new notion of ethics, a new theory of government and administration, and a new system of organized laws. They also imported a sophisticated art of painting and sculpture, a literature and even, at an earlier date, a written language. The colossal effect of this mass borrowing was as great as the importation of Western culture eleven hundred years later. It has no parallel in world history.

The remarkable thing about the age of the Great Change was that the Japanese, showing a unique genius for this sort of thing, were so well able to control their acquisitions. Having imported the civilization of T'ang China, they slowly and almost unconsciously rejected some of it, took some of it within their own culture, and changed other parts out of all recognition to what they had first received. This was something which a more speculative people might have failed to do. Here, for the first time, the historian could watch the Japanese, facing new ideas and institutions, untroubled by logical contradictions or philosophic paradoxes between the new systems and the old, judging all things only by their instinctive question "How does it work?" They seldom asked "What purpose is there behind it?"

With little bent for philosophy, the Japanese rejected, for example, the dry scholarship of Confucius' Analects, but concentrated instead on his doctrines stressing filial piety. The Confucian idea of the family was cemented into the framework of the Japanese ethic. It became the theoretical justification for the old system of clan loyalties. With the Japanese the Confucian family tie became all the more rigid and binding.

In a similar way, the Japanese, like the Chinese, brushed away the deep other-worldliness of Indian Buddhism. In Japan the yogi became a vested priest. Instead of conducting an ascetic search for personal enlightenment, the Japanese Buddhist made his religion a source of emotional comfort. The ideal of the Buddha was assumed to be too difficult.

The Japanese sects stressed prayers and ritual as the road to salvation. Hell never gaped very deep and horrible for the Japanese Buddhist, and the road to heaven grew progressively better paved. It is doubtful whether Gautama Buddha would have recognized the refinements of the Pure Land sect, an emotional revivalist brand of Buddhism, which finally taught that one faithful repetition of the slogan "Namu Amida Buttsu" (an almost untranslatable phrase meaning, roughly, "O, Holy Lord Buddha") was enough to secure paradise for the believer.

* * * * *

In practice, the imported political theories had their ups and downs. However much the eighth-century rulers of Japan were impressed by the organization of the Chinese Empire, they were unable to transfer it bodily to Japan. They were able to use the new devices of a controlled bureaucracy and sweeping imperial edicts to break down the power of the native clans. In the long run, however, the Confucian civil service proved too refined an article to be successfully imported. The clan feeling was far too deeply rooted in the Japanese—possibly because of their mixed origins, possibly because it is easier for factions to develop and continue in a country cruelly divided by mountains and unnavigable rivers. For the next nine centuries the history of Japan was a record of war and compromise, always with the pendulum swinging between the Chinese notion of a centralized state (or at least a notion that owed much to Chinese influence) and the original Japanese idea of a loosely organized federation capable of uniting only in the face of a national calamity, like the Mongol invasions of the thirteenth century or the inroads of European powers in the nineteenth.

For two centuries, the Fujiwara family, the first Japanese "Mayors of the Palace," kept up a central government reasonably faithful to the model of the Great Change. Unfortunately for themselves the Fujiwara, in the process, became too absorbed in court ceremonials and Chinese poetry contests to maintain much of an army. As a result two obscure military clans, the Taira and the Minamoto, inherited control of the land. To decide the supremacy, they fought a War of the Roses Japanese-style. It lasted intermittently for 25 years before the Minamoto won it—long enough to give Japanese minstrels material for centuries of poems and stories about the clash of the red banner of the Taira with the Minamoto white, Far Eastern equivalents of European epics like the *Chanson de Roland*. Other military clans succeeded to power after the Minamoto weakened. The story of their battling makes Japanese history, until the year 1615, something like the dream of every schoolboy historian—a round of pitched battles, hairbreadth escapes, and sudden gatherings of the clans. This perpetual *Morte d'Arthur* atmosphere was, needless to say, a little hard on the country.

Some of the feudal leaders were able statesmen as well as military heroes. Minamoto Yoritomo, the greatest of the early barons, founded an astutely governed military dictatorship within the framework of the empire that kept relative peace in Japan for over a century. Although the periods when these men could maintain a stable rule were brief—and the governments they raised necessarily conditioned on military, rather than civilian power—the memory from the Taika days of a settled and centralized Imperial Japan never died. It was cited and often copied by the successful soldiers. The Tokugawa Shogunate, the greatest of the military dynasties, lasted for 250 years. When it was overthrown, Japan's nineteenth-century reformers went not only to Europe and the United States to copy Western systems of government for the revived empire; they dug into their own history to bring back the old Chinese theory of imperial rule.

In tailoring this theory to fit their purposes, both in

1868 and 645, the Japanese made one very important alteration. This concerned the role of the emperor. The Chinese believed the emperor to be the son of heaven, with divine attributes. His divinity, however, was negotiable. He demonstrated it by his virtue; when this virtue was no longer present, or seemed not to be, the man who sat on the throne was considered no longer worthy of his job. The practical effect of this interesting theory was that the Chinese could substitute dynasties as they wished. Powerful rebels could openly and rudely separate a monarch from his throne, without harming the institution of monarchy.

The Japanese theory of kingship was very different. The dynasty was too hopelessly personal to every Japanese to be tampered with, too intimately bound with their basic notions of heaven and earth, too closely linked to their idea of invincible islandhood. The kingship was the rule of Amaterasu, a notion imbedded in the structure of the divinely founded nation.

This gave the Japanese monarchy a far different premise from the practical Chinese idea of the son of heaven, who enjoyed heaven's mandate only as long as he was virtuous. It was a divine right of kingship, more powerful than anything proposed by the Bourbons or the Stuarts. In Japan there was one inviolable ground rule observed by the military magnates throughout the period of feudalism—the dynasty is sacred. A reigning emperor could be forced to abdicate, exiled or starved into submission. But he could only be replaced by someone directly in the imperial line—generally a son, grandson or brother.

The only way for the feudal leaders to approach possession of the throne was by a kind of infiltration—marrying the daughters of one's house to the emperors or installing them as imperial concubines. In this way families like the Fujiwara or the Tokugawa managed to acquire a great many imperial relatives. But even Toyotomi Hideyoshi, the greatest individual ruler in Japanese history, at the height of his power, declined an offer to install his line as hereditary kings.

The Japanese emperor had his early development as a primitive priest-king. As the inviolability of his line impressed itself on Japanese tradition, the former function grew at the expense of the latter. As an absolute quality, the sacredness of the Japanese dynasty was a counterpart of the Catholic idea of papal infallibility. The emperor was a pontiff whose personal virtues or vices did not affect his right to reign. What mattered was having a member of the direct imperial line on the throne. The Japanese were not insistent, as the Chinese were, that he be a good or a powerful ruler. Very early in Japanese history, the exercise of actual power by the ruler became of secondary importance.

This philosophy of religious kingship resulted in strong kingmakers and weak kings. The Japanese imperial dynasty is the longest in history—so long that it has no surname. It is also the most undistinguished. Less than ten Japanese emperors can be called great kings. Three of them, Tenchi, Kwammu and Sanjo II, lived before the eleventh century, when a centralized government, organized on the adapted Chinese lines, ruled Japan. Two, Jimmu and Nintoku, are legendary. The Emperor Meiji was a real leader in the making of nineteenth-century Japan. Another, Daigo II, though less wise than the rest, is a favorite figure of Japanese romanticists. In the fourteenth century, he staged a 30-year fight to rule his country as well as reign over it—long after the rule of behind-the-scenes kingmakers had become a fixed policy. He was twice exiled by the Ashikaga Shoguns. Twice he escaped and raised powerful armies against them. At the time of his death, he had fought them to a standstill in a lingering civil war.

For the most part, however, the emperors were pawns of the kingmakers. When a military baron got control of the country, his first concern was to secure the person of the emperor and the imperial regalia—the mirror, sword and jeweled necklace of the Sun-Goddess—without which no member of the imperial family could hold the throne in good conscience. This done, he would then "request" the emperor to issue imperial decrees enacting all the laws which the baron thought necessary. The emperor, if he went along with this plan, was allowed to keep his court, judge his imperial poetry contests and officiate at his rituals, the titular master of the realm. If he objected, he was apt to be escorted to a Buddhist monastery, whence, if he knew what was good for him, he would sign a decree abdicating in favor of a younger and more pliable member of the imperial house. Then the barons would leave him in peace.

Since there was always the danger that a grown emperor, like Daigo II, might insist on ruling actively, this system led to a succession of child emperors, tiny puppets of the barons.* The child emperor was generally forced to abdicate as soon as he showed signs of independence—sometimes even earlier; the Emperor Chukyo was deposed, after a reign of 70 days, when he was three years old.

"Forced" is perhaps too strong a word. With the exception of the Hojo regents, all the Japanese kingmakers showed a scrupulous and generally a sincere regard for the imperial person. The emperor was always revered. A man who controlled all the real power in the country would be flattered, if the court bestowed on him some ancient, but empty title of court rank. The emperor might be power-

* Occasionally the child-emperors were puppets of their own relatives. The reign of the Emperor Shirakawa, a case in point, is an extreme example of the Japanese passion for governing indirectly. In 1073, at the age of twenty, Shirakawa became emperor. Thirteen years later he abdicated and went into retirement. From his secluded court, however, the ex-emperor continued to rule Japan. His son Horikawa, reigned from 1087 to 1107; his grandson, Toba, from 1107 to 1123; his great-grandson Sutoku, from 1124 to 1141: they were all powerless puppets. Until his death in 1141, Shirakawa, the "Cloistered Emperor," and his courtiers ran the affairs of the nation from behind the scenes.

less, but he was necessary, the weak but essential king on a political chess board.

In dealing with their emperors, the Japanese showed themselves the world's greatest masters of behind-the-scenes political management. To regularize their position, first the Fujiwara, then, in 1192, the great statesman Yoritomo, extracted from the emperors the title of Sei-i-tai Shogun—"the Barbarian-Conquering Generalissimo." Down to 1868 the real rulers of Japan held this position by hereditary right, just as the Mayors of the Palace did in eighth-century France. But, unlike the father of Charlemagne, no shogun ever thought of usurping the crown.

The title of shogun itself began to have such significance that weak shoguns were as seldom deposed as weak emperors. When the descendants of the Shogun Yoritomo showed themselves too weak to govern, Japan was ruled by the Hojo family. The Hojo had no wish even to disturb the titular shogunate. They took upon themselves the title of regent and left the shogun's palace and his empty title in the hands of his descendants. For a period of almost two centuries, the Japanese were thus governed by a regent who ruled the country in the name of the powerless shogun, who nominally ruled the country in the name of the powerless emperor. The Chinese, a more logical people, would have been horrified by an arrangement like this. But to the Japanese the forms of authority have always been sacred, from the time of the Emperor Jimmu to General MacArthur.

* * * * *

Beneath the gossamer of imperial sanction, the Japanese developed their peculiar web society—rigid and demanding on the people who lived inside it, but curiously pliant and assimilative when exposed to foreign influences Time and time again the Japanese showed themselves eager to acquire imports, cultural as well as material. Their technique for doing this reminds one of the alimentary processes of a boa constrictor: swallow whole and digest at leisure. In ancient and medieval times they adapted brilliantly—and, on the whole, more smoothly than they did later. The Chinese and Indian elements which they borrowed are now as much a part of Japanese culture as they are of their own—in the case of a religion like Buddhism, considerably more.

During their early borrowing, the Japanese were able to keep their cultural contacts with the outside world a one-way street, or at least a thoroughfare with only scanty traffic on the return route. While they gave little to the life of Asia themselves, they borrowed, if not wholly at will, generally by their own invitation. Sometimes the Japanese contacts with the mainland were military—like the frequent invasions of Korea; sometimes they were adventurous or mercantile, like the voyages of the pirates and traders who alternately terrorized and enriched the seacoast towns of southern Asia in the sixteenth century. Often, as with China, the Japanese sent their embassies out in a search for foreign culture, with the determination of a rural American women's club badgering its contacts in the cities for some new and inspiring lecturers.

In return the Japanese islands were too remote to excite much interest among the mainlanders. Even the British Isles, which owe so much of their fortune to their original isolation, were not nearly so fortunate in their location. No Roman legions came to Japan to develop tin mines; there were no Saxon or Danish raids, no Norman invaders. The only foreign invasion ever attempted—Kublai Khan's Mongol, Chinese and Korean fleets of 1261—was beaten off through the same happy combination of bad weather and military ability that enabled the British to destroy the Spanish Armada. Except for this attack, Japan's neighbors on the continent of Asia were either too remote to care about the forbidding islands to the northeast, or too continental-minded, like the Chinese, to give much thought to maritime expeditions of conquest.

By the sixteenth century the Japanese had taken the patterns borrowed from China and the rest of Asia, and blended them into the strong cross-weave of the web society. Some appeared intact, just as they had been loaned. Others were of course drastically overhauled. Still others were stored up in the national consciousness, awaiting further use.

Politically, Japan seemed at the beginning of its own Elizabethan Era. After centuries of long, punishing civil war the nation had at last become unified. Two men, great soldiers themselves, were the instruments of unification. The first, Oda Nobunaga, was a small landholding baron in central Japan. Although hardly a skilled politician, he was one of the best generals Japan ever had. By force of arms and character, he managed to put half of the Japanese provinces under his thumb before his death, by assassination, in 1582.

His right-hand man and successor, Toyotomi Hideyoshi, is the most remarkable figure in Japanese history—a history which has had more than its share of individual heroes. He was neither a *daimyo* (the title of a clan leader) nor a member of the hereditary nobility, the *samurai*. His father was a farmer named Nakamura, who happened to live in Oda's fief. By an appalling combination of bravery and shrewdness, Hideyoshi got himself into Oda's retinue, then went on to become his chief general. After Oda's death Hideyoshi consolidated his conquests and extended them until he held firm control of the entire country.

Hideyoshi's Japan was united, expansive and increasingly prosperous—the economic wounds of the civil wars were healing quickly. As a military power, it was possibly the most formidable in the Orient. Without straining his resources, Hideyoshi could send 195,000 troops across the Straits of Tsushima to invade Korea and China in 1592. (Tactically speaking, they won their battles—it was the lack of logistical planning and the brilliance of a Korean admiral that forced their ultimate withdrawal.)

Japanese traders and pirates sailed the South China Sea, while Hawkins was scourging the Spanish Main. They were equally known and feared as far south as the Malay Peninsula. Deprived of a chance to win territory at the expense of their neighbors in Japan, the feudal lords of the coasts turned to seafaring. In the inland cities, merchants offered heavy prices for luxuries of foreign make.

* * * * *

At this time two new elements thrust themselves—rudely and without invitation—into the lives of the Japanese. In the year 1542, some Portuguese traders, their ship tossed by adverse winds, landed on the island of Tanega, just south of Kyushu. They became friendly with the islanders and taught them the use of gunpowder. On August 15, 1549, another Portuguese ship landed Francis Xavier, of the Society of Jesus, at the rocky harbor of Kagoshima. He came to teach the Japanese Christianity.

Both the religion and the science of the West had a lightning development. In 1600 there were about 300,000 practicing Japanese Christians (all of them, of course, Roman Catholics; Protestant missionaries did not arrive in Japan until 1859). Churches were built in the leading cities of Japan and Jesuits, some of them Japanese, preached at the court of the Japanese rulers. In the same year, at the battle of Sekigahara, which decided the control of the country, a decisive proportion of the *samurai* who fought there were armed with arquebuses. In 1615, explosive mines were being used in the siege of Osaka Castle.

If Western innovations had followed the pattern of the Chinese, it might be expected that the Japanese, after rapidly swallowing these new importations, would have then gone through their leisurely period of digesting them. Christianity, we would assume, would have had to make some compromise with local customs—possibly to the extent of incorporating some Shinto and Buddhist observances into its calendar. Western science, similarly, would have had a peculiarly Japanese orientation—the Japanese might have been the first to put bayonets on their muskets.

Instead, after less than a century of exposure to contemporary Western culture, the Japanese dramatically threw it all out. In the quarter-century after 1600, 200,000 Christians were persecuted for their religion. Death and torture were commonplaces. In 1637 the last group of acknowledged Christians in Japan were besieged and slaughtered at Shimabara by the shogun's troops (who were assisted by the artillery fire of two Dutch ships). After that there were almost no avowed Christians left in Japan, except for a few hundred stubborn families, the "hidden" Christians, who practiced their faith in secret until well into the nineteenth century.

In 1636 the government decreed that no Japanese ship would be allowed to sail to a foreign port. Barring a trickle of goods from Dutch traders, there was no further import of Western articles, either guns or goods. The arquebuses grew rusty and the two-handed sword once again was the arbiter of Japanese politics.

The reason for this turnabout, as stressed in most histories, was the fear of the Japanese that they would be overrun by the fleets and the armies of European powers. The cross, the arquebus and a foreign army, in the Japanese mind, comprised a package deal—one could not be had without bringing on the other two. Relying on other sixteenth-century precedents, this theory had much truth to it. It was not, however, the whole explanation. While the Japanese, in running shy of the friendly seeming European traders, showed an astuteness which was not shared by the Malays, the Aztecs or the North American Indians, there was probably a deeper reason for their rejection than a simple fear of foreign conquest.

When Christianity first invaded Japan, its message was understandably confusing. It is doubtful if many of the first converts grasped the essentials of the religion they had entered. Many learned Japanese thought that the Christian priests were representatives of another, higher variety of Buddhism. (Their supposition was encouraged by the fact that the Jesuits, to fit better into the local scene, often dressed like Buddhist priests.) On the surface, since Buddhist priests, too, wear long vestments during their services and chant a complicated liturgy, the Christian observances seemed vaguely familiar. Oda Nobunaga himself welcomed the Portuguese Jesuits as allies against the warlike Buddhist monks who had opposed him.

After the Jesuits had solved their language problems and were able to communicate the Christian message in some detail, it became disturbingly clear that the likes of this religion had not been seen in Japan before. The worship of Jesus Christ, with its absolute moral values of good and evil, struck at the heart of the web society of feudal Japan. The Christians preached that a *samurai's* basic moral duty was not to his feudal overlord, but to Christ and the Church. If Caesar ordered the Christian to do a moral evil, the Christian was automatically absolved from his allegiance.

There was nothing in Christianity which permitted the easy compromise that Buddhism had made with the Shinto gods. In the preaching of the Jesuits, though minor compromises were made, there was no equivocation on one point: the gods of Buddhism and the ancestor-gods of Japan alike were false idols. The path of the Jesuits was literally strewn with the idols they denounced, as the new converts, to demonstrate their zeal, tore down the stone Buddhas and the lacquered Shinto ancestor tablets that stood in their houses and temple courtyards. For the first time in its history, iconoclasts had come to Japan.

Christianity had a deep and instant appeal. The poor and oppressed were moved by its insistence on the absolute equality of all men. Jesuits preached to the outcasts, the landless peasants and the slaves. In a society that was becoming more and more stratified, these people flocked to hear the comforting and revolutionary idea of the brotherhood of man. At the same time the priests presented a higher and nobler ideal to *samurai* who were already schooled in something resembling Christian austerity, but often dissatisfied with a code of ethics which set as man's highest goal an unthinking loyalty to superiors who were often demonstrably unworthy of it. By all their training, they were extraordinarily receptive to the idea of Christian sacrifice. Christianity became popular at the courts of Nobunaga and of Hideyoshi. Some well-known *samurai*, like Takayama Ukon and Konishi Yukinaga, one of Hideyoshi's best generals, joined the new church.

Neither Oda, Hideyoshi, nor Tokugawa Ieyasu, the dynast who succeeded to their power, were pious men. Oda was indifferent; Ieyasu paid lip-service to Buddhism; Hideyoshi was a Robert Ingersoll-style atheist. But both Hideyoshi and Ieyasu, without troubling to investigate the deeper meaning of the Christian religion, saw in it a revolutionary and uncompromising faith, which could well undermine the bases of their authority—the feudal loyalty of the *samurai* and the docility of the subject population of farmers and townsmen. As soon as he had thought this out, Hideyoshi acted to ban Christianity. Ieyasu later followed Hideyoshi's lead. Both men's motives are best explained in a passage in the letter which Hideyoshi sent to the Portuguese Viceroy of the Indies in 1591:

"In regard to religion, Japan is the realm of its native gods—the *Kami*, that is to say of Shin[to], which is the origin of all things; the good order of the government which has been established here from the beginning depends on the exact observance of the laws on which it is founded, and whose authors are the *Kami* themselves. They cannot be deviated from without involving the disappearance of the differences which ought to subsist between sovereign and subject, and of the subordination of wives to husbands, children to fathers, of vassals to lords of servants to their masters. In a word, these laws are necessary for the maintenance of good order at home and tranquility abroad. The 'Fathers of the Society' [Jesuits] as they are called, have come to these islands to teach another religion here; but as that of the *Kami* is too surely founded to be abolished, this new law can only serve to introduce into Japan a diversity of cults prejudicial to the welfare of the state. It is for this reason that by Imperial Edict I have forbidden these foreign doctors to continue to preach their doctrine. . . ."

Although Hideyoshi instinctively felt the dangers which Christianity held for his social system, he was also incapable of realizing the truly religious ends which the Jesuit missionaries were pursuing. They were foreigners, they had strange disruptive doctrines and they evidently worked hand in glove with the Portuguese traders—these facts made a good case for their being pure and simple agents of a foreign power. In the case of the Jesuits and the Portuguese, his political suspicions were baseless. After Spanish Franciscans from Manila shouldered their way into the Japanese mission field, however, his fears stood on firmer ground.

The hand-in-glove connection between the Spanish missionaries and King Philip's Viceroy was obvious. The occasional veiled threats of the Spaniards—temporal as well as spiritual—were enough to confirm the long latent suspicions that all foreign missionaries were advance agents of foreign landing-parties.

* * * * *

The expulsion of the foreign merchants came shortly after the downfall of Japanese Christianity. After 1636 the only link between Japan and the explosive changes in European technology was the sleepy Dutch trading post at Deshima, an artificial islet in Nagasaki harbor.* It was a

---

* Dutch traders arrived in Japan early in the seventeenth century, and there continued their Asiatic commercial rivalry with the Portuguese. As the Dutch refrained from propagandizing in favor of Christianity—or even professing it in public, the Japanese allowed

curt ending for the high hopes which Hideyoshi and his barons had once held of increasing Japan's trade with the world outside. Perhaps if Hideyoshi had been alive in 1640, the ban on foreign traders would not have been enforced. A strong man as well as a brilliant one, he was quite confident that he could control a new foreign trade to Japan's advantage. But his successor Tokugawa Ieyasu was more cautious. Not trusting the ability of the Japanese to handle a commercial invasion by the West, he decided to play safe by sealing the country off from even its old trading contacts, the Portuguese.

Caution was spelled out in every syllable of Ieyasu's policy. He was himself a man of great ability, second only to Hideyoshi in shrewdness and resource. He wisely held back from challenging Hideyoshi's interests during his lifetime. On Hideyoshi's death in 1598, however, Ieyasu quietly and deliberately took over the central power. He first developed and confirmed a large following among the Japanese nobility. At the Battle of Sekigahara, in 1600, he defeated most of those who still opposed him—chiefly the faithful partisans of the house of Toyotomi Hideyoshi. In 1615 Ieyasu stormed Osaka Castle, the last rallying-point of Hideyoshi's son, Hideyori. After that, there was no more opposition for him to scheme against.

Where Hideyoshi was intrepid, Tokugawa was cautious and intuitive. He concentrated his efforts on founding a stable dynasty of shoguns to rule Japan—always, of course, in the emperor's name. He moved first to keep any new and untoward influences from jiggling the feudal balance of power he had sustained in the country, next to erect a solid polity on its foundations.

---

them to remain after the Portuguese were expelled. But the conditions of their trading were rigidly outlined for them. At one point Japanese officials insisted on removing the rudders of Dutch ships, during their stay in Nagasaki harbor, as an assurance of good conduct. The small amount of commerce permitted them scarcely seemed worth the trouble—although the fact that the Dutch remained in Nagasaki proves that it must have been worth something.

Internally, Tokugawa and the first of his successors deliberately tried to freeze the social and political structures of the country at the exact stage they found it in. They codified the distinction between the classes of people, which before had been rather fluid. By a nicely timed policy of "divide and rule" they kept any of the feudal barons from getting too much power or influence. At the same time, they based their power on the maintenance of a rigid feudal structure. The wartime dominance of the *samurai* was transferred to a peacetime social system. The military clans were the pillars of their rule. As a result, all Japan was organized, by law, on the pattern of the old clan system.

The Tokugawa policy was essentially repressive, not constructive. It was the handiwork of a superb political poker player who, having won the pot, wanted only to freeze the game indefinitely, so that he might enjoy the position given him by his winnings. Having made themselves masters of Japan through their tested ascendancy over the other military clans, the Tokugawa dedicated themselves to preserving the familiar feudal organization which they controlled so well. They perpetuated this organization long after the conditions that had brought it into being, i.e., the wars and civil disturbances of medieval Japan, had vanished.

Given the premise of Tokugawa policy, it is easy to see how both of the Western influences that came knocking at Japan's doors would be declared anathema. Ieyasu, in fact, capped Hideyoshi's edicts expelling Christian priests with a cruel and sweeping persecution of all Christians. His hard and fast ban on foreign intercourse mocked Hideyoshi's policy of trade expansion.

An event of 1637 must have seemed to Ieyasu to embody within itself a capsule justification of all his repressions. Goaded by the bad government of a local *daimyo,* some Christian *samurai* and farmers, together with a great many non-Christians, revolted in Kyushu. Taken under siege by the Shogun's armies at Shimabara, they were for a time disturbingly successful. Although there were only a few professional soldiers in the Shimabara garrison, they held off five times their number of the best of the Kyushu *samurai* for weeks, before they were finally overcome and slaughtered. The fine morale of the Christians was itself a powerful weapon, but the physical key to their success was gunpowder. The musketry of the defenders took a terrific toll of the *samurai* swordsmen. It was not until the rebels ran out of ammunition that the besiegers were able to take Shimabara by storm.

Shimabara, and the increased use of arquebuses in other battles of the time, may have been an unhappy portent to the conservative Tokugawa. If a few peasants with guns could hold off a *samurai* army, the delicate balance of power based on feudalism was not long for this world. Guns and the other sought-after Western inventions—like large ocean-going ships—might bomerang embarrassingly. The Tokugawa decided to keep these imponderable or unknown quantities out of their existence as long as they could. They would have interfered with a proper clan consciousness.

* * * * *

As far as the modern Japanese remember their ancestors, they remember them as provincial clansmen. Admiral Shimizu can trace his descent back to a *samurai* named Ishida, who rode and fought in the train of Maeda Toshinaga, the Lord of Kaga. When Tokugawa Ieyasu defeated the barons who opposed him at Sekigahara, Maeda and his men fought beside him. The founder of the shogunate confirmed Maeda in possession of his fief, a rich farming land sealed off from the rest of the country on the east and the south by the Japanese Alps, facing the Japan Sea on the west. Ishida followed his master to his new capital at the city of Kanazawa and there built a house for his descendants, not far from Maeda's palace.

Sakaji Sanada's ancestor was not so fortunate. A farmer

named Watanabe, he came from central Japan. He stayed loyal to the house of Toyotomi, after Hideyoshi died. Farmer Watanabe fought bravely for Hideyoshi's son, Hideyori, in the defense of Osaka Castle, against the overwhelming forces of the Tokugawa. For one winter it succeeded. Then Tokugawa persuaded Hideyori to fill in the moat of his castle as a pledge of an armistice. As soon as Hideyori did this, Tokugawa attacked. In the slaughter that followed the castle's capture, Watanabe was one of the few who escaped. Ieyasu pardoned him, but took away his land and his name (he was evidently of *samurai* rank). Dejected, Watanabe wandered northward to the slopes of Fuji, where he settled on a small farm under the new name of Sanada.

The forbears of Hideya Kisei came from the south. They were *samurai*. The steel worker, despite his humble position and the poverty of his immediate relations, can claim a descent every bit as respectable as that of the ex-admiral. They lived in the wild mountain country of Satsuma, Japan's most southerly province, in the hills near the city of Kagoshima. Satsuma was rougher country than the plains of the north. The woods teemed with bears, wild boars and monkeys. The knights of Satsuma, cut off from the more cultivated north, were a hardier lot than the *samurai* of the main island. Their clan loyalty was proverbial—in the case of Kisei's ancestors, a loyalty first to the house of Saigo, then indirectly to the great family of Shimazu, the princes of Satsuma, who counted the Saigo among their faithful vassals.

It is not so extraordinary that, of four modern Japanese, two should be able to trace a *samurai* ancestry. As a class, the *samurai* were overpopulated. After so many generations of feudal warfare, the *samurai* multiplied. After each civil war there were hundreds of freemen soldiers who joined the military nobility, thousands of nobles of the defeated party who lost their positions and sank either to the status of small farmers, or to landless bandits, ready to give their swords to anyone who could feed them or give them land in return.

It is more remarkable that Shimizu, Kisei and Sanada are able to trace their ancestry back for over three hundred years. It is a good instance of the deep regard the Japanese have for family connections. Tadao Yamazaki is less interested in these matters than the others. He has no idea who his family was, or where they lived, other than that they came from the province of Echigo, the present Niigata Prefecture, far to the north of Kaga on the snowy western coast facing the Japan Sea. Possibly they, too, were *samurai*. Yamazaki has a fleeting childhood recollection of a portrait of his grandfather Sakuemon wearing the *chonmage*, the twisted topknot in which all *samurai* —and *samurai* alone—wore their hair. More likely, the Yamazaki family may have been part of the nameless millions of humbler Japanese, farmers and small artisans, who worked their fields patiently through the warring centuries, the helpless but loyal pawns of the *samurai* nobility.

Over a period of 250 years, the laws of the Tokugawa spun a fine, hard covering around their lives. Inside this man-made cocoon the web society of Japan developed. Its feudal structure was not unique. But its perpetuation in one fixed form was unique. Long after similar medieval societies of other nations had evolved into something quite different, the old family society of Japan remained snug in its chrysalis, untouched by invasion, migrations, or intrusive philosophies. It has remained, into modern times, the underlying basis of the Japanese social system.

The insulation of the Tokugawa was not altogether bad. Its greatest gift to Japan was 250 years of relative quiet, without any widespread breaches of a universal law and order. Literature and the arts nourished themselves. Internal trade was active. Not since the eleventh century had the Japanese enjoyed any such period of peace.

The men at the top of this society, however, had not inherited the genius of Tokugawa Ieyasu, its founder. What had been a cool and deliberately chosen effort to stabilize a national society in a given mold gave way to a blind insistence on the status quo. The degree of the isolation they imposed deceived them, the rulers, as fully as it deceived the ruled.

The Japanese people, sealed off by decree from any contact with the world outside, were kept as comfortable as the barriers and the extent of their walled cocoon permitted. The shock of the Renaissance, nationalism and the Industrial Revolution in the West was scarcely felt. The reports of what had happened, filtered through the Dutch trading post in Nagasaki, were listened to with only passing interest by the officials of the Shogun's court.

Ultimately, notwithstanding the Tokugawa's caution, some of the forces and shocks that were then changing the face and the mind of Europe gathered of themselves inside Japan. The cocoon they had devised was not insulated against violent change from within. If the laws remained static, the people who used them did not. pressures—social, economic and political—began to rise beneath the calm surface. They were made the more violent by the completeness of the vacuum in which they worked. Finally, with explosive force, the world of Tokugawa burst. The web society of feudal Japan faced the world, promising to turn into something quite different from what Tokugawa Ieyasu had imagined.

3
THE NATIONAL FACE LIFTING

> "Whatever progress the world may see,
> Pray, let us abide by the law of our Land,
> Which is of yore."
>
> *Emperor Meiji*

Just 83 years too soon for a ride in his grandson Hirohito's grey Cadillac, the Emperor Mutsuhito, then a soldierly looking boy of fifteen, journeyed north to Tokyo, over the broad and dusty track of the *Tokaido*. He rode in a specially built carriage, a lacquered palanquin hung with silk-gauze curtains to keep the crowds along the road from seeing his face. Four bearers of equal height and equal strength carried the palanquin on their shoulders, jogging along the eastern coastal plain of Shizuoka and the bare hill barriers to the north of the Izu Peninsula, at a fairly uniform rate of 12 miles per day.

As the imperial palanquin passed the new foreign settlements at Yokohama, the few Western traders and diplomats who had settled there looked on with the gape of visitors from another age. About a thousand soldiers marched around the palanquin, in ragged groups of from 40 to 200, some wearing snippets of Western-style military uniforms, others dressed in the cloaks and flowing trousers of the old *samurai* costume, with the two long swords of their rank fastened at their belts. There were several dissonant bands, playing odd patches of music which no one recognized—the Imperial Anthem of Japan had not yet been invented. As the Emperor passed, followed by the palanquin of his advisor, Prince Iwakura, and the retinues of several court nobles and provincial *daimyo*, the crowds along the way bowed deeply. No one spoke a word.

November, 1869, was the last time that Mutsuhito ever traveled in a palanquin. It was the last month of his residence in Kyoto, where his ancestors had held their court since the eighth century. He was coming to establish a new capital in the old moated palace which had been used by the Tokugawa Shoguns, in the city of Edo, which the first of the Tokugawas had founded. With his arrival Edo was renamed Tokyo, "The Eastern Capital." Mutsuhito himself took the imperial name of Meiji, which means "Era of Enlightenment." His trip symbolized the change over which he presided. It has been given his name—the Meiji Restoration.

The Meiji Restoration was probably the greatest national transformation in history. In the space of one generation the Japanese, by their own efforts, changed themselves from a stagnant feudal culture, powerless to defend itself against the machine civilization of the European West, into a modern world power, vital and vigorous, the arbiter of Asia's future. There is nothing quite comparable to it in history—the twentieth-century modernization of Turkey, the nearest parallel, falls far short of approaching it, either in scale or in efficiency. Its effects exploded in the lives of the Japanese—the fathers and grandfathers of Sanada, Kisei, Shimizu and Yamazaki—like a long-continuing series of quake and tremor, which has not yet ceased to disturb and confuse. But it was not a revolution. Its name "Restoration" was chosen well. It not only compromised with the structure of the Japanese web society, it succeeded through and because of that society. It is classic "evidence," as Sir George Sansom has put it, "of the way in which a society can decay and renew itself without changing its essence."

* * * * *

It is customary to say that Commodore Matthew Perry and his U.S. Navy squadron "opened" Japan to contact with the modern world in 1854, when they extracted from the Tokugawa Shogunate a reluctant agreement to open certain Japanese ports to foreign trade.* A quick look at the events of the Meiji Restoration, following so fast on the heels of Perry's entry and the arrival of other European and American ambassadors, has often led to the conclusion that the antiquated hermit society of Japan, stable enough by itself, was smashed and dislocated at the first impact of collision with the twentieth-century West. In reality, Perry's mission, and those that followed it, was only the detonator that set off the long pent-up energies for change and expansion, that gathered their explosive power during the years of isolation. The Meiji Restoration can be explained only in the context of the years that preceded it. How the upheaval happened, and what shape

---

* Perry's first letter to the "Emperor" of Japan, dated July 7, 1853, was a polite example of gun-boat diplomacy. An extract:

". . . The undersigned holds out all these arguments in the hope that the Japanese government will see the necessity of averting unfriendly collision between the two nations, by responding favorably to the propositions of amity, which are made in all sincerity.

"Many of the large ships-of-war destined to visit Japan have not yet arrived in these seas, though they are hourly expected; and the undersigned, as an evidence of his friendly intentions, has brought but four of the smaller ones, designing, should it become necessary, to return to Yedo in the ensuing spring with a much larger force

"But it is expected that the government of your imperial majesty will render such return unnecessary, by acceding at once to the very reasonable and pacific overtures. . . ."

The return was rendered necessary, although there was no further threat of military action. The treaty was signed in March, 1854.

it took—these were decided by a set of circumstances, both international and domestic, peculiar to the mid-nineteenth century. But that an upheaval would occur was made inevitable by what had gone on for over two centuries before.

The rigid clan system was the legacy of the shogunate that made some violent change inevitable. It had erected unscalable barriers between levels of society, arbitrarily chosen and arbitrarily maintained. The *samurai* came first, privileged noblemen who had the right and obligation to wear swords,* keep the peace and refrain from any degrading occupations like farming or trade. The farmers were next in rank, then the artisans and merchants. They all had relatively few rights, except what the *samurai* accorded them.

Forced by law into perpetuating this caste system, the Japanese found themselves drifting into the same three-cornered free-for-all that wrecked the harmony of medieval Europe—the nobility versus the farmers versus the rising merchant class. Within the framework of Tokugawa Japan, there was no possibility for averting this conflict, or for compromising, once it began. By the early nineteenth century, explosive but inevitable changes had taken place within the boundaries of each class group.

After two centuries of peace, the feudal nobility had become a parasite class. At the time of the Meiji Restoration there were two million people of *samurai* rank in Japan. There was no fighting for the *samurai* to do. In fact, the government watched them very closely to be sure that they were given no chance to lapse into the old feudal routine of clan battles. The provincial lords like Maeda of Kaga and Shimazu of Satsuma, to whom Shimizu's and Kisei's grandfathers owed their allegiance, were themselves kept as weak as possible, to forestall the possibility of any Tokugawa rivals. They were continually ordered to

---

* This included the right of *Kirisute gomen*, by which a *samurai* could cut down any commoner without fear of punishment, if he were displeased with him.

build expensive public works, so that their treasuries would never be full enough to plot a successful revolution. They were also, as was the Shogun himself, hobbled financially by the necessity of keeping their *samurai* retainers and their families.

After thus clipping the *samurai* wings, however, the Tokugawa insisted on keeping them caged. In a healthier society, the *samurai* would have gradually become small farmers or tradesmen, losing their identity as a class, as the changing times and their reduced economic circumstances demanded. This happened often in earlier times in Japan, when social distinctions—except on the level of the emperor and his court—were elastic. But the Tokugawa did not want to run the risk of the possible disturbances that might accompany any changes in the social structure. They had based their rule, at the first, on a policy of "divide and rule" towards the clans. As long as no clan or combination of nearby clans was strong enough to challenge it, the central government could depend on the clan structure to keep order, enforcing its commands by levies on the provincial rulers and the *samurai* at their disposal.

The weight of this stratified system fell heavily on the younger—and poorer—*samurai*. The inconsistency between their stratified position and their actual poverty and uselessness was clear. Many of them were able, fairly well-educated and certainly not resigned to continuing as a hopeless parasite class. Some, like the young Fukuzawa Yukichi, who later became one of Japan's greatest Western scholars, were openly rebellious. In his *Autobiography*, he cited an exasperating example of the restraints inherent in a clan society:

"Since all the *samurai* of small means keep no servants, they were obliged to go out and do their own shopping. But, according to the convention among the warrior class, they were ashamed of being seen handling money. Therefore, it was customary for *samurai* to wrap their faces with small hand towels and go out after dark whenever they had an errand to do.

"I hated having a towel on my face and have never worn one. I even used to go out on errands in broad daylight, swinging a wine bottle in one hand, with two swords on my side as becomes a man with *samurai* rank.

" 'This is my own money,' I would say to myself, 'I did not steal it. What is wrong with buying things with my own money?' Thus, I believe, it was with a boyish pride and conceit that I made light of the mock gentility of my neighbors."

As the *samurai* grew poorer and more numerous, they squeezed more from the farmer, whose rice was still the basis of the nation's economy. Working at the apex of an inverted pyramid of parasites, there was slight incentive for the farmer to till his soil. Thousands of farmers began to leave their land to flee to the cities, where they were swallowed up in the mobs of poor, sick and homeless begging for jobs as hangers-on of the merchants.

Many were goaded into open rebellion. Through the 250 years of the Tokugawa Shogunate, there were almost a thousand cases of peasant uprisings, all of them crushed with brutality. In the last 80 years of the Shogunate, the number and the pitch of these revolts grew very serious. The scorched land of the rebel, or the broken hut of the man who had fled were not unusual sights on the Tokugawa landscape. The ruin of Oliver Goldsmith's English Deserted Village was reproduced on a similar scale.

Some of the uprisings were protests against the high-handed policy of the government in removing feudal barons from their fiefs, or transferring them suddenly from one holding to another. A kind or a just master made a considerable difference in the living of the average Japanese farmer. But a farmer was generally driven to take arms by a more general disaster—his inability to buy the rice which he had grown in his own fields. In 1837 the armed representatives of some 1,400 farmers in the province of Settsu sent the following complaint to their governors:

"With both the high price of rice and the prevalence of epidemics, there have been many who have died. Since spring twenty out of every hundred have died of starvation and this fall, during the last ninety days, half of the people have died. We ask that just government be applied towards us." *

The farmer's misery was often the merchant's profit. In the trading centers of the cities a class of traders had developed, whose wealth grew far out of proportion to its humble place in the social scale. Like the brokers of medieval Europe, these men lent money to the *daimyo* and the *samurai* and acquired power over them. The wealthiest were able to buy titles. All of them, by their stranglehold on what little finances the country had, subtly built up their influence to the point where it was a factor that shaped the Shogun's policy. Some worked on a smaller scale, in the villages, loaning money to the hard-pressed farmers. They kept up their contacts in the cities, and fed the stream of trade that flooded the marts of Osaka.

These merchants were forcing the country from a rice to a money economy. They controlled the Shogun's treasury, borrowed and loaned among themselves through the great exchange houses that sprouted to handle their business, and stimulated the growth of commodity buying. The culture of the country showed their touch. Japan was one of the first nations, Oriental or Occidental, to fashion a vigorous bourgeois art and literature, gusty, affluent, and popular. The flashy beauties of artists like Kunisada and Kuniyoshi, sensual-mouthed women dressed in gay, gaudy clothes, are the monument of their great admirer: the prosperous town merchant, uninterested in politics, higher art, or what went on outside the trading marts, the *kabuki* theatres or the gorgeous brothels of Yedo and Osaka.

The merchants were the only contented element in Tokugawa Japan—and even this would be overstatement. The more ambitious among them were restless for foreign

* Quoted in Hugh Borton's *Peasant Uprisings in Japan*.

outlets, uncomfortable at having to channel all their energies and money-making abilities into the inland waters of the isolated domestic economy. The most intelligent saw that they sat on a flimsy social and economic structure, doomed to fall of its own weight.

* * * * *

It was an immense shock for this smoldering feudal society to find itself thrown face to face with the industrial West of the eighteen fifties. Fortunately for the Japanese, Perry represented a remote continental power which was interested more in trading privileges than in territorial acquisitions. This was not true of the Europeans who made their own treaties with Japan on the heels of the Americans. By the middle of the nineteenth century, the Victorian drive for empire had stretched past captured India to the Far East. Hong Kong was snipped off from China in 1842 and adventurous Englishmen were pouring into Canton to get rich quick in the opium trade. The French, who had already bombarded the coast of Annam, were not far behind the British in their marauding. From their colonies in the north, the Russians had begun to cast interested glances at the island of Hokkaido.* Adding up

---

* By the beginning of the nineteenth century, the Russians had already annexed several of the Kurile Islands to the north of Hokkaido, which were then inhabited and nominally controlled by the Japanese. Before the time of Perry's expedition, the Russians had also made some unsuccessful overtures at opening trade negotiations with Japan. On August 22, 1853, a Russian squadron appeared in Nagasaki harbor —just a month and a half after Perry's ships had anchored near Tokyo. The Russians asked, then and subsequently, for some trading privileges of their own. At the end of 1854, these were granted by the Japanese—but only with considerable reluctance, for the interest which the Russians had been showing in exploring the coasts of Hokkaido and the Kuriles made the Japanese very suspicious of their political motives.

It distressed the Russians to find Perry and the Americans successful in a task which they had been attempting since the time of Catherine the Great. They had hoped for a position in Japan, far more privi-

Japan's tangible assets at this time, there was nothing which could have prevented the traders and the gunboats of any Western power from doing business on their own terms. It seemed probable that Japan would go the way of India and China, and soon succumb to European colonizers.

From this fate the Japanese saved themselves. The margin of their escape was two qualities which the larger countries, although their cultures were older and richer, lacked: the genius for adapting foreign institutions, already proved in the great borrowings from China, and a deep, precocious sense of nationalism, not yet exploited, but needing only the right events and the right people to bring it to life. When the Westerners came to Japan, they found no blind native confidence of superiority, as they did in China, to keep the Japanese from studying and adapting Western institutions. There was no racial and cultural disharmony, as in India, to keep the Japanese from uniting under a tight political control. Where the older nations either fought the West directly, or stumbled on under its impact, refusing to believe that anything untoward had happened, Japan was resilient. The Japanese quickly realized that they could not expel the nineteenth-century traders in the manner in which they had dealt with the Portuguese of the seventeenth century. They accepted the new elements, learned what they had to teach, then worked hard at blending them with the national culture.

In the nineteenth century, just as they had in the seventh and eighth centuries, the Japanese readily went into the import business. But the new drive to swallow foreign institutions came from below. There was no Prince Shotoku to send emissaries to China, no sophisticated court demanding famous painters and religious teachers from abroad. It was the discontented young

---

leged than what the treaty of 1854 guaranteed them. It was probably lucky for the Japanese, again, that the Crimean War then temporarily took the attention of the Russian government away from expansion in the Far East.

samurai of the lower ranks, scattered in every clan of Japan, who now started the search after Western learning. Courageous and well-educated, but frustrated by poverty and the lack of useful occupations, they found an outlet for their ambition in Western studies. Even before Perry's expedition, a thin trickle of European books had seeped through the wall of Tokugawa isolation. Students came to talk and to study with members of the tiny Dutch trading mission in Nagasaki. They took their learning, and, occasionally, a few books away with them and in turn established schools elsewhere in Japan.

A few resourceful Japanese succeeded in escaping to the West, although the Tokugawa government strictly enforced the death penalty prescribed since 1636 for any attempt by a Japanese to visit the outside world. Jo Niishima was probably the most remarkable of these refugees. At the age of nineteen, he swam out to an American whaler anchored in the harbor of Hakodate, Hokkaido, and asked the crew members to take him to the United States. The captain of the whaler took him to New England, where he studied at Amherst College and Andover Theological Seminary. He came back to Japan, an ordained Congregational Minister, to found Doshisha University, the oldest Japanese Christian college, in 1866.

While Perry's squadron was anchored off Shimoda, in 1853, two young *samurai* named Isagi Kooda and Kanzuchi Manji, approached some of the officers from the U.S.S. *Powhattan* on shore and furtively handed them a letter:

"Two scholars from Yedo, in Japan, present this letter for the inspection of the high officers. Our attainments are few and trifling, as we ourselves are small and unimportant, so that we are abashed in coming before you. . . . We have, however, read in books and learned a little by hearsay, what are the customs and education in Europe and America, and we have for many years been desirous of going over the 'five great continents,' but the laws of our country on maritime points are very strict. . . . Our wish to visit other regions has only gone to and fro in our own breasts in continual agitation, like one's breathing being impeded or his walking cramped. Happily, the arrival of so many ships in these waters, and their stay for so many days . . . has also revived the thoughts of many years, and they are urgent for an exit. . . ."

The Americans had to deny the hopeful tourists their passage, and they were quickly imprisoned by the local Japanese authorities. But within the next ten years, the numbers of young men trying to reach some contact with the world outside grew too serious to be dealt with as a penal problem.

The first step in acquiring Western learning was to learn Dutch, since the Dutch merchants of Deshima were the only foreigners with whom the Japanese had any regular contact. Dutch grammars and dictionaries were the most valuable commodities in the country for the new scholars. Many sold their *samurai* swords to get money to buy or even to copy one. After getting the tools for further study, they turned to treatises on fortifications, gunnery or practical science written or translated into Dutch.

The appearance of European and American warships had stimulated a rather fearful curiosity about the Western engines of war, which the Tokugawa thought they had done with, when they expelled the Portuguese merchants. In 1863, after some *samurai* from the southern province of Satsuma had murdered an Englishman, a British fleet bombarded the harbor of Kagoshima, the Satsuma capital. In the following year, European warships shelled Shimonoseki, the principal port of the neighboring Choshu clan, after some attacks on Western shipping. These two embarrassing incidents gave the chieftains of Satsuma and Choshu a pressing incentive to study up on the new tactical doctrines. Soundly applying the theory "If you can't lick 'em, join 'em," the Japanese in Satsuma and Choshu became extraordinarily friendly to contact with Westerners, and the import of Western learning. They soon outstripped all the other clans in learning and applying Western military techniques.*

The industry of the new students was heroic. Probably for the only time in history, the zeal and traditions of a military class were hurled into a mass attempt to acquire book learning. Fukuzawa Yukichi tells how he and some fellow-students, at a school of the Western learning in Osaka, stayed up all night, frenziedly copying by hand the text and diagrams of the 150-page-long section on electricity in a Dutch science book, which they had borrowed for a day from its jealous owner. At going prices, the book was worth 80 ryo, the equivalent in those days of $200 now. Working literally from the books they read, they manufactured medicines and chemicals, dissected corpses, and experimented with modern iron-plating processes. They had to make even the pens and ink used for study. (Japanese ink was suitable only for brush writing.)

Fukuzawa himself is a good illustration of this da Vincian scope of interest. He taught his countrymen elementary geography and chemistry, the construction and handling of modern rifles, double-entry bookkeeping and the art of public speaking. He published one of Japan's first daily newspapers. In 1868 he founded Keio University in Tokyo, now one of the Big Three of Japanese educational institutions. Twice Fukuzawa traveled to Europe and the United States—first in 1859 as a member of the Japanese mission sent by the Shogun, to the United States, later as a representative of the new Meiji government in Europe. Further along in his *Autobiography*, he tells of his European trip:

"So whenever I met a person whom I thought to be of

---

* The British who gave Satsuma its lesson in naval tactics were equally practical about sharing their knowledge. After British naval gunfire had all but destroyed the city of Kagoshima, the Satsuma clan officials obediently apologized for the Englishman's murder and paid a heavy indemnity. Then the British diplomatic representative, Lt. Col. Neale, rather in the spirit of a vacuum cleaner salesman after a successful demonstration of his product, readily agreed to assist the clan in purchasing modern warships of its own.

some consequence, I would ask him questions and would put down all he said in a notebook. . . . For instance, when I saw a hospital, I wanted to know how it was run— who paid the running expense; when I visited a bank, wished to learn how the money was deposited and paid out. By similar first-hand queries, I learned something of the postal system and the military conscription then in force in France, but not in England. A perplexing institution was representative government.

"When I asked a gentleman what the 'election law' was and what kind of an institution the Parliament really was, he simply replied with a smile, meaning I suppose that no intelligent person was expected to ask such a question. But these were the things most difficult of all for me to understand. In this connection, I learned that there were different political parties—the Liberal and the Conservative—who were always 'fighting' against each other in the government.

"For some time it was beyond my comprehension to understand what they were 'fighting' for, and what was meant, anyway, by 'fighting' in peacetime. 'This man and that man are "enemies" in the House,' they would tell me. But these 'enemies' were to be seen at the same table, eating and drinking with each other. I felt as if I could not make much out of this. It took me a long time, with some tedious thinking, before I could gather a general notion of these separate mysterious facts . . ."

* * * * *

The Meiji Restoration, for all its Western innovations, was hardly a case of a progressive young faction with new ideas ousting a reactionary group with old ideas. If Westernization alone had been its goad and inspiration, such a violent national effort would not have been possible. Fortunately for their cause, the Western-minded opponents of the shogunate were able to call to their help a powerful tradition from their country's past. Throughout the late eighteenth and early nineteenth centuries, the abuses of corrupt officials, the famine in the fields and the fiscal bankruptcy in the treasury, the crumbling power of the shogun's armies had all ripped apart the mythical screen of Tokugawa invincibility. As the shreds were torn away, beneath them, partially disguised by the hindering mass of custom and religious observance which the shoguns had set up around it, stood the Japanese throne, still the center of the national polity, as intact and well preserved as the buried walls of Heinrich Schliemann's Troy.

Although the Tokugawa, following the precedent of earlier shoguns, never attempted to do away with the emperors, they did their best to hide the throne from view. The immediate ancestors of the Emperor Meiji lived and died in a brocaded cloister. They were kept under heavy surveillance and prevented by the shogunate from making any direct contact with the feudal clan leaders. Their civil lists were carefully pared, so that they were barely sufficient for keeping up a modest court life in Kyoto.

In Meiji's youth, however, the rumblings of discontent throughout the country could no longer be muffled by the palace walls. In 1864 they materialized into street fighting on the palace doorstep, when some extremist troops from Choshu tried forcibly (but unsuccessfully) to "rescue the Emperor from his bad advisors," a formula which later became quite prominent in Japanese politics. The Emperor was well prepared for crises like this by the realistic education which his father insisted he should have. His tutors, Prince Iwakura and Prince Sanjo, were two of the shrewdest leaders of the Meiji Restoration. As the shogun's police powers began to fail, they and other court noblemen broke the centuries-long isolation of Kyoto from the rest of the country and made contact and common cause with the restless leaders of the clans.

Outside the court, Japanese scholars had long since begun to revive the dusty doctrines of imperial Shinto with the enthusiasm of medieval schoolmen rediscovering Aristotle. Beginning as a reaction against the unexciting Confucianism of the Tokugawa, they ended by producing a definite restatement of Japan's divine mission and the divine ancestry of the Emperor. Seen by the light of this scholarship, which reached back to the days of the centralized government of Prince Shotoku, the Tokugawa were crude interlopers. The leader of these scholars, Motoori Norinaga, wrote in the late eighteenth century, "Our imperial country is the great center of all countries, and is their parent. Our just and true way has been given to us. . . . If you ask what kind of a way this is, I will answer that it is not a way that naturally exists in the universe. Neither is it a made way. I hesitate even to mention this way, depending as it does on our ancestral gods. It is called the Way of the Gods, because Amaterasu received it from Izanagi and Izanami and transmitted it to her descendants."

In the static air of the mid-nineteenth century, sparks like this finally caught fire. A revived loyalty to the emperor, so long underplayed in Japan, became the magic ideal which soldered together the strange alliances of Meiji. As the Shogunate, weakened internally, showed its inability to cope with foreign demands on Japan—now that the country had been "opened,"—the big "outside" clans,* led by Satsuma and Choshu, began to plot the overthrow of the Tokugawa. They were given the outright backing of the Imperial Court. They found their one rallying point in the person of the young Emperor Meiji, descendant of the Sun-Goddess, according to the scholars, and the symbol of Japan's divine nationhood. Tracts, books and speeches about the new role of the Emperor multiplied. A surge of wild chauvinism swept over Japan. Angry at the menacing gestures of the foreign warships, fearful of foreign conquest, the masses of Japanese

---

* The "outside" clans (*tozama*) were the fiefs of the 86 feudal chieftains who had submitted to Tokugawa rule only after the decisive Battle of Sekigahara (1600). Not friendly to the shogunate, they submitted grudgingly, and bided their time until they might be strong enough to accomplish its overthrow.

took up the imperial cause as the badge of anti-foreignism. "*Sonno joi*—Revere the Emperor and destroy the barbarians" became the war-cry of the clansmen. The foreign traders and diplomats who had recently arrived in Japan, were attacked in the streets. In 1863 British and French troops were landed to protect the new trading port of Yokohama.

In the rush of anti-foreignism, the young students of the West also suffered. Some of them were killed or assassinated. Fukuzawa himself had several bad times with ruffians in the streets of Tokyo. But they laid low, kept their heads, and ultimately used the enthusiasm of the anti-foreign mobs as a tool of their program to import foreign learning. It was a queer sort of alliance, as if the merchants and students of eighteenth-century England, inspired by the inventions and promise of the Industrial Revolution, had joined a revolutionary political movement which reasserted the divine right of kings.

Under this dual assault the shogunate crumbled. On the one hand it had been attacked as the barrier to Westernization; on the other, as the government which now made treaties with the foreigners, paving the way, as the anti-Western faction charged, for European domination of Japan. The clans were in open revolt against the Shogun, and there were too few troops and too scant popular support at his command to reassert any of his old authority. In 1867 the last Shogun, Tokugawa Keiki, publicly turned over his power to the young Emperor. After some confused last-ditch fighting between the Tokugawa supporters and the Imperialists, the change of government was completed.

On January 25, 1868, Meiji formally began his new rule. His *samurai* and court advisors, backed by the power of the great military clans, took over the mechanism of government. Before his journey up to Tokyo, Meiji pronounced his Charter Oath to the new officials in Kyoto. Its five articles held the promise of a great national revolution. They read:

1. Deliberative assemblies shall be established and all matters be decided by public opinion.
2. The whole nation shall unite in carrying out the administration of affairs of state.
3. Every person shall be given an opportunity to pursue a calling of his choice.
4. Absurd customs and practices of the past shall be discarded and justice shall be based on the laws of heaven and earth.
5. Wisdom and knowledge shall be sought all over the world in order to establish firmly the foundations of empire.*

It was doubtful, on the face of things, whether the great things which the Emperor promised could soon occur. To bring order out of the Japanese nation in 1868 required a strong and single-minded ruling authority. For this, the factions which had put Meiji on his throne—the Westernizers, the rockbound traditionalist *daimyo* from the provinces, the mobs in the streets shouting "Death to the foreigners"—were hardly the best harness-mates.

The men who here unified and saved Japan were the same lower *samurai* who had given most of their time to Western learning. They turned out to be as good statesmen, or better, than they were scholars. Of all the factions behind the Restoration, they alone saw the big issue clearly—the only hope for Japan as a nation was to transform itself into an industrial country with a politically advanced government, capable of resisting the threats of the European powers. They realized that the transformation must be made quickly. Some of the foreigners, watching Japan's ferment, had already begun to assert the views which they put into practice, when dealing with China. Sir Harry Parkes, appointed British Minister in 1864, at first ordered the officials of the new Japanese foreign of-

---

* The Japanese in which the five articles are written is involved and vague in its exact meaning. I have used here the version given by Chitose Yanaga, in *Japan Since Perry*.

fice to remain standing, during the length of their conferences with him.

There can be no exaggerating Japan's helplessness. There was no army or navy; until the disciplined Choshu Army imported good rifles in large quantity, the feudal *daimyo* still based their power on the two-handed sword. The administration of government had crumbled and the desperate condition of the farmers and the poor *samurai* was not relieved by the simple act of the Emperor Meiji moving his capital to Tokyo. The treasury was bankrupt. The new foreign trading had badly dislocated the economy. The shogunate's ratio of gold to silver, fixed centuries before, was still 1:5. The world's going rate, at the same time, was 1:15. When foreign traders found out about this, they rushed in to convert silver at the Japanese price. By 1868 the traders had milked Japan of most of its gold reserve, at tremendous profit. The Japanese looked on with the puzzled indignation of the dupe in an international shell game.

The lower *samurai*, taking over the government, perceived very sharply that international conditions did not permit the leisurely stone-by-stone process of setting up a new government and a new way of life for the nation. A revolution would have been fatal. The mechanism of the Japanese state had to be drastically reformed or changed. but it had to be kept running at the same time. The one aspect of Japanese life which the Meiji reformers wanted to preserve, was the renewed sense of imperial loyalty, now stronger for the change than it had been for over seven centuries. On this the reforms pivoted. The web society was pruned but resolutely retained—and all the physical changes of Meiji were fitted into its context. Deliberately the young leaders checked, stunted and disciplined the social transformations that might have come with their economic and political improvements—like the doting Japanese gardeners who make tiny, ageless dwarf trees from the seedlings of giant pines.

* * * * *

Installed in the new capital of Tokyo, the men who had started Japan's Westernization from below now enforced it from above. A series of edicts came crashing down on the heads of the bewildered Japanese. Western learning was introduced in the schools. In 1871, attendance at a new national network of elementary schools was made compulsory. Military conscription was introduced. The Gregorian calendar was substituted for the old Japanese system of lunar dates. In 1872 the First National Bank of Tokyo was founded. Six years later the Stock Exchange opened.

There was no part of Japanese life that was not touched, twisted, altered or destroyed. In 1870 the common people were allowed to use surnames (a practice previously unknown). In 1875 they were ordered to. The old feudal codes of Tokugawa times were abolished. The *samurai* were destroyed as a class. By decree the common people (specifically referred to as *heimin*) were given most of the basic freedoms then existing in the parliamentary regimes of the West. The old *samurai* topknot was banned and Western haircuts were forcibly popularized in the most sweeping barbering reform since Peter the Great made the Russians shave their beards. An orderly system of tax collection was installed, based on money, not on rice.

In Tokyo the Emperor Meiji appeared at all formal functions, dressed either in Western uniform, or in a swallowtail coat with a high silk hat. For the first time in a thousand years, an emperor appeared regularly among his people. The old palanquin was discarded in favor of a coach-and-four. In 1870, through his ministers, Meiji commanded the court nobility to discard the custom of shaving their eyebrows and blackening their teeth—a ritual which had survived since the eighth century.

To enable Japan to hold its own militarily with the industrial West, centuries of European economic evolution were accomplished by fiat. The Japanese built steel mills before they had perfected small cottage looms. To run the expensive new factories, the big merchants of Osaka and Tokyo formed government-subsidized trusts, beginning the strange interrelation of government and business in Japan, which lasted, in this form, until 1945. (See Chapter 10.)

The small farmers had to support this first wave of industrialization. It was not a happy role. Shocked and angered by the changes in their life, some farmers went out at night to rip up the new telegraph poles which the government had planted in their fields. Many refused to spare their sons from the work of the fields to attend the new compulsory public schools. The strong hand of the new government, however, kept them from continuing the open revolts of the Tokugawa days. Nor was there any focus or abstract justification for their discontent. However galling were the reforms of Meiji, they were carried out by the feudal *samurai* to whom the people owed their only immediate loyalty, and in the name of the system and the man, Meiji, on whom their loyalties and their morality were based.

Most of the younger *samurai* shared the enthusiasm of the new government. They found that here, suddenly, were boundless opportunities open for anyone with quick wits and ready intelligence. There was a surge towards Westernization like the rush of colonizers towards a newly opened frontier. The covered-wagon imigrants of the United States would have felt at home with the frontier spirit in the mood of Meiji Japan.

The men born into the frontier days of Meiji stayed in power to enlarge on the foundations they had laid. Rarely in the history of any nation has there been such a wealth of bold innovators, efficient administrators and statesmen who could so accurately take the measure of their own country and its international neighbors. As more able recruits joined the handful of young government officials around Meiji, they formed a loyal and capable bureaucracy, which, well into the twentieth century, made as well as executed the policies of Japan.

Ito Hirobumi, who was made a prince by the Emperor Meiji, may not have been the most brilliant or the most original of the Meiji reformers; he was certainly, however, the best-known Japanese statesman of that day and one of the great political men of his century. He began his career as a young *samurai* in search of Western learning, quite like Fukuzawa Yukichi. Unlike Fukuzawa, Ito kept all his talents reserved for politics and diplomacy.

In 1863 he and another Choshu *samurai* slipped out of Yokohama harbor in a British steamship, bound for Europe. Defying the Shogun's order against foreign travel—then still in force—they spent a year patiently studying the wonders of Western civilization. They arrived in Japan just in time to warn their feudal superior, the *daimyo* of Choshu, against firing on foreign warships at Shimonoseki. After the sharp defeat by the guns of the European punitive expedition, the Choshu clansmen had reason to regret not listening to them.

After the Restoration, Ito came into his own. At 29, in 1868, he was made governor of Hyogo (now Kobe), one of the few places officially opened to foreign trade. (In the same year, he interpreted for the Emperor Meiji during the latter's first audience with foreign diplomats.) In 1870, as Vice Minister of Finance, he spent a year in the United States studying the monetary system. Less than a year after returning, he was off again to the United States and Europe with the Iwakura mission, a select group of Japanese observers, sent to study the political functioning of the Western powers.

As Minister of Public Works in the early Meiji government, he set up a railway system and installed the telegraph in Japan. He saw to it that the machinery of the Hong Kong mint was purchased intact and shipped to Japan for use. During one of his trips to Europe, he arranged for Western technical professors to come to Japan, where they started instruction at the first Japanese engineering college. Back in Japan, he occupied himself with—among other things—the creation of a system of Western-style lighthouses and the introduction of new methods and machinery in Japanese mines.

As Europe and the United States came to know him, Ito was the prototype of the intelligent Japanese student abroad, the tourist with a purpose. More accurately, in the context of Japanese history, he was the spiritual descendant of the priests and court officials who bravely left Japan in the seventh century to learn all that might be learned of Chinese culture.

Inside Japan, where he was four times Premier, Ito grew into a precocious elder statesman. He dedicated himself to consolidating by caution what he and others had won through boldness. He consistently tried to hold down the new militarists who came on the scene with the growth of the modern Japanese army. He favored neither the rapid expansion which the generals wanted, nor the dictatorial style of government which suited them best. But he was no man of the people. For many years even the idea of political parties appalled him; such divisions seemed to imply factionalism and disrespect for the Emperor. Until his death in 1906, he fought a consistent delaying action against the advocates of a real and widespread democratic government.

* * * * *

The careers of thousands of humbler Westernizers followed a similar pattern. In 1867, at the age of seventeen, Fumio Shimizu's father, Takefumi, succeeded to the headship of his family. Takefumi had already, for the two years of his father's illness, represented his father—and the family—at the castle of the lord of Kaga. Each day, following the old rules of the *samurai*, he reported at the gates of the castle to see if his services were needed. His father, Yojiro, on his deathbed charged his son to keep up the *samurai* tradition in his family, despite the changed times which already had doomed the *samurai* as a class.

Takefumi found that there was little money left him. His father was a scholarly aesthete who spent most of his days in the study of classical Japanese arts and poetry, like the precise 31-syllable *waka* or the short, satiric *haiku,* in which he was expert. These hobbies had trimmed down most of the family's quiet fortune. As he was unmarried, Takefumi sold his family's house in the nobles' district of Kanazawa, and moved in with his sister, who had married a local doctor.

It was after a visit to the turmoil of Meiji Tokyo that Takefumi returned home to tell his sister and brother-in-law of a shocking new idea. He had noticed, he said, in Tokyo that not only foreigners, but high government officials were wearing smooth foreign-style leather shoes. Many Japanese admired these shoes, obviously to be preferred over the native sandals. Anyone who could make these shoes in Japan could name his own price. It was a sure way to retrieve the depleted Shimizu fortunes.

The family was horrified. Shoemaking involved work with hides and skins. Traditionally, under the feudal system, this was a trade reserved for the *eta,* a pariah class at the very bottom of the Japanese caste system. Takefumi objected that the Meiji Restoration had abolished the old feudal class system. Therefore, there was neither stigma nor distinction in working with leather. But his brother-in-law, reinforced by the outcry of other branches of the family, won the argument.

When the government established a medical school, on the foreign pattern, in Kanazawa in 1870, Takefumi's brother-in-law urged him to enroll. Medicine was a sure and honorable career. Awkwardly he consented to go. After his preliminary studies, he went on to Tokyo to enter the Medical Department of Imperial University. Probably due to overwork he contracted a lung ailment shortly before graduating. His doctors advised him to return to live in the country, if he wanted to avoid being consumptive.

In 1878, Dr. Takefumi Shimizu hung out his shingle in the large market-town of Sanno, in Tochigi Prefecture in northern Japan. The next year he married a girl of good family from Tokyo and settled down to raise a family. He grew contented and conservative. Fumio was raised in the same *samurai* tradition that his grandfather had wanted to prevail. But it was many years before Dr. Shimizu gave up his secret conviction that he could have made a killing in the shoe business.

* * * * *

A number of *samurai*, unlike Shimizu, were unwilling to compromise with foreign culture and failed to see the necessity to do so. In the slogan "Revere the Emperor and destroy the barbarians" they meant the last proposition as seriously as they did the first. They were chagrined, after the Meiji Restoration succeeded, to see their leaders fraternizing with the foreigners and openly copying their institutions, instead of destroying them. For several years, cowed by the authority of the Emperor and swept along in the rush of popular enthusiasm, they gave no serious trouble. But almost ten years after the Restoration, in 1877, they broke out in open rebellion.

The leader of this counter-revolution was Saigo Takamori, a ponderously built man, with a deep, heavy face, whose emotions were as violent and as powerful as his body. Saigo is the tragic figure of the Restoration and one of the most fascinating studies in Japanese history. Far better than Ito, the smooth, rational conciliator, Saigo dramatized the central problem of most of Meiji's loyal subjects: how to reconcile the ancient dynamic loyalties of the Japanese race with the new, disturbing dynamism of Western ideas and Western customs.

Saigo, a trusted clansman of Satsuma, was one of the

leaders in overthrowing the Tokugawa. He saw as clearly as any of the reformers the absurdity of the nineteenth-century shogunate and the necessity of reviving the emperor's rule. Like some of the others, he had made a trip to Europe and America to inspect foreign military establishments. When he returned he put the conclusions formed by his observations into the training of the new Japanese army. In 1876, when he resigned from office, he was the army's commander-in-chief.

The Western ideas, however, did not reach very deeply into Saigo's consciousness. He was not, like Ito or Fukuzawa Yukichi, a man who had understood and believed in certain Western theories of politics, economics and even society. Saigo's morals were deeply Confucian, guided by the teachings of Chinese philosophers, whom he continued to study. He was passionately loyal to the Emperor, more so than most of the other leaders. His loyalty was purely traditional, scornful of the suggestions that the Emperor assume some of the aspect worn by European constitutional monarchs. The only Western improvements which Saigo wanted were guns and military equipment for the army. Barring this, he wanted Japanese culture left alone.

In 1875 Saigo wanted to invade Korea. Without bothering to strengthen the country internally, he demanded that the Army set off immediately on Japan's divine mission to assert the Emperor's authority outside the islands. Earnest and impulsive, he had no patience with the waiting game of politics which Ito and Meiji statesmen were playing. Saigo and his men were first of all *samurai*. There was nothing which the *samurai* spirit could not sweep before it.

When he was outvoted in the Cabinet, Saigo resigned and returned to his home in Satsuma, the most aggressive and the most conservative of the clan territories. He set up a military academy, which drew hundreds of idealistic young *samurai* from all over Japan. Others arrived besides the students, and Saigo became a focus of the discontent at the foreign ideas and the constitutional government in Tokyo. His students began to agitate openly against the government. In 1877, forced by his own canons of loyalty to back up the actions of some associates, who had prematurely attacked and seized the government arsenal in Kagoshima, Saigo took the field. He led a disciplined army of 15,000 Satsuma troops, the finest in Japan, against the army of the Emperor.

The battles of the Satsuma Rebellion were fought on the inhospitable ridges and slim valleys of central Kyushu, near Mt. Kirishima, the spot where the sword of Ninigi-no-Mikoto, the grandson of the Sun-Goddess, was reputedly found. Fittingly for the last stand of the traditionalists, the Satsuma Rebellion was decided largely by the two-handed sword. In the battles and skirmishes, the new Imperial Army was not yet skilled enough in the use of firearms to ward off the Satsuma swordsmen, who continually charged at close quarters.

But Saigo's troops, outnumbered, were driven back to Kagoshima, the Satsuma capital. Near there, at Shiroyama, on September 24, 1877, they were destroyed. Saigo, the reluctant rebel, wounded and beaten, ordered one of his retainers to kill him.

One of the Kyushu *samurai* who fought at Shiroyama was Hideya Kisei's grandfather, Sozo. Sozo, like his father before him, was a loyal retainer of Saigo and the *daimyo* of Satsuma. He had grown up, like Saigo himself, in the implacable discipline of the Satsuma clan, which produced strong swordsmen and great hunters. Sozo's wife and women-servants had always to wash the men's clothes in separate tubs from their own—so strict was the discrimination between the sexes.

When Saigo rode against the government, Sozo Kisei unquestioningly went with him. He rode to the siege of Kumamoto Castle, where Saigo almost succeeded in capturing a good-sized government army. After the battle of Tabarazuka, Sozo fled southward with the remnants of Saigo's troops, to his home in Kagoshima. He was never the same after the defeat. He spent the rest of his life hunting in the mountains, or drinking home-brewed Satsuma *sake* with his friends. Gradually he frittered away the family fortune, which had been considerable, selling off lands and buildings bit by bit. He seldom bothered with the upbringing of his five sons. Probably all that he left them was a legacy of loyalty to his dead chief. Saigo is still one of Hideya Kisei's heroes.

Saigo, the unsuccessful rebel against the Emperor, has been universally revered in Japan. The Emperor Meiji gave his son a title of nobility, not long after Saigo's death. Before World War II, he was eulogized in the schools of Japan as one of the nation's greatest heroes. There were few houses in the Japanese countryside that did not have tucked away somewhere a portrait of Saigo—the short, cropped hair, the sharp eyes, the huge, bull-like face and the tight-fitting military tunic of Western design. In 1949, when the boys attending a Boy Scout jamboree in Tokyo were asked who their favorite hero was, most of them answered without hesitation: "Saigo Takamori."

Saigo's popularity is partly due to his personality. Saigo was the Japanese version of Chevalier Bayard, the *chevalier sans peur et sans reproche* of fifteenth-century France. He is the man who spared Tokyo, in 1868, during the fighting between the Imperialists and the Shogun's troops, in order to save the lives of the civilian population. He is the classic idealized *samurai,* stern and repressive in his own tastes and those of his family, generous and sacrificing to those outside. He is above all the symbol of *samurai* loyalty. When his chief, the *Daimyo* of Satsuma banished him during his agitation for the Emperor's restoration, he uncomplainingly submitted, and stayed in banishment for eight years, patiently studying. He returned only when the *Daimyo* called him back. When his followers precipitated the rebellion against the government, he loyally agreed to lead it, although he was enough of a realist to know that it had little chance of succeeding.

No Japanese of his day thought Saigo disloyal for leading his armies against the Emperor. He fought, honestly, not against the Emperor, but to save the Emperor from his advisors. He was not merely leading a clan rebellion, or the revolt of a special interest. Saigo's motive was that of a loyal subject bound to try, by whatever means he had, to rescue his sovereign and the divine mission of Japan. Yet he was the perfect representative of the clan spirit within the Japanese which had been warring with the idea of centralized bureaucracy since the struggle of Taika in the seventh century. Saigo with his two-handed sword was a symbol like Bonnie Prince Charlie with his claymore— the last rallying point of the uncompromising clans and the man who followed the threads of the web society, wherever they took him.

His loyalty was perfect loyalty—hence, in the web society, perfect morality. For his own purposes he did not die in vain. His spirit kept haunting the conservative guardians of the web.

* * * * *

With Saigo defeated, the middle-roaders of Meiji had for the moment won their fight. There was no more opposition. They evolved the pattern of their changes steadily, with a rare instinct for just how much the country would and could absorb at a given moment. Their concrete accomplishments were as close to the miraculous as human deeds can get. By 1885 the economy had found its sea legs. New factories were humming and the drift of men and families from the land into the cities at last had some purpose to it. Prince Ito's newly strung telegraph wires had extracted much of the terror and the inconvenience from the divisive mountains. The rivers were being turned into electric power, and harsh electric light bulbs sparkled in the new cities. As a seal of the new changes, the Japanese armed forces decisively trounced the Chinese in the Sino-Japanese War of 1895, giving the rest of the Orient some foreboding thoughts about the future.

The great legislative monument of the reformers was the new Constitution, which the Japanese received in 1889. This created and legalized a system of representative government for the first time in the history of the Asiatic continent. A Diet of two houses was established to pass on legislation, a judiciary to interpret it, and an executive arm with premier and cabinet, representing the party in power in the Diet, responsible for initiating legislation and enforcing it. Provision for safeguarding the rights of the individual and of property were written into the Japanese Diet, which could justly claim a Bill of Rights included among its early articles.

With all these forward steps, the Meiji Constitution was still a type of government that was "given" to the Japanese, not demanded or in fact written by them. There was no constituent assembly or constitutional committee of elected delegates to draft it. The government, after a good deal of agitation by the more democratic of the Meiji reformers, methodically set out to create a law of the land that would be democratic without being dangerous or disorderly, representative without being in the least republican. Prince Ito, who was entrusted with drawing it up, traveled at length in Europe, examining the parliamentary systems of the West, before he put pen to paper. His handiwork most closely resembled the modified parliamentary democracy of Bismarck's Germany. But it was even more vulnerable to capture by anti-democratic forces within its structure.

There was no pretense at sovereignty being a right of the people. In the Emperor Meiji's Japan, it was a restricted gift from the ruler to his subjects. In the preamble to the Constitution, this was flatly stated:

"The rights of sovereignty of the State, We have inherited from Our Ancestors, and We shall bequeath them to Our descendants. Neither We nor they shall in future fail to wield them, in accordance with the provisions of the Constitution hereby granted."

All power, at least in a formal sense, resided in the person of the emperor. What rights his subjects had were generally specifically hedged. Article XXVIII, for example, the Japanese version of freedom of speech, said: "Japanese subjects shall, *within the limits of law,* enjoy the liberty of speech, writing, publication, public meetings and association." Article XXVII, providing for freedom of religion, said: "Japanese subjects shall, *within limits not prejudicial to peace and order, and not antagonistic to their duties as subjects,* enjoy freedom of religious belief." Such wording was enough to stack the cards against the individual before play had begun.

The Meiji reformers, in their Constitution, rejected the Western and the Christian concept that the rights of the individual were God-given and existed independently and outside of any laws or social orders. In the context of their time and their nation, they could not possibly have accepted it. The freedoms of the Constitution, as Prince Ito put it, represented "a concession to the people of a most invaluable right." The concession came from the emperor, who embodied the only absolute rights and the only absolute sovereignty that the Japanese could imagine.

In a speech to some constituents at Otsu, in the same year the Constitution was promulgated, Prince Ito elaborated on the somewhat contradictory aspects of Japanese representative government. "It will be evident," he said "that as the supreme right is one and indivisible, the legislative power remains in the hands of the Sovereign and is not bestowed on the people. . . . But the Sovereign may permit the representative body to take part in the process of practically applying the legislative right. . . . Nothing being law without a concurrence of views between the Sovereign and the people, the latter elect representatives to meet at an appointed place and carry out the view of the Sovereign." For the next fifty years the latter part of this nice-sounding sentence—just what was the view of the sovereign and how it made itself known—was a baffling and unsolved problem in Japanese politics.

With all these limitations the Meiji Constitution did give Japan a system of government that was potentially democratic. Political parties began to contest elections as soon as the machinery for contesting them was set up. In the eighteen nineties, while Chinese mandarins were still groveling at the Manchu court, a good percentage of the Japanese were voting in fair elections. The Japanese version of politicians, election campaigns, political slogans and interested voters had begun its long and interesting history.

* * * * *

On July 31, 1912, the Emperor Meiji died. Sakaji Sanada was twenty-three at the time, a healthy farm boy, about to finish his three years of compulsory military service with the cavalry training division in Tokyo. A few days later, as the long funeral procession passed down the avenues of the capital, Sanada stood, tightly buttoned, at attention, one of the thousands of soldiers who guarded the route. He never forgot the large deputations of foreign diplomats and soldiers who had come to pay their respects. As one of Meiji's loyal subjects, this homage from overseas made Sanada feel very proud.

Meiji's grandson Hirohito was then only eleven. He did not know his grandfather very well, since, by old imperial tradition, he was raised and educated in a separate household. Until the age of four, Hirohito had lived in the house of Viscount Kawamura, an old court noble chosen for this honor as a result of his happy family life and good character. Kawamura had accepted the responsibility with mixed gratitude and foreboding. "The soul of a three-year-old child will live until one hundred" was a proverb frequently quoted in court circles.

At seven, Hirohito was transferred to the Peers School in Tokyo, then in charge of General Nogi Maresuki. Nogi was entrusted with the special task of instructing the Emperor-to-be and his younger brothers in the duties of semi-divine rulers. He was an old-school *samurai* cut from the same bolt of cloth as Saigo Takamori, austere, unsparing and wedded to his duty. In the Russo-Japanese War of 1904-05, he had become Japan's foremost military hero, the captor of Port Authur and Mukden. He gave his new teaching job the same rigid loyalty that he had enforced in the field.

The day before Meiji's funeral, Nogi visited Hirohito and his two younger brothers, Chichibu and Takamatsu, at their apartments. He explained carefully to the princes that he had asked for permission to see them on that day, since he would be going out of town immediately, as an escort to the Duke of Connaught, who had arrived for the funeral. He was particularly solicitous of Hirohito. "It is needless to say this again," he told him, "but now that you are the Crown Prince, please study even harder. You are now also the youngest of the officers of the Army and the Navy—and their future commander-in-chief. [On his grandfather's death, Hirohito, as the new heir-apparent, was given a commission as a second lieutenant.] Therefore please pay attention to your military duties. You will be very busy, but I ask you also to take care of your health."

As he finished this exhortation, the soldier's voice broke. He handed Hirohito a book of Confucian moral precepts, one—he explained—which he had always treasured. Then, with an encouraging word to the prince's younger brothers, he left.

The following day, Nogi and his wife committed suicide in their simple house in the Tokyo suburbs, in obedience to the *samurai* ritual of *junshi*, the suicide of a faithful retainer (and his family) on the death of his lord. Japan wept added tears for his parting. It was a glorious feudal gesture, all agreed—even if made at the death of the man whose reign had seemingly dealt a fatal blow to the old Japanese feudalism. By any reckoning, it was a fit ending to an era that had in it the great, the bizarre and the unexpected.

In his reign of 33 years, the Emperor had watched the

first explosive and tentative changes of the Restoration carried through to a success that few of his advisors had hoped for. The Restoration was a triumph over extremes. Its authors had taken the variant ideologies and techniques and synthesized them. The merger was successful. Their dwarf tree was sprouting. They had produced the most brilliant undertaking of nineteenth-century statesmanship.

But the roots of the tree were delicate, its seeds had come from different climates. There was the tradition of Fukuzawa, inquiring, flexible, critical. It was a spirit that wanted to adapt itself to the culture of the West, without fear and, in many cases, without discrimination. There was the great but limited political heritage left by Ito, dedicated to the tricky proposition that a bureaucracy should rule as well as execute. There was the ghost of Saigo, which defeat had not been enough to lay low, chivalrous but uncompromising, hostile to foreign innovation, accepting it only under the pressure of necessity.

The web society of Japan was intact. Men who wore morning coats and bowler hats turned out to have the same instinct for community, the same responsibilities and the same loyalties as their fathers, who wore *kimono* and carried swords. But it was subject to divergent strains. On the one hand, the new industrialization, the telephone, the motorcar and foreign books acted on it corrosively, threatening in time to eat away its strands. Against this, there was the new stress on loyalty to the emperor, belief in Shinto and the divine mission of Japan. This ideal of Meiji showed itself far stronger and more inflammatory than the clan loyalties of the Tokugawa days. In strengthening them, it tightened the bonds of the web, gave it a purpose and a discipline which it had never had before.

It was the tragic destiny of the Japanese that their history, for the next half-century, should reflect a desperate struggle between these divergent forces, a struggle which almost ended happily, but ultimately hurled the nation to disaster.

4

THE PARALYZED DEMOCRACY

"And who knows why with so much labor he builds his house or how such things can give him pleasure? Like the dew on the morning glory are man and his house, who knows which will survive the other?"

—*The Hojoki*

Late in the winter of 1912, long after the last sightseer had scrambled down the ashy slopes of Mt. Fuji, Private First Class Sakaji Sanada walked back to his father's house in Shimoyoshida, his three-year term of military service over. The mountain, now pure white, lowered above the town as grandly as ever, sending its cold winds down against the defenseless wood and thatch. But Shimoyoshida itself was not as Sanada had left it. The changes of Meiji had been swiftly realizing themselves in the rural prefectures. Even in the three years of Sanada's absence, a measurable transformation had taken place. Not since the mountain had last erupted—in 1708—had the face of the town been so sharply altered.

Electric lights sputtered at night in the streets. Most of the farmers had already possessed themselves of the stark, uncovered bulb, hanging by its cord from the ceiling, that would forever after make a mockery of the neat aesthetic of their houses. When Sanada, still wearing his loose blue uniform, walked down to the lumber yard, he joined the crowd gaping at the new electric buzz saw, which the proprietors had just imported. As he recalls, it came from America. There was now a coal-burning locomotive running as far as Otsuki, 10 miles away, on the main Chuo line which ran between Shiojiri and Tokyo. From Otsuki travelers rode in a two-horse trolley as far as Yamura, a prosperous silk-producing village less than five miles from Shimoyoshida. From Yamura to Shimoyoshida, however, the road was still the rough, curving track it had been since Tokugawa days. A horse-drawn carriage managed to make the trip daily between the two towns.

The industry of Shimoyoshida was changing, also. As long as Sanada could remember, his father and other farmers had raised silkworms during the winter. Although the climate in Shimoyoshida was too cold for extensive seri-culture, they had kept it up to pad out the bare living which they got from their upland crops. Lately, looms had been imported to Shimoyoshida. Sanada's father, Semmatsu, installed two in his house—rough machines, not yet powered by electricity, but by water-wheels placed beside the mountain streams that poured down the slopes from Shimoyoshida to the plain below. The farmers now got their silk yarn in Otsuki, where silk culture was more profitable. By the early nineteen hundreds, with the rapid rise of foreign trade and a widening commodity market at home, they were turning out lining material for Japanese *haori*, as well as for Western style suits and topcoats. They made umbrella fabric and silk damask for export to Korea and China.

The rush of new objects and ideas buoyed Shimoyoshida to a level of aliveness it had never felt before. The streets still echoed from the delirious lantern parades that celebrated the battle of Tsushima, the capture of Port Arthur, and the victorious end of the Russo-Japanese War. Sanada and other recent army conscriptees jabbed their neighbors' curiosity, telling about the strange-looking craft they had seen flying in the skies during the military maneuvers of 1909. Merchants, for the first time, were able to travel down the mountain and ride the smoky railroad coaches to Tokyo. The parliamentary government had been cautiously extending the franchise. By 1900 all male citizens who had paid a property tax of at least 10 yen were eligible for the franchise. Semmatsu Sanada, as a respected elder statesman, was asked to watch over the campaign funds for the local branch of the *Seiyukai*, Japan's most popular new political party.

* * * * *

The activity which shook Shimoyoshida was only the distillation of a hectic popular awakening that took place throughout Japan. The Meiji *samurai* had instinctively counted on the disciplined web of Japanese society to act as a stabilizer through a brutally fast transition period. But new sights and new ideas apparently rushed to the brains of Japanese as readily as to Russians, Frenchmen or Americans. Socialist theories circulated widely, fed by the example of the rising revolutionaries in Russia. Proletarian parties were formed. In 1910 horrified police uncovered an anarchist plot to assassinate the Emperor.

The workers in the cities and the new factories began to organize to protect their rights. In December, 1911, the streetcar workers of Tokyo went out in a five-day strike, paralyzing the commerce of the city. They won it. Their demands were granted, plus a 100,000-yen bonus. Public opinion was growing as loud and as explosive as public opinion in the constitutional states of the West. There were riots in Hibiya Park, in Tokyo, not far from the Emperor's palace, to protest unpopular government actions like the Treaty of Portsmouth ending the Russo-Japanese War, which the average Japanese felt was too lenient to Russia and unfair to Japan. The bureaucracy which ran the government hurriedly tried to brake the swift course of reform, which they had started. The horseless carriage of Meiji seemed to be running out of control.

The epicenter of the new movements was Tokyo. There, in 1885, Fumio Shimizu arrived to study at the Engineering Department of Imperial University. He was nineteen years old, and had already spent three years studying at the Kagoshima Technical School, in Kyushu. Since the death of his father and his elder brother, he had also had to take over the responsibility of heading his family. Before moving to Tokyo, he rented a small house in the Meguro district. His mother, who had been left alone in Tochigi, the old family home in the north, came down to keep house for him.

At Teidai (the popular abbreviation for Imperial University) the gusts of Marxism, Benthamism, pacifism and ultra-nationalism were blowing with gale force through the new-planted ivy on the university walls. Although a large minority of the students still wore the native flowing Japanese dress of *haori* and *hakama*, with large wooden clogs, most had changed into the expressionless black uniforms, with high-collared tunics and small caps, like German *Studentenmütze*, which their sons still wear today. They had already taken on the characteristics which Japanese university students still have—noisy, emotional, idealistic, fanatic in their pursuit of new classroom theories, eager to find a barricade to defend them on outside. All the currents which agitated Japan could be found in microcosm on any university campus.

In Shimizu's time, echoing the revolutionary rumble from Russia, Marx was the great messiah. Although Shimizu was in the Engineering Department, a section of the university which he gratefully recalls "required no dreaming of wild dreams or arguments in its laws," he was not untouched by the enthusiasm of young Marxists studying Law and Literature. He read the commentaries on Marx that jammed the bookshelves in the shops near the university's tree-lined entries. His mother sometimes worried about him, back in their house, as he stayed at the university to join in the all-night gatherings of students who argued constantly over politics, philosophy, and sometimes, as he looks back, over "apparently nothing." Once, fresh from his university arguments, he tried to share his knowledge with outsiders. On a trip to the country near Kyoto, he delivered a speech on "Humanism as taught by Marx" to a patient group of country people. He remembers with embarrassment, "They didn't understand what I was talking about."

The intellectual pressure on Japanese students in those days was even greater than it is today, when they are still expected to assimilate the finer points of two cultures, the native Eastern and the Western, in an atmosphere muggy with German-style rote scholarship. Although almost all of the professors were Japanese, they had learned their subjects from Europeans and Americans, at a time when intellectuals cherished a great contempt for native scholarship. The professors took their own student prejudices into their new classrooms. Except for his own pleasure, Shimizu during his student days never read any books in Japanese. All of his Engineering textbooks were written in English. In Literature, English shared the honor of a teaching language with French. The faculties of Law and Medicine, however, leaned heavily on German. Professors generally gave their lectures in foreign languages. Half the words written on any blackboard were sure to be either English, French or German. If a student wanted to get a well-rounded education at Teidai, sooner or later he had to master at least two languages besides his own.

Most did this with gusto. Any book written in Japanese was felt to be automatically inferior. The same feeling extended to personalities. No matter how effective a Japanese professor seemed, his students shared a suspicion that they were only getting the new learning from him "second-hand."

The fascination for things foreign was often ludicrous, but even the students most affected by it kept a knife-edge distinction between foreign ends and foreign means.

The students at Teidai, in their way, were the descendants of the young *samurai* of Meiji, fascinated by foreign ways, but seldom forgetting that they must bolt down as much of the foreign learning as they could—for a fixed objective: the progress of Japan. The university student's greatest ambition was to become a civil servant, one of the bureaucracy which had raised Japan to its present place. His motive was not the security that drove so many European students later to prize the life of the *petit fonctionnaire*. It was an active desire to participate in the growing family life of the country.

Shimizu's own ambition took a slightly different bent. In 1915 the Japanese Navy advised all the universities that there were some openings for officer-technicians. This fit in with an idea of his own. In early 1914, at school in Kagoshima, he had heard of the Siemens bribery scandal, involving peculations by navy technicians. He decided at that time to apply for a job as a navy technician himself, partly to compensate by his own honesty for the disgrace which the others had brought upon Japan, partly from the practical consideration that, with so many officers cashiered in the bribery scandal, there would be a great many openings in the service. He was accepted. In 1917, as soon as he had been graduated from Teidai, Shimizu took the two-hour train trip from Tokyo, down the steep winding coast along the bay, to the naval base at Yokosuka.

He began his naval service with three months of basic training—"the only period during my entire naval career," he recalls, "when I engaged in anything which resembled soldiering." He was commissioned a *chui* (lieutenant, junior grade) at the end of his indoctrination, and sent to Kure to begin his career as an engineering technician at the arsenals there. For the next five years he supervised work at arsenals and ammunition plants in Kure and Maizuru, the northernmost of the four major Japanese naval bases.

At Kure all the machinery in Shimizu's ammunition plant was British made. In the Meiji era, the Japanese

Government had hired British technicians to supervise operations there—it was only a few years before he arrived, that the last British technicians had left. In the fall of 1923, Fumio Shimizu got a coveted chance to inspect the source of the machinery, the technicians and a major part of the foreign influences that had acted so strongly on him and his fellow-students in Tokyo. He received orders from the Navy Ministry to proceed to the Vickers Armaments Factory, in Dartford, England, to study the manufacture of machine guns.

In the early twenties most Japanese still regarded the act of going abroad as a great and rather fearful adventure. The awe of foreign travel instilled by the Tokugawa took a long time to die. The steamship companies, accordingly, offered the outgoing passenger—and his immediate family—free railroad tickets to Ise, where they could pray at the Grand Shrine for a safe voyage. Shimizu, an easy-going skeptic in matters of religious faith, was not interested in the free train trip. But his mother, a pious believer in Nichiren Buddhism (the most intense of Japanese popular Buddhist sects), insisted that he go. It was the first and last time that he visited the severe wooden buildings at Ise, rebuilt every sixty years by ancient order, the holiest shrine of Japanese nationalist religion. Moved by his mother's worries, he prayed for a few moments himself.

In November, impatient to get to his destination, Shimizu sailed from Kobe. He traveled in the tradition of Fukuzawa, Ito and others of the two generations before him, fascinated by the externals of Western civilization, and earnest about discovering what combination of human chemistry had produced them and made them succeed. He was the envy of his brother-officers. A trip to England meant a kind of spiritual pilgrimage for whoever took it— from the rising "island country" of the East to the old established island empire of the West.

Shimizu's route stretched along the props and outposts of the British Empire—Singapore, India, the Red Sea, then through the Suez Canal, into the Mediterranean, past

Gibraltar to England. The effect was not lost on him. "All along the route," he thought, "I have seen nothing but evidences of the might of the British Empire. The English have been strong, because they have had such an abundance of raw material resources." He realized, however, that they must be a "great people" to have made those resources theirs in the first place. "It was a terrific lesson," he recalls. "Japan was an island country like Britain. Britain was powerful. What better model could Japan have?"

He arrived in London on the day before Christmas, 1923. His reactions were orthodox: he found the city foggy, deep and chilly. But he liked the mood of the people—happy and prosperous, recovering after what at first glance seemed a successful war. He formed an impression of a nation that was solidly industrious and intensely virile. He was surprised, however, to find that his ultimate destination, the Vickers plant, was old and dirty-looking—"very poorly planned." It was explained to him that the modern plant, built during the war, had been closed down for economy reasons, since this, the old one, was adequate for the limited postwar arms output. His guides cheerfully told him that their plant was a good example of how not to get the utmost efficiency out of a factory. He was amazed at their frankness.

Shimizu spent most of the next six months at the Dartford plant, with only occasional visits to the bright lights under the Bovril sign in Piccadilly. He admired the weapons which Vickers produced, and their standard of workmanship. Talking over theoretical problems with their technicians, he found that Kagoshima Technical School and Imperial University had in this instance prepared him well—he could easily hold his own. It was in working out actual production problems in manufacture that he found he was far behind them. "The Japanese," he decided, "theorize too much." This led him to make his one professional generalization of the trip. The British, he concluded, had succeeded industrially because of their "incessant and serious efforts to parallel theoretical progress with advances in application." He was doubtful whether the Japanese could catch up with either the British or the Germans in this respect. He had no worries, however, about being able to surpass the French and the Italians.

On the way home, Lieutenant Shimizu pondered on what he had seen. His first impression that Britain was the model for Japan had been a thousand times reinforced. The people of that "cold and dreary" island had gone out and wrested vast dominions for themselves, which supplied them with comforts, luxuries, in fact their livelihood. What one island people could do, he dreamed, why not another?

In August, 1924, his ship, returning by the same route, through Suez and Singapore, nosed into its dock in the port area of Kobe, a thin strand of houses, people and streets wedged between the high green hills of Hyogo Prefecture and the clean waters of the Inland Sea. The richer for his new dreams, Shimizu was hurt by reality. "As the ship passed through the Inland Sea," he thought back, "I felt suddenly disillusioned with the vast number of tiny houses crowded against each other in the hills. In the ports, there seemed nothing but thousands of tiny human beings scurrying around. I had seen the buildings of the West. There seemed suddenly to be an unbridgeable gap between Western progress and Japanese. I remember feeling then the Japanese must work harder or they would never become a great nation."

* * * * *

At the time Shimizu's pessimism seemed without warrant. The tiny human beings whom he watched from shipboard had gone further than he supposed in bridging the gap between Japan and the West. The struggles of Western man to improve his life and material surroundings had found a quick echo. In 1921, a year before his trip to England, 30,000 of the tiny humans had marched through the streets of Kobe in demonstrations connected with the Kawasaki Shipyard strike, the largest ever organized in Japan. In 1920, 24,000 men had struck at the government steelworks in Yahata. Their strike was not orderly. They had attacked the furnaces after they left them and battled with reserves of police and troops. But the strike had been effective enough to gain its objective. The government tripled their wages and cut the twelve-hour working day to a normal eight.

Two hundred unions were active in Japan by the beginning of 1926, almost all of them less than seven years old. Their membership did not begin to include all of Japan's two-million-man industrial-labor force, but its rise was in direct ratio to the new feeling of freedom and civic rights which was slowly coming over the Japanese people. Through the end of World War I, conditions in Japanese factories had been frequently as brutal as in the first sweatshops of the Industrial Revolution. After the workers, and some liberal capitalists, had begun to change these conditions themselves, the government gradually responded by setting up a labor bureau in the Ministry of Commerce and Industry, and by promoting legislation like the Health Insurance Law of 1926.

Popular agitation made its mark on Tokyo. In 1918 Takashi Hara became premier, the first commoner in history to head the government. In 1925, Premier Takaaki Kato, another liberal statesman, put through the Diet a law granting universal male suffrage, with no property qualification. Japanese democrats had been fighting for something like it since 1902. Throughout the twenties, for the first time since the Restoration, the country was run by party governments, which were at least as sensitive to public opinion as they were to the wishes of the old Meiji bureaucracy and the *genro*—or Elder Statesmen—the tiny group of imperial advisors who had made and unmade cabinets since the eighteen seventies. The liberal wing of the Meiji reformers seemed to have won—

Fukuzawa's ideas had conquered Saigo's, and, to a great extent, Ito's as well. It was the high-water mark of native Japanese parliamentary democracy.

It was an age, too, of trade and industry. The monopoly system of Japanese capitalists, led by the *zaibatsu*, the four great combines of Mitsui, Mitsubishi, Sumitomo and Yasuda, reached out for world empires. The overseas departments of the Mitsui Bank or the Yokohama Specie functioned like auxiliary foreign offices. The Nippon Yusen Kaisha and the Osaka Shosen Kaisha, carrying trade and passengers around the world on their smartly serviced ships, formed a vast civilian navy. University students in the decade after Shimizu's graduation no longer had the same overwhelming ambition to serve the government. The 1925 graduate of Tokyo Imperial University —even more so the graduates of the great private colleges, Waseda and Keio—was out to get a job as a junior engineer with one of the large civilian construction firms, or as a teller or customer's man (Japanese style)* in one of the big financial houses in Kabuto Cho, the four-block-square cluster of light, new office buildings in downtown Tokyo that offered Wall Street's services to Tokyo and the hinterland.

The civilian had come into his own. The soldier-hating courtiers of the tenth-century imperial court could rest happily for once, for not since their time had the prestige of the Japanese military sunk so low. Army and Navy officers took to wearing civilian clothes off duty. A uniform was no longer an asset. In 1924 the Kato Cabinet chopped four divisions from the Army and sent 2,000 regular officers into retirement. The Navy took its lumps in turn at the disarmament conferences concluded in Washington and London.

Japan's foreign policy during the twenties was peaceful

---

* Due to the wild and woolly character of Japan's unregulated stock exchanges, where small investors operated at their peril, a "customer's man" in a Japanese brokerage office could best be compared with a croupier at a loaded game.

and forward-looking. It was forgotten, in the furor that followed Yosuke Matsuoka's walkout from the League of Nations in 1933, that for a decade after the founding of the League, Japanese statesmen had played a highly constructive part in its proceedings. At the Treaty of Versailles, Baron Makino, the Japanese delegate, earnestly seconded by Wellington Koo of China, had presented a racial equality clause to be inserted in the League Covenant. "The equality of nations," it read, "being a basic principle of the League of Nations, the high contracting parties agree to accord as soon as possible, to all alien nations of States, members of the League, equal and just treatment in every respect, making no distinction, either in law or fact, on account of their race or nationality." In 1920 the same nations which later sponsored the Atlantic Charter, and denounced the immorality and barbarity of the wartime Japanese, turned this proposal down. The British and the American delegations, prodded by the premier of Australia, Willie Hughes, one of the louder advocates of white supremacy, could claim the credit for defeating this just and moral statement.

Japan's policy in China was sincerely based on the Open Door. Premier Hara and his foreign office held that a stable and independent China was all that Japan wanted, to permit the trade which was the lifeblood of their islands. On January 21, 1926, Foreign Minister Kijuro Shidehara told the Diet that responsibility for preserving order in the eastern provinces of China was no concern of Japan's. "Taking that course," he said, "we should forfeit our national honor and pride."

* * * * *

Nothing better symbolized the drive towards swifter Westernization at home and a peaceful rapport with foreigners overseas than the six-month visit of Crown Prince Hirohito to Europe, the first time in history that the heir apparent to the Japanese throne had made an overseas journey. On March 21, 1921, Hirohito and his suite boarded the old battleship *Katori*, in Yokohama harbor. They sailed out to Europe along the same route that Fumio Shimizu took shortly after, with stops at way stations like Colombo, Hong Kong and Port Said, on an itinerary carefully designed for "study and observation."

At twenty, the Crown Prince had grown into a thin-faced, rather handsome young man who took his responsibilities very seriously. Although not yet officially regent, he had begun to take the place of his father, the Emperor Taisho, at state occasions.* Court officials were fond of remarking on his resemblance to his grandfather Meiji, although Hirohito's face, betraying the effort of his concentration, had already taken on a slightly scared expression which had never been noticeable on Meiji's.

The relations between the Crown Prince and his subjects who accompanied him on the trip were far from the ideal behavior pattern of the modern constitutional monarch (British model) which his Westernized advisors hoped he might grow into. Even the imperial intimates kept a touch of almost religious awe in their manners and references to him. The official diary of the trip, written in English by Count Yoshinori Futara and Setsuzo Sawada, has a typical entry, describing the visit of Hirohito and the Imperial Prince Kanin to *Katori*'s engine room, following the accidental death there of two stokers:

"Their Highnesses visited the engine room today, followed by several members of their staff, wearing sailors' rough working clothes. In spite of the heat (over 130 degrees F.) the Princes, covered with oil and perspiration, clambered up and down the hot iron ladders. They made enquiries concerning the whereabouts of the spot where

---

* Taisho, whose personal name was Yoshihito, was not of sound mind. As his brain weakened, he became progressively more embarrassing to his court officials. Possibly the last straw occurred when the God-Emperor, at a formal convocation of the Imperial Diet, rolled up the manuscript of the message he had come to read and peered through it at the distinguished audience.

the stokers had been scalded to death. This visit from their Highnesses stimulated and encouraged the crew to an unimaginable extent."

For all the awe in which Hirohito was held, his trip shattered all imperial precedents. After sampling the colonial receptions of the British Empire en route, the Emperor-to-be went on a round of "informal" state visits in Western Europe in the manner of a friendly Western constitutional ruler consorting with his peers. It was the kind of grand tour that could only have been made in the twenties, one that Hirohito would often look back on. To Europeans it may have seemed commonplace, but conservative Japanese found the spectacle of their 124th Emperor tripping off his pedestal, at the least, shocking. Between formal calls and official dinners, Hirohito went to the London theatre and spent a holiday fishing in the Scottish Highlands. He visited Eton, played golf in public, talked scouting with Lord Baden-Powell and sat for a portrait by Augustus John. In Amsterdam he went to see "The Night Watch" at the Rijksmuseum and in Rome he had an audience with Pope Benedict XV and an informal lunch with President Thomas Masaryk, of Czechoslovakia (who happened to be there at the same time). He celebrated the 100th anniversary of Napoleon's death in Paris, and toured the battlefield of Verdun with Marshal Philippe Pétain. In Paris, Hirohito, finally, went off shopping on his own one afternoon, an extraordinary departure for a prince whose family was traditionally protected from sordid things like the handling of money.

Backed up by a zealous and efficient staff, Hirohito performed all the evolutions that were required of him intently and correctly. No detail was overlooked, from presenting a bouquet of flowers to the leading lady of a London show to asking Premier David Lloyd George earnestly to "take good care" of himself, "not only for the good of this country, but also in the interest of the whole world." He made a good impression. He was so obviously sincere. He made his public speeches and private comments with the touching courage of a shy man irrevocably committed to a public occupation. (Except for the most formal statements, he generally spoke in French.)

En route to Europe, the Prince had spent most of his time studying the history and politics of the countries he would visit. He pursued his researches, for himself and for others, with a humorless directness. While *Katori* was anchored at Gibraltar, one afternoon, he noticed some officers leaving the ship for a trip across the bay to Algeciras. "Gentlemen, where are you going to visit?" Hirohito asked. When they told him that they planned some aimless sightseeing, he advised helpfully: "It was at Algeciras where the conference on the Morocco question was held; the delegates met at the City Hall. If I were you, I should take advantage of this opportunity to visit the historic room."

"A counsel," concludes the diary of the trip, "which the sightseers did not fail to take."

Only occasionally did Hirohito give some evidence of the despairing load he had to bear. In Rome one of his attendants found him busily writing some letters to Japan at the height of a hot summer afternoon. He urged Hirohito to follow local custom by taking a siesta. The diary then records:

"The Prince appeared rather embarrassed, and said:

"'Oh, that's all right. I only mean to do as much as I can. As I have no time of my own, I can't take a rest. Really, I have no time. Why, you know that I haven't time, don't you?'

"The Crown Prince put down his pen and looked at him with a bright countenance as if expecting an affirmative answer, and the author could say nothing further to His Highness."

Early in September *Katori* dropped anchor in Yokohama harbor. Hirohito, who had gone shopping in Paris, visited the London theatre and attended a lecture at Oxford, returned to the country where it was a criminal offense for anyone to look down on the reigning monarch from an upper-story window. The shock of returning was cushioned. Since the Crown Prince had grown used to cheering crowds in Europe, it was arranged beforehand that the Japanese crowds in Tokyo should do the same. But when he appeared in front of Tokyo station, an American observer recalls, his loyal subjects forgot their coaching. There was only the deep, awed hush that had always greeted the arrival of the Sun-Goddess' descendant. Finally, the crowd had to be intimidated into shouting their "banzai"s by a claque of well-trained police guards.

* * * * *

Neither the humanization of the Emperor, the deliberations of the League nor the shouts of the factory strikers were fully appreciated by Sakaji Sanada and his fellow farmers. The scholarly buzz of Professor Sakuzo Yoshino and his fellow jurists, busy explaining the proper rights and duties of democratic citizens, was inaudible outside of small radii around Tokyo, Osaka and Kyoto. But the feeling for people's rights was growing in Shimoyoshida and hundreds of other farming communities. It was fed by a new insecurity in the lives of the country people. For all the improvements in farming techniques and the mechanics of government services, the land remained overcrowded and overtaxed. It had also become dependent on factors far beyond the farmers' ken. In 1866 or 1870 a war in Europe meant little or nothing to the Japanese farmer. In 1914 it meant that Sanada and his friends were cut off from their supply of German dyestuffs for the cottage looms. (The government, incidentally, had hastily organized the Japan Dye-Stuffs Company during World War I to remedy this deficiency.)

In the summer of 1927 the machine age of Tokyo ground a little closer to Shimoyoshida. A hydroelectric development company in the capital drew up plans to construct a power plant at the base of Mt. Fuji. The plant would utilize the considerable supply of mountain water, draining all the streams of the Fuji uplands. Shimoyoshida was horrified at the idea. Draining the upland water would take away most of the water the farmers needed to grow their few hardy crops. But the project was a hard one to fight against; it was backed by the *Seiyukai*, the largest political party, which relied on just such pork-barrel projects to justify the campaign contributions of its rich businessmen supporters.

Three hundred farmers got together at a protest meeting in Shimoyoshida, to demand that the hydroelectric project be withdrawn. Sanada, who had inherited his father's prestige in the town, was one of their leaders. The village officials and local representatives of the *Seiyukai* promised them that only surplus water would be drained off. "How could there be any surplus water," Sanada yelled at them, "if the plant was constructed above the farmlands?"

When they got no satisfaction in Shimoyoshida, the farmers decided to make a "long march" to Kofu, the capital of Yamanashi Prefecture, which is 25 miles to the northwest. In March, 1928, they set out—on foot. When they reached the main highway to Kofu, they found it barricaded by the police. The worried town officials had called in higher authorities to stop the farmers from "exciting a riot and creating a disturbance." Peaceably the farmers withdrew. They decided to split up in small groups and make for Kofu over the back roads. Sanada and two others were selected to cross Lake Kawaguchi, one of the five lakes at Fuji's base, the shortest and fastest route to the capital.

Sanada found a farmer with a boat, who ferried them across the lake. As night fell, it began to snow, and the quicksilver surface of the lake was scuffed for a while by some threatening waves. Sanada was a trifle worried, but the stormy setting gave him some historic courage. He began comparing himself to Sakura Sogoro, the peasant leader of the early Tokugawa days, when he made his winter journey to Yedo, to appeal to the Shogun on behalf of the oppressed farmers of Chiba.*

After a day and a night of traveling, Sanada and his neighbors got together in Kofu, where they staged a sit-down strike in front of the prefectural capital. Three members of the Prefectural Assembly, all of them wearing the *Seiyukai* party emblem in their lapels, came out to discuss matters. They promised that they would do everything in their power to uphold the rights of the farmers in Shimoyoshida. Sanada wanted them to put the promises in writing, but the others were content with a verbal agreement. The project went through, but Shimoyoshida's water supply was not interfered with. "In the long run," Sanada concluded, "it turned out to be a victory for us."

* * * * *

Sanada's victory spoke well for the growth of a better informed public opinion, conscious of its rights without being revolutionary. But it also showed in microcosm the hidden defect of the showy new Japanese democracy. There was no growth of leaders or basic expansion of the government structure to match the rising stature of the people. There had been no official channel through which Sanada and his neighbors could legally voice their discontent. The town officials were practically powerless,

---

* Fortunately, Sanada did far better on his mission than his exemplar. Sogoro was a headman of Kozu village, east of Tokyo, in an area whose farmers had been cruelly taxed and exploited by the local *Daimyo*, Hotta Masanobu. In 1644, he traveled alone to Yedo, as representative of 300 others, to present a petition to the Shogun, asking for some redress. The Shogun received the petition and ordered the *Daimyo* to the capital to explain the situation. The *Daimyo* obeyed, and was later punished. Before this, however, he took a decisive vengeance on Sogoro. After watching their children beheaded before their eyes, Sogoro and his wife were crucified shortly afterward. Since his death, he has been something of a patron saint to Japanese farmers. There is a temple to his memory in Kozu.

moved mainly by the bureaucratic fear of any disturbance in the established order. There was no representative whom the people of Shimoyoshida could expect to champion their grievance, either in the local assembly or in the Diet. The great political parties, the *Minseito* and the *Seiyukai*, had become the creatures of large financial interests. The farmers of Shimoyoshida spoke to the three *Seiyukai* assemblymen in Kofu more as petitioners begging a favor of a governing authority, than as a sovereign people demanding justice from its servants, the representatives.

The Meiji democracy proved itself to be only half a democracy. Crudely put, it was a paralytic with an excellent brain, finely developed arms and torso, but unable to depend on its twisted, weak pair of legs. The agencies of government—the bureaucrats and administrative technicians—had grown mature in their efficiency. There were capable men in the Diet. The trappings of representative government were all new and glossy. But the motive power of representative government—the direct-as-possible contact between the people and their elected administrators—was wanting. Japan was a democracy without a sovereign people. Japan was an awakening people without tribunes to represent it.

The idea that Ito stressed in the Japanese Constitution, that it was a document given to the people by the emperor, not needed or demanded or instituted by the people, had molded the concept of government in Japan. The elected official absorbed the bureaucrat's conviction that public office was a right and prerogative of the public official, given him by the emperor. There was little feeling of duty about it. The only duties of a politician were the familiar duties of men in the web society—above to the emperor, his superiors and the politicians or businessmen who put him in office. Below him, his loyalties to the electorate were far less clear. There was no precedent in Japan for the responsibilities of a democratic representative to his constituents—as distinguished from a leader to his men. The responsibilities, if they existed at all, were generally a watered-down survival of the noblesse oblige tradition of the feudal web society.

Often mutely and without realizing what it attacked, public opinion railed against this perpetuation of the web society in politics. It secured reforms, alterations, but never change. No frontal attack was made on the web society. As a result the progress of democracy in Japan could only be a gradual loosening process, chipping away at the bonds until freedom of movement was secured, trying for a workable compromise on the way with the imperial mission and Ito's Constitution.

This process succeeded during the twenties. It made the age literally a golden one for Japanese democrats. The success might have continued. But during its greatest triumphs an undertow of basic weaknesses and unhappy events had already begun to carry Japanese democracy away from shore. A major cause of the failure lay in the queer, doctrinaire type of Japanese liberal, the product of a university system hopelessly infatuated with the nineteenth-century German philosophers—Hegel, Marx, Nietzsche and Schopenhauer. The liberals tended to fall into Socialist or Communist extremes, to provoke clashes with authority prematurely and often without necessity. Given a choice between the flag-waving, yelling university students and the stolid policeman on the corner, all Japanese who were not already flag-waving university students preferred the policeman. Agitation played into the hands of governments like the Tanaka Cabinet of 1928, which could hunt out and destroy ten honest trade unionists or believers in a real parliamentary democracy for each Communist or left-wing Socialist, who publicly provoked it.

Another blow to Japan's democratic development was the sagging economy of the late twenties and the early thirties. As a nation that lived on trade, Japan was tragically vulnerable to the coughs and sputterings of the world's economic systems. After the financial panic of 1927, hardship and insecurity pressed upon the small farmers and factory workers. Like the *Kleinbürgertum* of Central Europe, they began to lose confidence in their cold-hearted civilian government, ever more closely allied to the great financiers of Tokyo and Osaka.

* * * * *

Hideya Kisei started his life as a workingman in the grip of this depression. He had since his childhood never known prosperity. His father Kanefusa had inherited less than one and a half acres of paddyland and some five acres of upland from Hideya's disillusioned *samurai* grandfather, hardly enough to support a family of seven. To give his children enough food, he rented an extra two acres of land as a tenant farmer. Three of his brothers, denied any of the family inheritance by the law of primogeniture, also hired themselves out as tenant farmers, bound to a treadmill existence of low returns and high rents. They were deathly poor, but the townspeople of Kurino still pointed them out as former *kizoku* (the descendants of *samurai*).

Shivering in the unheated rooms of their farmhouse, battered by the cold sea winds from the coast, Hideya dreamed of going to the city to make his fortune. Some of his schoolmates had already gone. At fifteen, after he had finished the compulsory eight years of primary schooling, he poured out his plans to his mother. He was too fearful of his father to ask his permission. His mother, like many Japanese women, was docile, submissive and self-effacing before her husband, but dedicated with all the power of a strange inner toughness to helping the lives of her children. She scraped up enough money to get him to the city and keep him there for a month or two. Not long after he had told her, in the summer of 1930, Hideya crept out of his father's house and boarded the train that winds north along the cliff-hung bays of eastern Kyushu for the daylong trip to Yahata and the steel industry. He was deeply bothered about the secrecy of his departure. He swore that he would return a successful man or not at all.

For two months Kisei walked the streets of Yahata and the neighboring city of Kokura, a factory town of equal drabness, trying to find the job. He has never forgotten the crowds of ragged men patiently waiting in long queues before the employment offices of every company in town, most of them come from small, crowded farms like his. His mother's money did not last him long. Like most of the ragged men, he grew dirty and hungry. But the vow he had made on leaving home kept him from any thought of abandoning his search.

Towards the end of the year, his perseverance won through. He got himself a job as a recorder at one of the blast furnaces of the Yawata Steel Company plant. His wages were 70 sen a day—the equivalent, in those times, of 33 cents. "At last," he thought, "I am on the road to future success." The words sound forced and overdramatized, but Japanese have a habit of stating things that way. The heat of the furnace never fazed him. He had too much ambition to notice it. For his mother's sake, and for his family's, he could not fail.

Kisei started going to the night school at the plant, run by the steel company. He spent as much money as he could spare buying books and magazines. He hoped, with more perseverance, to go on to another company school where specialized study of the industry was conducted. This would have assured him promotion—possibly, at some time, to the manager class.

Three months after he joined the company, however, Kisei was transferred to a shift stoking the furnace. He worked as part of a regular three-shift gang, an arrangement which left him no time to go to school. He resigned himself to learning and reading in his spare time. He bought more books on industry and labor, studying them whenever he could get back to his room in the long wooden company barracks. Occasionally, he got letters from home. His mother wrote that Kanefusa Kisei had been very angry at his son's unannounced departure. After he got over his first burst of rage, he never mentioned Hideya again. He grunted noncommittally when his wife told him of Hideya's vow never to return unless as a successful man.

By the time Hideya Kisei arrived at Yahata, the trade-union movement there, once among the most promising in Japan, had been stifled. Since Yahata was government-owned, the management had had an easy recourse to the Army and police, whenever the workers grew obstreperous. Although the 1919 strike had been, in a sense, won by the workers, it scared the government into prompt suppression of anything that looked like a repetition. Under threat of wholesale dismissal, the union disbanded. All that was left, by 1930, was a "discussion council," composed of a few representatives of the labor force in the various plants at Yahata. This council met regularly to negotiate with the company on wages and working conditions. It was weak. As Kisei recalls, "It could register protest and apply for better conditions, but could not force them, if management didn't feel inclined. And management didn't."

As he pored over his books and talked to older men in the mills, Kisei grew very interested in the old 1919 strike. He was thrilled by the thought of the strength which so many men, acting in unison, had shown. He grew bitter at the police and the government managers, who had used force to put this movement down. "It was about this time," he remembers, "that I got my deep conviction that industry was able to progress because of labor—and that, consequently, labor should be given first consideration. It wasn't as clear-cut as that then. I only felt a deep frustration and hatred for the management and the social conditions, which allowed labor to be exploited." There was a painful likeness between the conditions of city laborers and that of the poor tenant farmers in Kurino, from whose lot he had fled.

At this early age, Kisei came to some further conclusions about the nature and the failure of the Japanese labor movement, that had gone on its way so firmly in the early twenties, only to fall, bound and mute, even before the militarists took over the country several years later. Although the workers, like Sanada's farmers, had been awakened to the possibilities of equity in a democratic society, ten years, or, at the most, the thirty years of the Japanese labor movement had not obliterated what Kisei calls "a blind obedience to authority, from the long years of Japanese environment." An old-timer at the mill had sadly told him that the greatest difficulty of the early labor organizers was not from the government, but from the workers themselves.

Essentially the Japanese worker, in the mass, realized too late that in the factory system he had entered into a new relationship, not covered by the codes and obligations of his old web society. There were an unusual number of "enlightened" capitalists in Japan, who unconsciously kept up with their employees an outmoded, but upright relationship of the benevolent master, responsible for those who served him. But these were outnumbered by the counterparts of the new bureaucrats, men who in the spirit of Ito's constitutional charter, felt their authority and their rights far more than they sensed their responsibility and duties. These employers, perversely attracted by the worst kind of Western capitalism and perversely won over by Western ideas, had in effect partly jumped out of the responsibility codes of their own social web—at least as far as their duty to the workers was concerned. Once this was done, oddly like the Japanese troops who later invaded Nanking, there were no moral codes to restrain them. It was a cruel joke on the workers. Simple people, they thought the bonds of the web held true for everything.

* * * * *

As the thirties began, the well of bitterness deepened between the small farmers and laborers and the capitalists who ran their government. The world depression, complicated by new stirrings of nationalism in Europe, continued to have its effect on Japan. The governors of Japan, heedless of their risk, continued to prune the branches of their dwarf tree, using the police and the weight of the bureaucracy to suppress the continuing popular movement towards a real political and economic democracy. There was no thought that the stunted half-growth of Japanese democracy, thus restricted, would never be strong enough to resist its enemies. The enemies profited. Since the darkest days of their humiliation, two generations of Spartan militarists had been plotting and preparing behind the barracks walls, waiting for the chance to destroy the embryo democracy outside. It came very quickly.

On the night of September 18, 1931, a bomb exploded on the tracks of the South Manchurian Railway near Mukden, in the area, according to an agreement of long standing, occupied by Japanese troops. Within two days after the explosion, Japanese troops had occupied all of southern Manchuria. By January of the following year, the entire area of Manchuria had been absorbed by the Japanese Army. The smoothness of the occupation left no doubt in anyone's mind that the occupation was a carefully planned job, worked out in long conferences between the leaders of the Kwantung Army in Manchuria and War Ministry headquarters in the dingy buildings on the top of Kudan hill in Tokyo.

The military, after sitting through the twenties in silence, had taken the offensive, at home and in Manchuria, at a time when the opposition was weakest. It was a ripe moment to exploit the straitened finances of Japan, the insecurity of its trade, the overcrowding and the basic frustration of a brave, idealistic people in a drab moment of its history. The Frankenstein that had always been latent in the structure of Meiji Japan had burst out of its dungeon, with no one brave enough or energetic enough to thrust it back. The big Japanese capitalists, on the contrary, speedily saw the Manchurian conquests as Japan's golden field of raw-material expansion, as essential to the economy as the lands which Britain had taken to itself in similar fashion less than 75 years before. The rank and the file of the Japanese people listened to the new sounds of drums and bugles—and found that it took their minds off their troubles.

Once on the march the modern *samurai* did not stop. The cliques and cabals of young officers, angry sons of poor farm families, kept pushing the Army ever further along the road to a military dictatorship. They were abetted by civilian rightists and nationalists, including many onetime Socialists. In the minds of many young students the doctrinaire mystique of Marx was conveniently and comfortably superseded by the similar mystique of National Socialism, a faith that blended the new discontented nationalism of Europe with a revived cult of Shinto and the *samurai* virtues. By the middle of the thirties, after one especially bad uprising of young officers on May 15, 1932, and several abortive ones, it was difficult even for the generals to restrain their subordinates.

In February, 1936, Tadao Yamazaki, then eleven years old, was attending the last year of primary school in the city of Ogaki, a middling textile manufacturing center in Kyushu, where his father was teaching at the local commercial school. The morning of the twenty-sixth was gray and flecked with snow. Yamazaki arrived at school early and began, with a few others, to scrub the school floor, a task which the students performed each day.

Just as the classes were settling into their usual routine, a teacher appeared and puzzlingly told the children to remain calm. They should not, he said with some emotion, believe the rumors that were floating about or jump to hasty conclusions. Until the government made an official announcement they should not let their emotions get the better of them. Tadao and his schoolmates, after hearing this advice, went back to work wonderingly. The rest of the day passed without incident.

The next day Yamazaki and his classmates, with their families, began to get an inkling of the cause behind their teachers' concern. A few days later, when order was restored in Tokyo, the whole story leaked out to the public. Fourteen hundred troops of the First Army Division, stationed in Tokyo, had revolted under the leadership of the same young officer cliques who had staged the brief revolts and assassinations in the past. They had occupied the War Ministry, the Diet Building and several other points in midtown Tokyo. They had assassinated three cabinet members—Finance Minister Takahashi, General Watanabe, the Inspector General of Military Education, and Admiral Saito, Lord Keeper of the Privy Seal. Admiral Okada, the Premier, had barely missed death himself by hiding from the assassins in his official mansion.

It was the beginning of a three-day revolt, an attempt to achieve what the young officers called the Showa Restoration, after the name of the Emperor Hirohito's reign. Their objectives, to cut down the last remnants of moderate and civilian opinion in the government and create a military dictatorship, were close enough to the grand policy pursued by the army generals to cause, for a moment, the most desperate kind of confusion in the armed forces.

When the revolt broke out, Shimizu, then a commander, was in Yokohama. He received orders early in the morning to prepare trucks and arm them, as best he could, for despatch to protect the Navy Ministry in Tokyo. When the first false rumors filtered through that Admiral Okada had been killed, the officers at Yokosuka were shocked. Okada was a navy man—far more moderate in his views, like most navy officers, than the steel-helmeted *samurai* of the Army. Yokosuka was full of fight, less indignant at the affront to the legally constituted government of Japan than eager to get a fighting crack at the Army, which every good navy man detested, in a rivalry that was far deeper than the friction between the two arms anywhere else in the world.*

The revolt failed. Martial law was declared in Tokyo. Loyal troops surrounded the rebels. Air-dropped leaflets and radio broadcasts appealed to them to surrender, in obedience to an imperial command. This had the desired effect. Four days after it began, the revolt of the 26th of February, called in Japanese—after the dates involved— the *"ni ni roku,"* ended without any further blood spilt.

Although the *"ni ni roku"* embarrassed the Army high command, its swift suppression, which only the generals had been capable of carrying out, ironically fastened the grip of the Army on the country. After February 26 no government official dared to oppose militarism publicly. On July 7th of the following year, the Japanese Army, in full strength, invaded China.

The *"ni ni roku"* rebels had attacked the imperial government in exactly the same way and for the same motives that Saigo Takamori had attacked it in 1877—to save the Emperor from his advisors. If they had got to the Emperor, or occupied Tokyo in greater force, it is quite possible that they could have succeeded. It was not hard to capture Japan, from Tokyo. When Admiral Shimizu re-

---

* The rivalry originated in feudalism and geography. The southern clans of Satsuma and Choshu, the most powerful in Japan, insured the success of the Meiji Restoration of 1868 by their military power. Satsuma, spread out along the rocky seacoast of Kyushu, was historically a maritime community. After the shogunate was overthrown, Satsuma *samurai* took over the direction of the new Japanese Navy. Choshu, across the Straits of Shimonoseki from Kyushu, had an equal reputation for land warfare—the Choshu clan was the first in Japan to arm and organize its troops on the pattern of modern military forces. Choshu men, naturally enough, occupied and held a leading position in the new national Army.

The *"Sat-Cho"* rivalry that had existed when these were semi-independent clan territories was transferred to a brisk inter-service dispute between the rival groups of leaders in the Meiji era. Long after army and navy officers had ceased to be selected by geography, the clan tradition of animosity between the services continued itself.

flected on his conduct in the incident, he made a deeply revealing comment. "I am sure that if the order had been for the benefit of the rebels," he said, explaining his reactions on being told to arm the Yokosuka trucks, "we at Yokosuka would not have worked so willingly." The implication was plain: they would have worked and obeyed nonetheless. The old web society was a peculiar instrument. Capture the center, and every filament on the periphery would fall into place.

1937 to 1941 were a continuum. With big business either subservient or discredited, the labor movement crushed, the politicians and bureaucrats well intimidated, the Army was able to run the country to its own liking. Cabinets rose and fell on the orders of the militarists, who were now able to use without the need for discretion one of the fatal flaws in the Meiji governmental structure—the stipulation, enacted in 1895, discarded and later revived, that the war minister and the navy minister must both be officers on active service. Since no general could take office against the wishes of his superiors, and since no cabinet in turn could be formed without a war minister and a navy minister, this gave the armed forces a blunt veto power over their political adversaries.

The war party stayed in the ascendant. On September 26, 1940, Japan formally became a co-partner in the Rome-Berlin Axis. On October 12th, Premier Fuminaro Konoye presided over the founding of the Imperial Rule Assistance Association, a totalitarian-type structure that superseded all the old political parties. The following July, Japanese troops debarked at Saigon, to take over military control of French Indo-China. Late in 1941 Konoye tried and failed to head off the impending war with the United States, which the militarists threatened. He was quickly replaced. On October 18, 1941, the Minister of War, Hideki Tojo, a cruel and stubborn dynast, assumed the office of Premier and the attitude of a military dictator.

Shimizu, Sanada, Kisei and Yamazaki were not only numbed by these swift changes, but, like their fellow-citizens, powerless to oppose them—even if they wanted to. Not long ago, with hindsight, but good hindsight, Shimizu delivered a short epitaph on his political brother officers: "They were ill-equipped for dabbling in politics and the economics of a nation. Military men are notorious for their directness and short-tempers. Politics called for patience, diplomacy and a give-and-take spirit. That they would make a mess of things was a foregone conclusion."

5

THE WILL TO WAR

"We deserted our wives, we parted from our children, we left our aged parents uncared for, all to obtain this one head. What an auspicious day is this. . . ."

Chushin Gura

As dawn broke on December 8, 1941, the 64,000-ton battleship *Yamato* was under way in the Inland Sea, headed for the naval base at Kure. The sky was cloudless and only a slight swell ruffled the sea. At her normal cruising speed of 23 knots *Yamato* glided past the round green islands sprinkled off the Shikoku coast. A few fishing boats, in a ragged convoy, had just put out from the ports behind the islands. Dragging their nets between them, they gave *Yamato* a wide berth.

Admiral Shimizu, aboard the battleship, was a proud and satisfied man. *Yamato's* firing tests, held in deep water off eastern Kyushu, had been an unqualified success. Whenever he looked above the deck at the sweep of the 18-inch gun barrels, he could not help feeling a bit triumphant. It was eighteen years since his apprenticeship at the Vickers factory. Now, guns which he designed were far and away the most powerful shipboard armament in the world.

At 0700 the crew lined up beneath the guns for morning colors and the reading of Emperor Meiji's Rescript to Soldiers and Sailors, a daily ceremony on every navy ship and army post since 1882. After the Rescript had been read, Admiral Shimizu walked leisurely aft to the senior officers' wardroom, where he sat down for his morning tea, chatting with some officers from the ship's company.

At 0830, suddenly, the *Navy March* roared out over the ship's public address system. The admiral looked up from his tea, mildly interested, expecting to hear about a routine victory in the China War. He got more than he had bargained for. "At 0320 this morning," * the announcement began, "Aircraft of the Special Naval Attack Unit attacked and destroyed the United States Pacific Fleet at Pearl Harbor. . . ."

"I was petrified," he remembers, "then I felt a cold shiver pass up my spine. *'Erai koto ni natta,'* I thought— 'A fine mess we're in for.'" Worriedly, he had the bare statement confirmed by the staff officers from Combined Fleet Headquarters, who were aboard. They had known, unlike Shimizu and *Yamato's* crew, that an attack was in the planning stage. But neither had any of them suspected that it would come so soon, or come at all.

The crew of Japan's—and the world's—biggest warship received the news with a hum of whispers. There was more surprise than jubilation. No message was read to the crew in honor of the occasion. No toasts were drunk in the wardroom. There was no wild cheering. A few of the officers talked about a great master stroke. But, to the admiral's recollection, "most of us thought that we had bitten off more than we could chew. The general feeling among the officers was one of grim resignation."

* * * * *

In the Army, less cautious and worldly-wise than the Navy, there was less of the Navy's reservations. Private

* This was Japanese time; in Pearl Harbor it was 0750, December 7th.

Second Class Hideya Kisei at that moment was somewhere off the Yangtze estuary, jammed in the hold of an Army transport with some 3,000 of his fellow-conscripts. A few minutes after ten, the order was passed for quiet. Kisei's company commander, a first lieutenant, yelled the news of Pearl Harbor at his men through an open hatch cover. In an instant, there was an uproar of babbling voices. Then the first cheers of victory began to break from the smelly darkness below decks.

"At first," Kisei said, "we were stunned with surprise. But, a few seconds later, we felt delirious with joy and pride. We had blind faith in our leaders and in the invincibility of our armed forces. There were very few who had any doubt about winning."

The surprise that Kisei felt at hearing the news was somewhat mitigated by the odd circumstances of his departure, three weeks before from the port of embarkation, near Hiroshima. At the barracks, summer khaki uniforms had been issued. Then, under rigid secrecy, the men had been marched to their ship, destination unknown. They all knew, as Kisei puts it, that "something was afoot." But nobody suspected such a "gigantic stroke."

Less than an hour after the announcement of Pearl Harbor, the ship weighed anchor and headed due south. A few days later, Hideya Kisei's signal corps detachment, wearing their new summer uniforms, walked down the gangplank at Bangkok.

* * * * *

On the home front, the shock of the Greater East Asia War hit equally deep. Sakaji Sanada heard the news over his radio. For a few minutes, he sat stunned and motionless in the large living room of his farmhouse, while the tinkling bells of the newsboys carrying the war extras and the low murmur of his fellow-townsmen in the streets dinned their way into his consciousness. At first he could not believe his ears—war with the United States was something on a dimension outside his understanding.

After the words had sunk in, he finally got up and walked outside to talk to his neighbors—to reassure them, in fact, since he had a position to maintain in the village. "It was an agonizing feeling," he says in retrospect, "but, since it had begun, there was nothing to do but perform our duty. We must do our job at home, tighten our belts and work harder."

* * * * *

Tadao Yamazaki heard the news with his classmates, at Tokyo Commercial University in the capital. "So it has finally come," he thought. There was more enthusiasm in the classroom than there was on the farm or, for that matter, aboard the battleship. Later, characteristically, Yamazaki had more to say about his feelings than the others: "My thoughts were good and clean cut. I did have some doubts as to whether we would be victorious in the long run. But, by this time, everyone was burning with the spirit that we were the liberators of all Asia. Our pent-up abhorrence for Western imperialism was suddenly unleashed. I firmly believed that this war was thrown upon us and that we had no alternative but to fight —fight to free all Asia or die in the attempt." Most of his fellow-students felt the same—and generally in an even more pronounced way.

* * * * *

At the hub of this suddenly activated military machine stood one of its less willing cogs. Hirohito agreed to the war with great reluctance, but he now had little power to check the drive of the militarists at its zenith. On the day of the Pearl Harbor attack, he issued a formal declaration of war, a statement—in contrast to the bombastic communique of his generals—which had at times a concessive quality about it:

". . . It has been truly unavoidable and far from our wishes that our Empire has now been brought to crossed swords with America and Britain. More than four years have passed since China, failing to comprehend the true intention of our empire. . . .

"Patiently have we waited and long have we endured in the hope that our government might retrieve the situation in peace, but our adversaries, showing not the least spirit of conciliation, have unduly delayed a settlement and in the meantime they have intensified the economic and political pressure to compel our empire to submit. . . .

"This situation being such as it is, our empire, for its existence and self-defense, has no recourse but to appeal to arms and to crush every obstacle in its path. . . ."

* * * * *

And so they went to war. With the suddenness of an earthquake, the citizens of Japan fell upon the West. As they recovered from the first shock of their contact, individual reservations and lonely doubts were swallowed up in a common drive to victory, as irrevocably as bits of paper houses in Kyushu are torn from their roots and sucked into the air by the typhoons from the China Sea. Hirohito, looking less myopic in uniform astride his white horse Shirayuki, saluted as the soldiers jerkily goose-stepped past his palace. Sanada's son, Mitsu, banzaied his way up the beaches at Lingayen. Hideya Kisei, sweatily fingering his rifle, pitched through the Burma jungles. Fumio Shimizu kept his technicians feverishly working to feed more disciplined steel into the typhoon's progress. Tadao Yamazaki got a rough buck private's training with his university classes. No one paused. In all its strengths and weaknesses, the web society of Japan seemed to have been made for total war.

Certainly there was justification for calling the Japanese

a nation of "fanatics." The single-mindedness of the Japanese war effort, its frenzy and its cruelties, seemed to the Westerner anachronisms beyond explanation. The Japanese militarists did not have to bribe their people to greater efforts by keeping up a steady flow of consumer goods and creature comforts, as Hitler did for the Germans. The Japanese fought without reward. They also fought without giving or seeking quarter. Although the scientific extermination schemes of the Germans were far more horrible, Germans at least would surrender, if surrounded in battle. If not humane, most German Army prison camps were at least correct. There seemed no other way, however, for foreigners to explain either Japanese prison camps or the incredible last-man defense of islands like Saipan and Tarawa, except to conclude that the Japanese were in fact a mentally arrested nation in arms, each soldier welded to his rifle by every tradition of his history.*

The foreign critics were partially correct. No historian can ignore the military elements in the Japanese tradition. Moreover, the shape of prewar Japanese society, as it had grown through the centuries, was very favorable to developing a single-minded "nation-in-arms." But it was a dangerous gloss to conclude that Japanese society was essentially militarist, irrevocably feudal and hopelessly fanatic—all these expressed in European terms. Sanada, Shimizu, Yamazaki, Kisei and Hirohito—these men cannot be called essentially "warlike" by any stretch of the imagination. Their tragedy was that they were heirs to a society which had its morality and ways of thinking first critically misshapen by six centuries of civil war, then artificially frozen in their deformed state by three centuries of isolation.

* In the years immediately following World War II, after the Germans had been accepted (rather incautiously, it would seem) as pillars of European defense, the postwar Japanese were still looked on with distrust. Europeans, in particular, wondered how soon the Japanese would return to their "old ways."

* * * * *

From 1870 to the early 1930s, the Japanese had made considerable efforts to build their country into a modern democracy. Possibly, if a few strong men had been found to carry through the peaceful intentions of the greatest Meiji reformers, there would have been no Pearl Harbor, no Marco Polo Bridge.

Going further back, the historic roots of the Japanese tradition are not militaristic but stable and peaceful. In the eighth and ninth centuries, when only the desperate warnings of a few priests kept Europe from falling into militarist anarchy, Japan was a unified, peaceful kingdom with a considerable civilization. While the Saxon and German chroniclers were still recounting the primitive verses of *Beowolf* and the *Nibelungenlied,* in Kyoto the Lady Murasaki Shikibu was leisurely writing the Tale of Genji, and Sei Shonagon her Pillow Diary, both polished and intuitive novels of polite society, the like of which European writers could not produce until some 800 years later. The land was prosperous and well-ruled. The governing nobles of the Nara court, like the Chinese of their day, looked down on the warrior as intellectually and socially inferior. There were no *samurai*. The military codes of *Bushido* ("The Way of the Warrior") which Japanese soldiers handily resurrected in the nineteenth and twentieth centuries, would have been targets of sophisticated amusement, if they had been recited a thousand years before.

Then disaster came. After the military house of Taira took the rule of the country away from the emperor's courtiers, Japan became a nation governed by the sword. It remained that way for the next six centuries, while the Minamoto and other feudal dynasties succeeded the Taira.* Power was the warrant of their legitimacy. Although the tradition of imperial rule never died, as the events of the Meiji Restoration proved, a strong code of

* See Chapter 2.

power politics established itself among the Japanese, deeply grounded and difficult to eradicate.

In an odd way, Japan's secluded geographical position here worked against internal union, instead of for it, by helping to continue this rule by feudal leaders. Invasions—or the fear of successful invasions—from outside have unified many countries. Japan had few outside threats like this to reckon with. Only once was an invasion attempted—by the Mongols in the thirteenth century. To help defeat it, the Japanese did put down their local quarrels to unite under the emperor's direction.* The menace past, they picked up their feuding where they had left off.

The logical conclusion of this feudal quarreling was anarchy. It began in the late fifteenth century and lasted for a hundred years. During this time, which the Japanese call "*Sengoku Jidai*—The Age of the Warring Country," central rule collapsed completely. Like feudal Europe centuries before, the local barons were absolute rulers of their territory and knew no law outside. The *samurai* was king, galloping over the country resplendent in his horned helmet and rich, brocaded armor, two swords slung at his side. For his landmarks, wherever his expeditions took him, he had the smoke of burning cottages, the pillars of ruined temples, the rot of desolated fields.

Sengoku Jidai was the worst, but not the only period of feudal anarchy. The century that preceded it was almost as bad, and, long before that, the people of Japan had become used to the rigors of civil war. If the Thirty Years War—which lasted little over one generation—sowed the seeds for the troubles of modern Germany, how much worse was the effect of centuries of feudal wars on Japan!

---

* The invasion was badly crippled by the destructive typhoon which wrecked part of the Mongol fleet off Kyushu. The Japanese called the typhoon "*kamikaze*—Divine Wind"—and the Emperor Toba II, a very God-fearing man, thanked the Buddhist priests in their temples for averting disaster with their prayers. He spent the rest of his life, and most of his subjects' money, trying to satisfy the priests' resultant demands for bigger and better temples.

The Chinese scholarship that had been imported to study poetry, philosophy and legal theory, was put to work translating the classic Chinese books on military strategy. The work of the peaceful artisans of the Nara period was eclipsed for centuries. In their place the swordmaker raised his trade to a respected art. Thirteenth-century Japanese swords, probably the finest blades that anyone has ever turned out, were the principal export in the country's limited trade with China.

Even Buddhism was transformed to fit the needs of a military time. The Zen sect of Buddhism, which stressed a Spartan self-discipline, individual meditation undisturbed by long systems of rites or a complicated theoretical philosophy, became the religion of the *samurai*. More directly, the Buddhist monks in the large imperial monasteries themselves became soldiers of a sort. At first, like the original Knights Templar of the Crusades, they fought only in the name of religion—usually to punish the adherents of a competing sect. Ultimately, by the middle of the feudal period, the Buddhist monks of monasteries like that on Mount Hiei, just outside of Kyoto, were virtually corps of unruly mercenaries, whose military strength frequently decided who would possess the capital.

The effect of this military age was entirely to change the mental outlook of the Japanese on soldiers and soldiering. The Confucian courtiers who openly laughed at the clumsy *samurai* in the early days of Japan, now expressed their contempt only in veiled whispers. The despised *samurai* appeared at court, and were given high titles by reluctant emperors. The tradition of contempt for the professional soldier, which still persisted for centuries in China, was completely lost in Japan. With his two-handed sword, the feudal *samurai* cut down the scholars, the court nobles and the farmers from their exalted positions on the social ladder.

Japanese feudalism was not the same as the feudalism of Christian Europe. There were of course surface points of comparison: the relationship between lord and vassal, the value put on courage and sacrifice. But Japanese feudalism lacked anything of the abstract Christian morality which so often dignified the cult of chivalry. There was no stern command to help the weak, or, especially, to protect defenseless womanhood. The only virtues were social virtues. Loyalty was the greatest. The loyalty of a vassal to his *daimyo,* or the responsibility of the *samurai* to someone who served him, became exalted to religious proportions—a natural enough development through centuries where life or death depended on the loyalty of one's lord or comrades. It was this loyalty, as has been pointed out, that became the cornerstone of the whole Japanese web society. And it was essentially a military virtue.

In the seventeenth century, Tokugawa Ieyasu conquered his rivals and set up his shogunate. The rigid caste system which he and his successors riveted on Japan was the order of a military society. To justify a social system, which even in peacetime kept the military man at its apex, the code of *Bushido* was elaborately worked out and the Shogun's scholars tried to give it a complicated philosophy of its own. Later, after the Meiji Restoration, the founders of Japan's modern army revived *Bushido* in another form. The emperor was substituted for the clan chief as the focus of the soldier's loyalty. *Bushido,* now buttressed by the revived Shinto religion, became a kind of religious patriotism.

Western historians may be correct when they say that both varieties of *Bushido* were artificial inventions. But only the codes needed to be invented. The military idea behind them that loyalty, courage and sacrifice for one's clan or country were the highest virtues was by that time imbedded deep in the Japanese tradition. Since the twelfth century military loyalty and morality had been almost synonymous to the Japanese mind.

The old *samurai* virtues were of course most strictly remembered among the descendants of *samurai* families. As a boy, Fumio Shimizu remembers sitting for hours on the straw mats at home, listening to his father lecture him on the virtues of fortitude and sacrifice. There were terrible thunderstorms in the hills of Sanno, where he then lived, but persistent beatings from his *samurai* father taught Fumio and his brother never to flinch or cry out, when the lightning crackled outside their windows. Even when he was being thrashed, any outcry of pain was forbidden. Hideya Kisei, in Kyushu, also got this part of a *samurai's* education. None of the boys in his family was allowed to use hot water for washing, since their father felt this was unmanly. He remembers once leaving their cottage with a small string of his outer coat improperly tied. That evening, when the child came home, his father gave him a sound beating.

Families who were not themselves *samurai* had nonetheless taken over the *samurai* system of ethics for their children's education, just as they had adopted *samurai* surnames for their own, when the Meiji reformers had ordered the bulk of the population to get themselves family names. Centuries of popular Japanese literature exalted the military virtues. For the classicist, there was the *Heike Monogatari*, a ballad-like tale of derring-do written in the twelfth century, which is still sung by minstrels in country districts of Japan. In the theatres, audiences year after year sighed, wept and shouted at the eighteenth-century *Chushin-gura* of Takeda Izumo, the story of the Forty-Seven Ronin who dedicated their lives to avenging their master.

The Forty-Seven Ronin are still heroes of a sort to the Japanese, although since World War II the idea of mass suicide had lost much of its appeal. When their lord, Asano Naganori, assaulted the Shogun's master of ceremonies, Kira Yoshinaka, for insulting him, the Shogun ordered him to commit suicide. With Asano dead, the Forty-Seven became *ronin*, "wave men"—homeless *samurai* who had lost their estates. They swore in a temple to avenge his death by killing the official. After two years of plotting, they fought their way into Kira's palace early one morning, killed him and deposited his head on their master's grave. Then they peacefully awaited their punishment. Although the Shogun himself was personally sympathetic, as were most Japanese, to this supreme example of loyalty, he reluctantly authorized their execution—since they had unfortunately broken the law of the central government, in a way too public for the government to ignore it. The story is well known. But there is no better example of the Japanese idea of military loyalty.

Admiral Shimizu was personally conversant with a similar case. His grandfather, Kojiro, inherited the name, title and court position of a *samurai* named Shimizu, another retainer of the lord of Kaga. The title fell vacant early in the nineteenth century, when the original Shimizu and all his family committed mass suicide, to atone for some slight they had offered their feudal master.

Outside of this context of feudal loyalty, military rule and recurrent civil war, it is impossible to understand the frenzy, the bravery and the blind obedience of the Japanese fighting man. It is precisely here that the gulf was widest between the twentieth-century West and the prewar web society of Japan. The European version of feudal loyalty, already tottering, had been mocked to death in 1605, when Cervantes published Don Quixote. It was 300 years before it occurred to a Japanese author to mock his homegrown ideals of knighthood. Ryunosuke Akutagawa, a brilliant satirist, wrote his biting story, The General,—a thinly disguised attack on the popular hero General Nogi, in 1922. It was by no means capable of laying its target low.

* * * * *

However stunned individual Japanese were at the time of Pearl Harbor, they rallied rapidly and fiercely to support the war. Shimizu, Kisei, Yamazaki and Sanada now describe those war experiences from the vantage point of defeat and occupation, although their reactions, to begin with, were probably slightly more temperate than the average. None of them would deny, however, that once committed to a war, the *samurai* tradition behind them made it inevitable that they fight it through to the bitter end. Whether the end meant victory or defeat was irrelevant. The modern militarists, after they seized power in the thirties, were able to draw on the resources of this tradition, and the sympathies it evoked. The *samurai* loyalties within the Japanese were strengthened by every trick of modern propaganda, their emergence made doubly inevitable by the accidents of geography and world politics. The way to Pearl Harbor was well charted.

Tadao Yamazaki and his generation grew up in an insularity less vicious, but far more complete than that of the Hitler *Jugend* or Mussolini's *Ballila* boys. The Japanese military riveted their hold on the country with relative ease, because they were bringing nothing alien to Japan. Capitalism and parliamentary government were alien things, which had to be understood with an effort. But the loyalty of the web society of Japan, its cohesiveness, its clan spirit—these were ready tools for the generals to exploit. They now offered Japanese a real-life version of the traditional *samurai* stories, with a new cast of characters—the advancing Imperial soldiers banzaiing their way across the China plains. For the popular old dramas of brave men standing their ground against base enemies, they substituted a more potent image: Japan, the brave "island country," making its way to its destiny against the treachery and the conniving of a hostile foreign world.

Yamazaki grew up in Saga City, in Kyushu, a conservative provincial capital which has produced some of Japan's greatest military leaders. General Ginzaburo Masaki, the man who engineered the February 26th revolt against the government in 1937, was a Saga man. So was Lieutenant General Akira Muto, one of the makers of Manchukuo. The Three Human Bombs—the soldiers who blew themselves up with a land mine to breach the Chinese entrenchments at Shanghai in 1931—they were Saga men, and their statue, new and shining, stood in the town square.

Another great popular hero was Major Noboru Kuga, called the "flower of Japanese soldiery." In the same Shanghai Incident, Major Kuga, while wounded and unconscious, was taken prisoner by the Chinese. After his release he committed *harakiri*,* since he felt that only his death could erase the shame which his capture had cast on the tradition of *Bushido*. A classmate of Kuga's, Major Kairen Kan, sometimes came to the school at Saga to lecture the students about Kuga's heroism. "We thought these men were more than heroes," Yamazaki remembers. "They were the epitome of courage, loyalty and devotion to one's country."

At school Yamazaki learned the *"samurai* spirit" as thoroughly as Russian children were learning the "Leninist-Stalinist spirit." During Saga's snowy winters, the boys were marched out into the yard, stripped to the waist, for bruising calesthenics. Anyone who wore gloves or mittens was ridiculed as a *"yowamushi*—a weak worm" by his classmates. The new *samurai* had to be tough— and the archaic Spartan training which Shimizu and Kisei's feudal fathers had insisted on, was now given en masse to all Japanese children.

The indoctrination was not wholly cruel. Oddly enough, another popular Saga hero was Taneomi Soejima, the founder of the Japanese Red Cross. But the art of healing was not so glamorous as The Three Human Bombs. With the tide of the twenties now completely reversed, each Japanese boy had one great ambition—to strap on the heavy, awkward sword of an army officer and to fight for his country's glory.

In 1938, in his second year at Middle School, Yamazaki had his own hopes in this direction blunted. After a routine medical checkup, he was told that he was physically unfit for military service in the Regular Army. It was a

* This ritual of suicidal belly slitting is more commonly known in Japan by its other pronunciation of *"seppuku."*

major crisis in his life. Reluctantly, he decided to become a scholar or a teacher, a tragic comedown in his ambitions.

In those days, as the ruthless silk curtain once again dropped over the islands, every disturbing bit of foreign influence was quietly muffled within its folds. Foreign movies were disappearing. Foreign words were discouraged in conversation. The free press of Japan got its death blow in 1937, on the day when troops, on military orders, purposefully smashed the printing presses of the Osaka *Asahi*, Japan's most respected newspaper. Everything that Yamazaki and his classmates read—books, newspapers, magazines—was in some way devoted to furthering the militarists' plans. The few moderates left in government posts were unsparingly attacked. Every day the students read in the newspapers how the civilians were "holding Japan back" in its efforts to bring stability to East Asia.

When Japanese troops marched over the Marco Polo Bridge in 1937, Yamazaki had no doubt about their righteousness: "I firmly believed that Japan had every right and responsibility to punish the insolent Chinese. I felt sorry for the Chinese people. On the other hand, I believed that this was the only way to help the Chinese straighten out their country." He felt no special hatred for the United States or the other European powers at that time, only a deepening distrust. The distrust was abetted by what he learned about the exploitation of the natives in Western colonies like Burma, Indo-China and the Dutch East Indies.

His teachers were as aggressive as the young officers of Saga about spreading the idea of Japan's new destiny in Asia. New maps previewed a tempting political entity—the Greater East Asia Co-Prosperity Sphere. New books revived the Shinto theories of Japan's divine nationhood, to keep pace with the advance of Japan's human armies. The primary schools were not neglected. Six-year-olds, wearing their first dark-blue uniforms, sat obediently in their classrooms, learning the words of a popular childrens' song:

> *"Shoulder to shoulder with my elder brother,*
> *I can go to school today,*
> *Thanks to the soldiers, thanks to the soldiers,*
> *Who fought for our country, for our country."*

In the first lesson in the Japanese school readers, they read this:

> *"March on, march on,*
> *Soldiers, march on.*
>
> *The sun is red,*
> *The rising sun is red.*
>
> *The flag of the sun!*
> *Banzai! Banzai!"*

In the streets of Japanese towns and cities, there were old-fashioned parades with lanterns and banners to celebrate each new victory. For some the victories cost dear. Already, unobtrusively, rows of white boxes with ashes inside them were traveling in special railway cars from the ports into the interior of the land, each nicely lettered with the name and unit of the farm boys, accountants and students who would never join in the victory celebrations. Few of the people who got these small boxes made any outcry. Most of them accepted this ending quite stoically, convinced that it was of the order of things that it should happen.

* * * * *

Those who were prosperous—and many who were not—managed to travel to Tokyo, where they streamed through the stark black Shinto gates of Yasukuni Shrine, the plain but awesome monument on the Kudan hill in Tokyo, not far from the buildings of the War Ministry. The crowds of Yasukuni walked silently beneath its cool trees to worship before the black and gold-lettered tablets inside the sanctuary. The spirits of the honored soldier dead were here enshrined, in the Shinto pantheon that grew more important in the life of the nation, as the way of the soldier was more stressed.

Yasukuni is not an old shrine. It was founded on the present site in 1869 by the Meiji government, as a memorial to the imperial soldiers killed during the civil wars of the Restoration. Gradually the shrine became more meaningful. By the time of the Russo-Japanese War, it was regarded as the spiritual resting-place of all those killed in action. In a poem written then, Emperor Meiji expressed this feeling:

*"The souls of heroes whose bones whiten in foreign lands,
Have even now returned to the Capital."*

Although English-speaking Japanese generally protested that Yasukuni Shrine was no more than a Japanese equivalent of the Lincoln Memorial, popular belief ran much deeper. Shinto priests taught, and millions of Japanese believed that the soul of a slain soldier was instantly transported to the sanctuary of the shrine, where it hovered about with the other honored dead, tutelary deities of the nation. Yasukuni was at the same time a pious monument and a Valhalla taken literally. It was the heaven-on-earth of the militarists' Shinto religion. Its gaunt wooden gates were served up as a symbol to recruits going into battle in China. Similar to the teachings of Islam and, if only superficially, to Christianity during the Crusades, Shinto taught them that any Japanese who died in battle calling the name of the emperor, would automatically become one of the blessed of Yasukuni. The emperor's war was a holy war, and those sacrificed for victory—no Japanese war, by Shinto definition, could end in defeat—were its slaughtered saints.

* * * * *

On the 19th of October, 1938, a cool Monday evening in Tokyo, Hirohito drove to Yasukuni for a special ceremony—the solemn enshrining of the 10,334 officers and men who had thus far been killed in the China Incident. The old Shinto rites were conducted in darkness and in utter silence. Although the shrine precincts were crowded with the widows and families of many of the slain, there was scarcely any sound but the reedy voices of the Shinto priests reciting the *norito*, the ritual prayers for the sanctified dead, and the rustle of dead leaves around them in the autumn breeze.

The English-language *Japan Times* wrote an editorial the next day describing the ceremony's meaning:

". . . Enshrined as *Kami*,* [the soldiers] become deities to guard the Empire. They are no longer human. They have become pillars of the Empire. As they are enshrined at Yasukuni, they retain no rank nor other distinction. Generals and privates are alike. They are no longer counted as so many military men, but so many pillars.' It is because they are the pillars of the nation that they are worshiped by the Emperor and the entire populace . . ."

The supreme Shinto pontiff, who officiated at this memorial, was by now well used to his traditional role. When he ascended the throne in 1926, Hirohito looked and behaved like a reasonably accurate model of a constitutional monarch. The lessons of his triumphant tour of Europe were fresh in the minds of his Europeanized advisors. They felt that the Japanese monarchy would soon become in fact what the more liberal of the Meiji reformers wanted it to be. But they and their plans were defeated by the fall of Japanese democracy. The ascendant militarists wanted an emperor starchly dressed in his

* The same type of national god with a small "G" as the Emperor was declared to be.

Shinto regalia, whose traditional divinity would be dinned into the consciousness of the Japanese people as loudly as the memory of their *samurai* past.

The Crown Prince who had played deck games with his suite abroad the *Katori* became an untouchable presence, gradually cut off from all contact with his subjects. His insulation behind palace walls was the twentieth-century version of the old Japanese custom: solidify power through the authority of the Throne, but keep the emperor himself from wielding it. The twentieth-century militarists however, differed in one important respect from the shoguns, who had used the same system before them. After coming to power, they kept the concept of imperial authority alive for their own use—instead of letting it quietly lapse. They believed so strongly in the emperor system, in fact, that their usurpation of the emperor's power was almost unconscious.

Japan's new emperor-worship reached Ruritanian extremes. In 1934 there was a national crisis when a police inspector named Juhei Honda detoured the Emperor's car through a street not on his official route. Under the tension of the Emperor's visit to Kiryu (a silk-manufacturing center north of Tokyo), Honda had steered his procession down a side street. The street had not been properly swept for the Emperor's coming, and the passersby there were not properly dressed for the occasion. As a result of the wrong turning, the Emperor missed an official reception party and arrived at his destination 30 minutes early.

By his chance mistake, the unfortunate Inspector Honda had committed the cardinal sin. By the standards of the web society, such an affront to the Emperor, its guiding figure, was an offense against morality itself. Although guards were posted around his house, Honda made a desperate attempt at suicide—the only way a member of the web society could atone for such a misstep. He only wounded himself in the effort, but the resultant hospitalization forced the whole story into the open, after the newspapers had been kept from printing a word of it for three days. The Premier offered personal apologies to the Emperor for Honda's error. There was popular awe and indignation, and tension among Diet representatives and Cabinet members. The Home Minister, who included the police among his responsibilities, was almost forced to resign.

The Emperor's person was held in more awe than his opinions. He had little sympathy with either the China Incident or the drift towards war with the United States, but he had neither the force of character nor the training to throw back the forward march of the Army. The old Meiji statesmen who instructed Hirohito in the work of kingship had taught him all too well the duties—and the restraints—of a constitutional monarch. He was not to interfere directly in government, as his grandfather often had. He was to preside, but not to act. The moderates around him, including his cautious distant relative, Premier Fuminaro Konoye, were equally ill-equipped for a showdown with the Army (if, in fact, they ever wanted one). None of them had any positive program to offer Japan in place of the new militarism. At the same time, the rising fortunes of Germany before and at the start of World War II made it seem that militarism paid heavy dividends on relatively moderate investments.

In the circumstances, Hirohito contented himself with registering slight disapproval at the course of events. He was mildly skeptical when Foreign Minister Yosuke Matsuoka, in 1940, carefully explained to him that the Tripartite Pact with the Axis powers had been necessary, to avoid an international boycott of Japan. Later the Emperor remarked to his chamberlain, Marquis Kido, that though avoiding boycotts was wise, he felt it unfortunate that the government had so little "insight" concerning the United States.

At an imperial briefing session on September 5, 1941, Field Marshal Gen Sugiyama assured Hirohito that Japan could complete the capture of the "southern areas" within three months, whether or not the Americans interfered. Hirohito answered, in language unusually direct for him: "That's exactly what you generals told me when you started the China Incident. You said it would be straightened out within three months. However, it has already taken four years. Are you not now calculating more or less the same way?"

On the day following, while the Japanese Ambassador, Admiral Kichisaburo Nomura, and the special envoy Saburo Kurusu continued negotiations in Washington for a peaceful settlement in Asia, the Cabinet and the General Staff chiefs had a meeting to discuss war plans, in case the negotiations with the United States failed. Hirohito presided. There was a deep conflict between the military and civilian members. The military men virtually set a date for an attack against the United States. The civilians protested that the diplomatic ways of settling differences were being ignored. The Emperor sided with the civilians. He pulled a piece of paper out of his pocket and read to the conference an old poem of his grandfather's:

"Though I consider the surrounding seas as my brothers, Why is it that the waves should rise so high?"

"I have always read and appreciated this poem," he said, "and kept in my heart the Emperor Meiji's spirit of peace. It has been my wish to perpetuate this spirit."

Hirohito voiced this sentiment obliquely, in the devious, allusive language he had been trained to use. Its meaning was well understood—and the military men, for the moment, were awed and shocked. With polite court officials, the suggestion might have had the force of a permanent command, enjoining Japan from making war. But the gentlemanly Emperor of Japan was now dealing with men like General Hideki Tojo. They were not gentlemanly people.

* * * * *

While Hirohito worried in Tokyo about the consequences of Japan's military ambitions, Farmer Sanada, from the uplands near Mt. Fuji, could see nothing but the victories and the festivals which they brought. "We were living," he says now, "in a long festival-feeling. There was an endless string of victories. And each victory meant another celebration. To win isn't exactly a bad feeling, you know."

Sakaji Sanada was perhaps the only one of the five not seriously affected by the wave of changes that overtook Japan. In the newspapers and the broadcasts that came to him over his new radio he heard the same phrases that the Emperor muttered in his speeches and the zealous teachers taught to their eager students. Although the festivals were familiar, the new words had a slightly disturbing quality. A feeling of unrest sometimes came upon him. But he could not identify it. Sanada accepted the changing mood of his time as unquestioningly as generations before him had accepted the wars of the *samurai*. In accepting it, he strengthened it, and the solid, uncomplaining acquiescence of millions of Sanadas formed the base on which the new *samurai* fashioned their empire.

In 1937 Sanada got a more personal stake in the Greater East Asia Co-Prosperity Sphere. His son Mitsu, twenty-one, was ordered up to the 49th Artillery Division in Kofu for military training. The following December he was sent to Manchuria, where he spent a year with the border patrol. In 1940, back in Japan, he entered the training school for *Kempei*, the Japanese gendarmerie who combined the duties of military police and secret service men.

In August, 1941, Sakaji Sanada got a telegram from Mitsu asking him to meet him at the Aoyama Divisional Headquarters in Tokyo. Now a corporal, Mitsu told his parents that he was about to leave for overseas—where, he did not know. Before they parted, he gave his mother a lock of his hair.

* * * * *

In Yahata, Hideya Kisei was more intimately engaged in Japan's preparation for war. The steel works shifted to a 24-hour day. The shifts overlapped. Kisei's crew found themselves working a steady twelve to sixteen hours a day. He came to his house only to sleep and to change clothes. He was not able to do any of the chores set for him, as a householder, by the local neighborhood association. (It was then that his friends in the adjoining houses sympathetically urged him to get a wife.)

No one came to lecture the workers at Yahata in the turbulent thirties; there was no specific attempt to convince them of the justice of the new Japan. Kisei, as did his fellow-workers, got what he learned of the world news from hearsay and the local newspapers. This was enough. "We heard," he said, "that the West was trying to throttle Japan out of her rights in Asia. We felt angry and frustrated. This feeling of hatred for the Western nations grew stronger as the Pacific war came closer."

Hatred and power politics meant longer hours and no extra pay. At times, after long hours of shoveling the molten steel into the big vats, Kisei angrily thought he was being degraded to the status of a slave laborer. He was not cheerful about the extra work. But he did not complain. "I guess we were pretty much blinded by the war propaganda," he says now.

When the web tightened he was as powerless as Sanada to resist its bonds. If he thought of Japan's new conquests, it was hardly in terms of aggression. "It didn't occur to me that we were engaged in aggression," he remarked, "I only knew that Japan was poor and that she needed more land for her ever growing population. The moral aspects of these actions didn't interest me."

There was enough truth in what Kisei said to offer a good excuse for a program of conquest. Since the Meiji Restoration, Japan had become a partly industrialized country, certainly the only one on the continent of Asia

—dependent for her raw materials on the world outside. In the grand tradition of international buccaneering, Japanese had always been tempted to go outside and assure their sources of the raw materials by capturing them. For a country so slighted by nature, so dependent on precarious foreign markets for its livelihood, so conscious of foreign suspicion in the form of anti-Japanese tariffs in the British colonies and anti-Japanese exclusion acts in the United States, armed possession of a place seemed the one way to assure a supply of its products. When the militarists wanted to put their argument on logical grounds, they needed only to point to one or two of these facts. Every Japanese, however ignorant, knew that his country was overpopulated and must import food. Most Japanese knew that their country lived or died by trade. A growing number of Japanese realized how precarious the state of international trade was.

* * * * *

Admiral Shimizu, when he was stationed at the Japanese naval base of Yokosuka in the prewar days, used to look wistfully at the navy tankers heading out of the bay, high in the water, on their way to pick up oil in Borneo or the Middle East. Without going so far as to think how, exactly, this oil could be obtained, he would daydream about the Japanese Navy one day sitting on top of its own oil supply. "It was," as he says, "an unconscious dream of all navy men."

Shimizu was far more worldly-wise than the other four gentlemen of Japan in his approach to Japan's problems in the nineteen thirties. He could almost feel the silk curtain being pulled over the islands—although he seldom worried much about it. At the same time he wondered just where the line was drawn which legalized aggression. Shimizu and his friends used to discuss these matters at the Yokosuka officers club, the *suikosha*, a comfortable building that stood high on a rock-ribbed hill overlooking the broad semicircle of the bay. "Peter the Great," he recalls arguing, "swept into East Asia and made Siberia and Saghalien Russian. The English moved into America and took the land away from the Indians. The British then swept through the world and established colonies. The doubt in my mind was what date or era could be picked as the border line between justified conquest and aggression. If Holland could take Indonesia from the natives, why could we not take Indonesia from the Dutch? We needed oil just as much or more than the Dutch did."

Shimizu, like many navy men, had little zeal for the Army's great adventure in China. When his depot in Yokosuka received an urgent order for large supplies of bombs for use against Shanghai, he felt strong misgivings. Talking with his brother officers, Shimizu held the view—not unusual in navy circles—that the best thing for the Japanese would be to hit hard at China, get a good peace, then pull out after about six months of fighting. He had no illusions about the propaganda of Japan's new *mission civilisatrice* in Asia—in fact, he always considered the Chinese a more sophisticated and politically sounder people than his own. He was convinced that the land mass of China, like that of Russia, was a mouthful too big for any single conqueror to swallow.

The growing hatred of the West, in the nineteen thirties, did not find much of an echo in the circles that Shimizu moved in. The West, he reasoned, was able to frustrate Japan's more extravagant plans because it was more powerful. This was a matter of fact, not emotion, to be regarded soberly, if not fatalistically. Fact, through all these years, was what concerned him most. He had an engineer's impatience with any quality that could not be measured by a slide rule, or any situation which could not be expressed in a plan or a blueprint. Like many professional soldiers in the old German Army, he kept his eyes resolutely fixed on the technical quality of his guns.

The change-over to military rule in Japan did not particularly escape him—he just avoided thinking about it.

"I knew nothing about it at the time," he insists, "and probably cared less." The technician was happy in his work. Scrupulous in what might be called the tactical side of life, Shimizu was a good citizen, a happy family man and a just superior, well-liked by almost everyone who came in contact with him. But his morality did not press him to consider the strategy of aggression abroad and the stifling of opposition at home. He did not choose to examine the basic premises of his country's policy, and whether they were good or evil.

Ironically, it was Shimizu, as a technician, who could feel most acutely the quickening pulse of Japan's militarization. If he was unwilling to think about the ultimate change in his country's national policy, he could measure its growth every day in his arsenals and on his drawing boards. Fumio Shimizu and the men like him—engineers, government bureaucrats, international traders—paved the path to war, each of them concentrating almost embarrassingly on his individual section of the road, afraid to look at the major pattern, almost as the Japanese artist prefers painting sensitive pictures of small, restricted scenes, afraid to abandon himself to the chaos of a large theme on canvas.

Late in the thirties, the slowly moving machine of Japanese mobilization leaped ahead to full speed. From 1937, Shimizu realized that he was part of "an all-out effort." Army and navy officers, coming back from inspection trips overseas, walked into the board rooms of Japanese industrialists, holding catalogues of foreign machinery products. Peremptorily they demanded that production on this and that type be started in Japan. War production plants began sprouting everywhere—in Yokohama, Kawasaki, Osaka and Tokyo. Nagoya, a sleepy-eyed provincial capital, became transformed, during those days, into a hub of factories producing airplanes, guns and motors. The pace of expansion reflected the strains of a newly industrialized country. Some factories had to be stocked with imported machinery from Germany or the United States. Others, like the Aichi Aircraft plant in Nagoya, had to fall back on oddly primitive distribution methods. The last American consul in Nagoya grimly watched from his windows, as new airplane fuselages were carried through the streets on oxcarts.

In Yokosuka, while working on problems of ship armor plating, gunnery improvement and ammunition manufacture, Shimizu was promoted in 1937 to the rank of captain. The same year he was transferred to the Tokyo Ordnance Center, to work on the Japanese Navy's key project, the building of the twin super-battleships *Yamato* and *Musashi*. He was concerned with the plans for the battleships' ordnance, which as yet had scarcely reached any concrete dimensions, although experts had been working on them since 1934—two years before the lapsing of the London Naval Treaty, in which Japan had promised to stop construction of any capital ships.

By 1937 there was an air of desperation at the ordnance center. The military advances in China and the new resolution for war had put an almost unbearable burden on the perspiring technicians. Key men in the Navy were working with an average of only two days' leave from duty during the year. There was continual pressure from flag officers for greater output. Already many of the engineers were complaining among themselves at the loss in quality production forced on them by the speed-up.

Working nights at Tokyo was a small matter to Fumio Shimizu. His job was something that naval architects and gunnery specialists had been dreaming about for twenty years—building the first 18-inch shipborne guns in history. The theory behind them was fairly sound. The battleship admirals at Combined Fleet Headquarters realized that they could not hope to catch up with Britain or the United States in sheer volume of tonnage. Their classic naval strategy had turned towards producing big ships, of superior firepower, so that one Japanese capital ship could give a good account of itself against the smaller guns of two American or British. It was realized that American battleships were limited to main batteries of 16-inch guns, since ships large enough to mount a bigger gun could not make the trip through the narrow locks of the Panama Canal.

Shimizu got a blue-ribbon priority for everything he needed in the production line. The guns, however, were of such a size, that new facilities had to be built to construct them. In April, 1941, his plans completed, Shimizu moved to Kure to supervise the casting of the guns and their installation. It was April, 1942, before *Yamato*, fully equipped, was put into active service. She was the most powerful battleship the world has ever seen: outclassing even the German *Bismarck*. Today, seven years after *Yamato* was sunk, Shimizu can still quote the statistics of her size from memory. Her dead weight, fully equipped, was 64,000 tons. Her speed was 27 knots. The engines produced 150,000 horsepower. They were protected by 20 centimeters of deck armor and 41 centimeters of armor plating on the sides of the hull. The nine 18.1 guns had a range of slightly over 25 miles.

Shimizu insists that, at the time *Yamato* was planned, no naval officer had any idea of using this firepower for "aggressive purposes"—another of those sentences which probably turns on the definition of the word "aggression." Personally, at least, he did not. But he did take an honest pleasure in turning out something far superior to anything produced by either the British or the Americans.

Captain Shimizu could sit back in his office in Kure, late in 1941, and reflect that the technical side of Japanese naval warmaking, with the exception of electrical matters, was well on a par with the rest of the world. Only a few things disturbed him. A few months before December 8, he saw pictures of H.M.S. *Prince of Wales* in New York harbor, on her way to the Far East. He noticed some strange electrical equipment topside, which he had never seen before. It puzzled and worried him. Later, he found out what it was: shipborne radar.

6

THE DEFEAT OF GLORY

"The sound of the bell of Jetavana echoes the impermanence of all things. The hue of the flowers of the teak tree declares that they who flourish must be brought low. Yea, the proud ones are but for a moment, like an evening dream in springtime. The mighty ones are destroyed at the last, they are but as the dust before the wind. . . ."

Heike Monogatari

The Germans began World War II with an excellent chance of winning it. The Japanese on their own merits and resources could not possibly have won the Greater East Asia War, barring a general German victory over the European Allies and the United States. The Japanese Navy, in 1941, still needed years to prepare itself for the giant task of winning an essentially naval war over waters stretching from the Indian Ocean to the Bering Sea. The Japanese Army was undermechanized and backward in its grasp of modern tactics. The Japanese industrial machine (as witness Chapter 9) was not only fatally bound to its communications, dependent on overseas sources for everything except low-grade coal, wood and water power; it was organizationally unprepared for supporting a major modern war effort.

The fact that Hideki Tojo and his militarist followers started this war is a classic case of men imprisoned by their own propaganda. They were able so successfully to evoke the armored ghost of Japanese feudalism and the *"samurai* spirit" because they firmly believed in that spirit themselves. They were unregenerate militarists, whose lives had been spent in an atmosphere of shrines and army camps, superbly insulated against the mellowing effects which international intercourse had on the nation as a whole. Like Saigo Takamori, who wanted to attack the Asiatic mainland in 1870, before Japan had built its first steel mill, they were convinced that *"seishin"*—Japanese "spirit"—was enough to win battles. Their motto—abridging Tennyson's Sir Galahad—could have been, "Our strength is the strength of ten, because our hearts are pure Japanese."

In *Verdun,* his pictorial novel about the first World War, Jules Romains has his hero chuckling over an old quotation from Foch's staff doctrine: "Charge the foe and let cold steel decide." This saying, in the Japanese Army, would never have been laughed at. It would have been, rather, in the best traditions of the service. Tojo's army swept down on its enemies with a religious fanaticism that the West itself had not experienced since the Seventh Crusade. The bulky *samurai* swords—long, curved, beautiful weapons—which every one of its officers carried, were not just a showy part of the uniform. They were used in battle. They were a reminder that, in its spirit, there was very little difference between the Japanese Army of 1941 and Hideyoshi's clan *samurai* or the Forty-Seven Ronin.

In their indoctrination programs the military leaders were able to mobilize every tie of duty and loyalty, which existed in the old web society of Japan. With this they created in their Army an extreme and vicious caricature of the national society. "Be resolved that Honor is heavier than the mountains," the old Imperial Rescript to the troops read, "and death lighter than a feather." "Duty should weigh with us as the mass of a lofty mountain," echoed the slogan of General Aritomo Yamagata, the founder of Japan's modern Army. "Against it, our lives resemble the swan's down in lightness." This was the sort of training maxim that produced Kamikaze suicide pilots and Human Bombs. Blind obedience and unscrupulous devotion to the nation was what the generals wanted. Since the world's current extensive experience with Communist fanaticism began, it is no longer quite such a puzzle to understand how years of this sort of indoctrination could produce a single-minded soldier, whose only morality was an army command.

Japanese military orders themselves are the most lurid literary specimens of their kind. A prosaic directive for building field entrenchments would as often as not be climaxed by a paragraph or two praising Japanese military *"seishin"* and exhorting the soldiers, in a very religious manner, to close with the enemy. Again, these orders were were not written solely to impress the soldiers who read them. They honestly expressed the sentiment of the officers who wrote them.

These modern *samurai* regarded death in battle or an honorable suicide as the only way to atone for defeat. The militarists tried to beat this conviction into every Japanese soldier. In most cases they succeeded—often even with civilians. The most tragic example of this was the desperate death of hundreds of Japanese civilians in the Marianas, who hurled themselves over cliffs into the sea shortly after the end of Japanese military resistance there, since soldiers had convinced them that this was the only proper way for loyal Japanese to take defeat.

A classic wartime suicide was the death of the leaders of the Japanese 32nd Army, which fought a brave and well-planned campaign against the American invasion forces on Okinawa, in the spring of 1945. By mid-June, after two and a half months of last-ditch fighting, the 32nd Army's tactical units had been all but annihilated. A few hours after dawn, on the morning of June 22nd, the army commander, Lieutenant General Mitsuru Ushijima, and his chief of staff, Lieutenant General Isamu Cho, walked out of their final command post, a cave in the wet cliffs on the southwest coast of the island. They had just finished having a quiet farewell party with the surviving members of their staff. In honor of the event, Cho had passed around the last of a case of Black and White Scotch, which his orderly had salvaged in the retreat from their old headquarters.

Followed by the staff, the generals climbed down to a small cleared space in the rocks, just above the sea. Ushijima was dressed in a formal black *kimono;* Cho wore his best dress uniform, heavy with ribbons and aiguillettes. After a last greeting, first the commanding general, then the chief of staff, ripped open his belly with a dagger, in the traditional upward thrust of *harakiri*. As they fell forward, a staff officer cut off their heads with his long sword.

Before his suicide Cho had despatched a last official message pouch to Tokyo, carried by an officer courier who managed to slip around the American lines to the islands north of Okinawa. The most important item in the pouch was not an action report of the Okinawa fighting, but a small four-line poem, addressed—through the medium of the Emperor's poetry teacher—to the Throne. It read:

"Beside the Emperor I die a warrior;
My blood stains heaven and earth,
Although my body falls in the far south,
My soul returns to protect the Emperor's country."

The author had followed through to the end his country's peculiar tradition of knighthood.*

---

* At this late stage of the war, when the Japanese morale had been slightly weakened by repeated defeats, many rank and file soldiers were not quite so keen on the idea of ending their lives, as the World War II newspaper stories, both Japanese and American, suggested. Sometimes, officers had to order it. Late in the same Okinawa campaign, some four hundred survivors of the Japanese 24th Infantry Division were trapped in a series of caves in the south-central part of the island, which had been used for division headquarters. When American intelligence officers called down (in Japanese) asking them to surrender, the division commander, Lieutenant General Tatsumi Amamiya, commanded his men to commit suicide. He stationed

* * * * *

Into the barracks of the militarists, at various times, marched Shimizu, Yamazaki, and Kisei, and both Sakaji Sanada and his son Mitsu. They have the same memories of their training, all unpleasant. Recruits in both the Japanese Army and Navy were under the direct charge of the privates first class and the lower non-commissioned officers. They were trained to obey these men implicitly, and also to wait on them. If a recruit made a mistake, he was kicked, slapped and beaten often enough so that he would not make the same mistake again—this was the Japanese theory of discipline. Brutality was encouraged—as an impromptu toughening-up process. Although commissioned officers did not frequently deal out blows themselves, life in the barracks or below-decks was a literal round of "the sergeant hits the corporal, the corporal hits the private first class, the private first class hits the recruit." As the recruits got promotions, they kept up the system which had humiliated them, as studiously as American college sophomores hand down the practices of hazing freshmen.

There was no redress from this brutality. It formed the boundary of a cruel, desperate world all its own. During the thirties, it was not infrequent for draftees to crack up mentally, or even to commit suicide from the strain of accepting military life. Sanada and Kisei came to the Army from the rough surroundings of a mountain farm and a steel mill, so that the transition was not too difficult for them. But Tadao Yamazaki, a city boy with a considerable knowledge of the world outside the farm and the barracks, was shocked at his navy recruit's training in 1943. "Seamen weren't treated like human beings," he says drily, "not even as Japanese for that matter."

---

guards at the caves' entrances to prevent anyone from reconsidering this blanket decision on his own. Within a half hour, all the survivors had blown themselves up with grenades. General Amamiya himself took an easier way out. He had his orderly give him a painless intravenous injection.

This kind of indoctrination had its effect. It coarsened the minds of soldiers, as well as their bodies. It encouraged the private soldier or sailor, beaten by everyone in authority above him, to be in turn merciless in his treatment of enemy prisoners or foreign civilians. At the same time, the constant emphasis on death, duty and devotion to the Emperor had its own effect. Soldiers idealized their loyalty as a compensation for their brutal surroundings. Even as perceptive an observer as Yamazaki, when ordered to the fleet, could talk lyrically about "dying a beautiful death" for his country.

There was no doubt that Admiral Shimizu had this conception of duty and honor at all costs ingrained in him, as well. The urbanity of many Japanese navy officers, in this respect, was deceptive. The same men who chatted so sociably in Washington or London drawing rooms in the twenties or thirties let themselves be cut down leading futile "banzai" charges in 1944 or 1945, or committed suicide rather than be taken prisoner off their sinking ships or ruined command posts.

The state of mind which made fanatical fighters out of Tojo's armies, led them into battle inadequately equipped for modern warfare. Japanese officers always in their hearts preferred a bayonet charge to an artillery interdiction as a means of disposing of the enemy. Their wartime performance showed it. The army which they led, with its successes and failings, was the last great infantry army of modern times.

As an infantry army, the Japanese were rough, tough and efficient. The troops were aggressive and courageous. They kept their discipline perfectly—Japanese atrocities were only perpetrated when commanding officers, knowingly and deliberately, let their men off the leash. No one could ever call the Japanese a parade-ground army, however. It will not be remembered, as the British and German armies, in terms of gleaming files passing in review. The Japanese, on parade or at war, had very little spit and polish to them—just lines of clean, but rumpled-looking troops, marching jerkily and loosely behind serious men with mustaches who carried long, preposterous-looking swords.

The lack of parade-ground elegance gave some foreigners an unfortunate contempt for what the Japanese Army could do in action. The contempt was not shared by people who had seen them fight, from the American military observers who watched Japanese infantrymen storm the Russian lines in Manchuria in 1905, to the Marines who wrenched the jungle of Guadalcanal from their sons in 1942. The Japanese, in a tactical sense, were well officered. They knew standard infantry tactics and had a few favorite fillips of their own. Until the end of the war Allied infantrymen were trying to work out a foolproof defense against Japanese night infiltration. When on the defensive, the Japanese made a black art out of the technique of making their stand on the reverse slopes of hills.

It was popular, during World War II, to assert that the Japanese fought like a batch of robots, incapable of thinking for themselves as individuals. Aside from this being a charge which Americans tend to level at almost everyone else, it was not strictly true. The fault frequently did not lay with the Japanese soldier, but with his commanders. The senseless "banzai" charges and the continued uncoordinated attacks were more often than not the results of weak planning at headquarters. Unfortunately for the Japanese, the philosophy of "charge the foe and let cold steel decide" was no incentive to good staff work.

The military men who ran the Japanese Army, with few exceptions, were the most conservative group of professionals in the world. Their insistence on making modern *samurai* out of their men crowded new developments in warfare out of their attention. Because the Army was successful in China, using against a weak enemy weapons and tactics not too different from those of the Russo-Japanese War, their conservatism grew stronger. There were many shrewd professional soldiers in the Japanese officer corps in 1941. But few of these were over fifty, and their opinions during the next four years were generally smothered beneath the weight of gray hair and gold medals in the higher staff offices.

Japan was the last of the great powers to begin mechanizing its armies. In 1938 and 1939, when the Japanese and the Russians fought an exploratory little border war with each other, in divisional strength, at Nomonhan and Changkufeng, the conservative military men got a bad jolt. The Japanese troops, armed with their standard infantry and artillery weapons, were badly pushed around by Russians using armor, massed artillery and tactical bombers. Hastily the General Staff gave the green light to the lonely band of armor specialists at Imperial Headquarters, for organizing a tank division. Hobbled by material shortages and only grudging support from the generals, they did not get far. By the end of World War II, only two such divisions had been fully trained and equipped. The First Armored Division, intended for use as a unit on the broad Manchurian plains, was scattered piecemeal among Japanese garrisons in the Pacific. The Second Armored Division was sent to Luzon late in the war. There it, too, was committed piecemeal against the advancing Americans, and was annihilated piecemeal and without difficulty, a last memorial to the inability of the Japanese high command to adapt its thinking to new techniques of warfare.

Since the Pacific war was decided by sea and air power, the Japanese Army was strategically beaten by 1943, when the Navy was. Its outposts had been left isolated and incapable of reinforcing each other, even before it began large-scale tactical operations against the American Marines and Army. Nevertheless, many of its last-ditch campaigns were conducted with great skill. At Peliliu a Japanese infantry force of less than two regiments badly hurt the First U.S. Marine Division and tied up the 81st Army Division and supporting troops for nearly two months, before its last effective fighting units were put out of action. Without any direct air or naval support, Generals

Cho and Ushijima kept up a skillful defense of Okinawa under the pressure of American air power, naval bombardment and army and marine forces over twice their army's size.

But even in their best defensive operations, Japanese staff officers had their planning badly crimped by the insistence of most troop leaders on attacking—in the *samurai* spirit—wherever possible. When Japan's meager military planning resources could be concentrated on a successful offensive, as in the early campaigns of 1942 in Southeast Asia, or when troops were committed to a simple, bitter-end defense, as units of the Special Navy Landing Forces* were at Tarawa, the modern militarists were at their best. Otherwise their strategy had no flexibility. It was critically taxed by unforeseen enemy maneuvers. In this way the modern Japanese resembled their ancestors who fought against the thirteenth-century Mongol invaders—formidable, with their familiar two-handed swords, when able to attack at close quarters, but at a loss how to deal with Mongol cavalry and long-range archery attacks, a new type of warfare.

* * * * *

The admirals who commanded the Japanese Navy did not share this backwardness of the army generals. This is not to say that they were iconoclasts—navy recruits got almost as much indoctrination in Japanese "military spirit" as the soldiers. But, both by tradition and experience, the Navy was far more closely connected with the world outside the Japanese islands. Because their trade was more complicated, navy men kept up their reliance on foreign shipyards and foreign instructors in the nineteenth century, long after the Army had struck out on its own. Admiral Togo, Japan's Nelson, learned his seamanship at the Royal Naval College in Greenwich, England. Admiral

---

* U. S. troops and correspondents often mistakenly called these navy detachments, trained for land fighting, the "Imperial Marines."

Uriu, Togo's most famous contemporary, was an Annapolis graduate. Long after this active collaboration with the Western sea powers had ceased, pleasant memories of the association lingered. Fumio Shimizu, in his early days in the service, used to chuckle at older officers who still admiringly referred to Britain as *"Waga Eikoku*—Our England."

From their cruises around the world in the twenties and thirties, Japanese Navy officers also brought back a considerable respect for the industrial capacity of Europe and, especially, the United States. Although fleet exercises and war games in the Pacific were always planned with something strongly resembling the U. S. Pacific Fleet as the hypothetical enemy (and vice versa in the case of the U. S. Pacific Fleet), the admirals were none too eager for an actual showdown. Japan, they argued, must first build its Navy up to something at least the equal of American fleet strength. They were not gambling men.

In the military councils of the thirties, it was the admirals who were dragging their feet. The Army, goaded by its victories in China, dreamed of building a huge continental empire in Asia. All the generals asked from the Navy was transportation for their troops and insurance against the U.S. Pacific Fleet interfering with the gains in Asia, before they had been consolidated. By this time, the army bosses predicted, the Americans, lacking the "spiritual" strength of the Japanese, would be tired of the war and willing to accept a negotiated peace. This was the premise on which Tojo gave the word to attack Pearl Harbor.

The very Navy which sent its planes to bomb Pearl Harbor was least sure of successfully finishing what it had started. Despite the happy memories of Annapolis and "Our England," the admirals' reservations about the Army's war plan were not sentimental ones. Control of Southeast Asia, with its oil and rubber, appealed to them as much as running Manchuria did to the generals. They flinched, however, at the practical aspects of the Army plan.

In the Navy's view, it was visionary to hope for a negotiated peace. Admiral Isoroku Yamamoto, the commander-in-chief of the Combined Fleet, was badly misquoted in his famous 1942 remark about dictating peace in the White House. He was not talking from arrogance. What he actually said was that only by the complete defeat and occupation of the United States, which peace in the White House implied, could Japan escape defeat itself.* Weaker than the Army and without its prestige, the Navy could not make Yamamoto's view prevail. In 1943 Admiral Yamamoto, a brilliant naval strategist, was shot down by American fighters over Rabaul. He was thus not around in 1945 to give his army friends a cheerless "I told you so."

Once committed, the Navy gave a far better account of itself than the Army did. The original carrier attack on Pearl Harbor was almost flawlessly executed. Had the planes of Admiral Nagumo's First Carrier Fleet caught the U. S. Pacific Fleet's carriers, as well as the battleships in port, the Pacific war might have taken years longer for the Allies to win. If any more proof of Japan's naval prowess was needed, it came with the sinking of H.M.S. *Prince of Wales* and H.M.S. *Repulse,* drastic confirmation that the day of the battleship was over. The early Navy operations in Southeast Asia, ranging from transporting troops to Corregidor to capturing the airport at Menado in the Celebes with navy paratroopers, went off with equal smoothness. Some brilliant defensive actions were fought, as well. The undetected evacuation of 5,183 Japanese troops from Kiska, on July 28, 1943, un-

---

* In a fragment of his memoirs, published in the newspaper *Asahi* at the end of 1945, the late Prince Konoye records the comment which Admiral Yamamoto made to him about a Japanese war with the United States:

"If I am told to fight regardless of consequences, I shall run wild considerably for the first six months or a year, but I have utterly no confidence for the second and third years of the fighting. The pact with the Axis has been concluded and we cannot help it. Now that the situation has come to this pass, I hope that you still try to avoid an American-Japanese war."

der the nose of American search planes and destroyer screens, was another classic of its kind.

When American and Japanese fleets traded blows in the Solomons on relatively equal terms, the Americans, who had tended to look down on Japanese proficiency in a fair fight, got some unpleasant surprises. At the battle of Tassafaronga, in November, 1942, Rear Admiral Raizo Tanaka and his eight transport destroyers were attacked by a greatly superior American force of five cruisers and six destroyers, while performing a supply mission for Japanese troops at Guadalcanal. In a night torpedo attack, Tanaka sank one American cruiser and crippled three, at the cost of only one dead destroyer of his own. The cruiser battle of Savo Island, fought in August of the same year, was a smashing Japanese victory. In a battle of roughly equal forces, the Japanese sank four Allied cruisers, without any serious losses of their own.

Looking at the war as a whole, there were of course few Japanese naval victories. Even before the weight of their naval power became overwhelming, the Americans had proved themselves slightly better ship handlers and far better strategists—again, planning was the Japanese Achilles' heel. But, especially as cruiser and destroyer men, the Japanese were hard to beat. Their brilliant torpedo attack tactics, for example, caused American staff officers ruefully to revise their own cruiser doctrine.

The Japanese admirals, when they had sat around in the red-brick Navy Ministry building in Tokyo, planning the war, made two specific mistakes. The first was ultimately fatal. They failed to reckon with the aggressive submarine war waged by the United States Navy. The submarines sank five million tons of Japanese shipping, ultimately cut the sea lanes between Japan's colonies and homeland, and were the greatest single factor in the American victory in the Pacific war. The second mistake was exactly the converse of the first: the Japanese used their own submarines badly. The undersea fleet that could have played hob with the widely scattered lines of sea communication between the battle areas and the U. S. Pacific Coast, was tied down for most of the war, either used for fleet scouting or transporting men and supplies to isolated garrisons.

Speaking more generally, the admirals lost the war for exactly the reasons they had feared: they lacked the ships, the trained sailors and pilots (and Japanese naval aviation, incidentally, was far superior to the Army's), and the building facilities to keep up a punishing naval war with the world's greatest maritime and industrial power. For their limitations, they fought well. But, by 1943, the admirals were beaten. Some of them knew it, others pretended not to. Few of their fellow-citizens at home suspected it.

* * * * *

At home in Japan, the first year of the Greater East Asia War was sweet. Reports of one victory after another—Manila, Singapore, Hong Kong, Bataan—came crackling over village radios and neatly folded in the pages of the ubiquitous *Asahi, Mainichi* and *Yomiuri,* the three national circulation newspapers. Despite the air raid drills and the extra working hours, Sakaji Sanada and millions like him were basking in a "festival-feeling" intensified. Crowds packed the theatres in downtown Tokyo to see the newsreels of the bombing of Pearl Harbor. Every Japanese could find a thrill of identity linking him with the fur-helmeted fliers, looking down through their bomb sights at the United States Fleet. The man in the street was puffed up by thoughts of the new national dignity. It was enough to make the tight web existence of the island country, with all its stiflings, seem justified. The slogan *"Hakko Ichiyu*—the four corners of the earth under one roof" (an ancient Japanese equivalent of *"Ein Reich, Ein Volk, Ein Fuhrer"*) appeared to be coming true. From the low-class *kasutoriya*—the literal gin mills of Tokyo, to the factory streets of Kawasaki and the scented geisha houses of Kyoto, the whole nation was humming and believing the words of a new prize patriotic song:

See, the sky opens over the Eastern Sea,
The Rising Sun climbs higher, radiant in its flight.
The spirit of Heaven and Earth is throbbing with vigor,
And hope dances through the eight islands of Japan. . . .

With an unbroken line of Emperors
We are blessed with light and eternity.
We the people, all of us,
Conforming to the Divine Mission of the Virtue of
* His Imperial Majesty,*
Go forth to make the eight corners of the world
* Our home. . . .*

At college Tadao Yamazaki and his classmates were reading translations of *Mein Kampf* and Alfred Rosenberg's *Myth of the Twentieth Century*, to help keep up with the Schmidts on the other side of the victorious Axis. In Shimoyoshida, three or four times a month, the postman brought Sakaji Sanada letters from Mitsu, who had landed in Manila. Mitsu liked Manila. He described it as a city "where peace had returned." The Filipinos, Mitsu said, welcomed the Japanese occupation. To reinforce his description, he sent back a few postcards of Philippine scenes and copies of his army propaganda leaflets.

On the tip of another Japanese Army spearhead, Hideya Kisei's Signal Corps detachment had marched across Thailand. After some shakedown training, they were attached to an infantry regiment moving in on the heels of the retreating British in Burma. On all fronts the tide of victory kept rolling in. Even Shimizu, who had just been made a rear admiral, could not help being "pleasantly surprised" at the progress his comrades were making. Perhaps, on the eighth of December, he had been too pessimistic.

166   *Five Gentlemen of Japan*

* * * * *

On the fifth of June, 1942, for a small but significant group of Japanese, the sweetness of victory began to turn sour. The carriers and battleships of the combined fleet steamed towards Midway Island to complete the destruction of the United States Pacific Fleet. But the Battle of Midway was a Pearl Harbor in reverse. Four first-line Japanese carriers were sunk by planes from the same U.S. Navy carriers which Admiral Chuichi Nagumo, the victor of Pearl Harbor, again had hoped to take by surprise. The margin of Japanese naval superiority was cancelled. Admiral Yamamoto, the commander-in-chief, steaming westward in *Yamato*, away from the scene of his carriers' defeat, realized that the chances of dictating peace in the White House were gone forever. The Japanese admirals at home shared every bit of his concern. At Tokyo, where he was in command of the technical center, Admiral Shimizu's pessimism returned. "After the early victories," he said, "Midway was like a dash of cold water."

Midway was the high-water mark. For the next two years, the Japanese generals, as forgetful as some American generals of the fact that the Pacific war was a naval action, blustered about a "thousand-year war," if necessary, to secure the gains of Japan's new empire. But the admirals had lost their race to snuff out the U.S. Pacific Fleet before it grew to unmanageable proportions. The victory announcements which Imperial Headquarters spokesmen kept making after Midway and the loss of Guadalcanal had a false ring to them. They were as ineffectual substitutes for the real thing as the barley and soybean paste which Japanese civilians were now begining to eat in place of their old rice and sweet potatoes.

* * * * *

Sanada's euphoria was speedily dissolving under a regimen of austerity and hard sacrificing work. As 1943 gave way to 1944, the failings of the Japanese military machine were intimated to him in very personal ways. He knew that Japan was desperately short of metal and other raw materials when the Army confiscated the four steel looms, which had been his most reliable source of income. He quickly replaced them with wooden looms, but towards the end of the war he could only use two of those, because of the shortage of yarns. He had no illusions about Japan's food shortage. His fellow farmers elected him chairman of the local *Nomin Hokoku Sai-shintai*—literally translated, "The Farmer-Citizens' Patriotic Propulsion Corps." In accordance with his duties to help increase local food production, Chairman Sanada distributed leaflets to all the families of his district, giving information on the economies possible both in growing food and eating it.

Embarrassingly enough, Sanada, despite this honor, was unable to meet his own rice quota—the amount of food that his farm was judged capable of contributing to the war effort. When the authorities dressed him down for this, he was resentful. "If a man has tried his best and failed," he protested, "he is still just as good a citizen as the man who meets his quota without even trying."

When he was not working around his own farm, Sanada was out with his neighbors doing "voluntary" labor service. In 1944 they helped build a nearby airfield. Nearer at home, they dug local air-raid shelters and tried to patch up the rutted mountain roads that climbed around the village and past the ashy base of Mt. Fuji. Until 1937 these roads had been well kept. Japan at that time threatened to have a far better highway network than most of Western Europe. But, since then, most of the road-building funds had been allotted for other purposes. Now it was up to the farmers to fix them.

Sanada and his neighbors did not enjoy their new work. And the spurious victories in the war news each day grew more suspect. At home, he said despairingly to his wife, Hie, that the Japanese were fools for trying to do the impossible. Japan was losing the war. "Now, now, Father, you mustn't think that way," Hie would caution. His thoughts continued, but outside the home, he kept them to himself. As the crisis became graver, his feeling of national loyalty continued to be despairing but deep. "Whether I liked it or not," as he says now about his war work, "I had to go and I went and did all I could." This was a good capsule summary of a widely shared point of view.

* * * * *

While Sanada fixed the mountain roads, Tadao Yamazaki was performing some "voluntary labor service" of his own. In the summer of 1943 all Japanese were drafted for this work. (By October, 1944, some two million students, from the university level down to primary school, were engaged in compulsory war work.) Yamazaki was shipped to Hokkaido to work on an airfield at Chitose. The location of the field was another tacit admission that the admirals in Tokyo soon expected to do some fighting near their home bases. This lesson was not lost on Yamazaki. He now had begun to wonder seriously whether Japan could escape utter defeat. This doubt did not prevent him from working hard and loyally in school and at the airfield, consoled by his own form of resignation. "Fatalistic submission" is how he now describes it.

It was very difficult, at this stage, to remain a student. By army order, the Education Ministry had reduced the length of preparatory and college study from six years to five, and military training and part-time labor service constantly interfered with classes. Surprisingly, the courses which were still taught were not drenched with what Yamazaki remembers as "the absurd, fanatic political propaganda" of the time. His old English-language instructors, who were British, had naturally been replaced by Japanese; aside from this, there were no essential changes.

There was no insulating the university from what went on outside, however. A third of Yamazaki's classmates had to leave college to take over family responsibilities, due to the departure of brothers or fathers in military service. Those who stayed behind were continually being taken from their work by military training programs or labor service. No one was starving, but food was scarce. At work in Hokkaido, the students stuffed themselves with cheap, sweet bean soup and rice cakes—in lieu of something more substantial. As a result, some of them suffered constantly from diarrhea.

* * * * *

In 1944, driven by the desperate orders of admirals who were fighting a war without enough ships or planes, and generals who were fighting a war without enough mortars, tanks or artillery, the workers whom Hideya Kisei had left behind him at Yahata sank all their hatred and their resentment at wartime privations into an effort to feed the furnaces more quickly. Kisei's wife, Kiyoko, now worked in the company store at Yahata. More and more women had come in to work with her, taking the place of men who had gone away. Quiet and serious, wearing shapeless baggy trousers called *monpei* instead of Western-style dresses or the fragile and impractical *kimono*, they handed out goods over the counters or clicked out sums on the abacus in the bookkeeping department, doing their work without question and without enthusiasm.

Kisei himself was deep in the Burma jungles, working frantically with his fellow signalmen to keep up the thread of military communications in a maelstrom of hills, rivers and jungles. The victory shouts of Pearl Harbor day and the first westward advance had long ago become dim echoes. After pushing to the borders of India, the divisions in Burma had been thrown back, then slowly pushed eastward in turn by a growing weight of Allied men and machines, Kisei's detachment along with them.

In 1944, Kisei's unit was surrounded and cut off in the disastrous counter-offensive at Imphal. With 39 others, he fought his way eastward through the jungles towards his own lines. After a two-week nightmare of dodging British patrols, desperately foraging for food and floundering without maps or compasses through unknown territory, Kisei and eight others reached the outposts of their main forces. He remembers those days as the most horrible experience of his life.

* * * * *

In July, 1943, the battleship *Mutsu* was blown up during a routine passage through the Inland Sea. No one ever discovered what caused the explosion. It was one of those accidents which happen once in a thousand times aboard a warship, like the fatal chance shot from the *Bismarck* that blew up H.M.S. *Hood* in a matter of seconds. The navy investigators, however, immediately suspected sabotage. Admiral Shimizu, notwithstanding his high rank, was accused of complicity in the sabotage attempt. He had never made a secret of his distaste for the Greater East Asia War. In the growing atmosphere of panic among the Japanese military leaders, it was probably natural that they thought he had done something concrete to express his protests. He was brought before a court martial, tried and acquitted.

The very fact of the court martial was a deep blow. Although Shimizu had not tried to hide his opinions, "they did not," as he protested with his engineer's logic, "interfere with my activity as a naval technician." Harassed by overwork since he had begun building the guns for *Yamato* and her sister ship *Musashi*, he had a serious physical breakdown. After the trial he stayed at home, on sick leave, for four months.

When he returned to duty in November, 1943, he was given command of the Toyokawa Arsenal, east of the city of Nagoya. The navy staff must by then have repented of the court martial against him, for the Toyokawa factory was the biggest navy arsenal in Japan. It was now quite clear to Shimizu that Japan was despairingly on the defensive. Hope had been abandoned for long-range construction jobs like battleships and aircraft carriers. Significantly, the man who had designed battleship guns in 1941 was concentrating in 1943 on machine guns and small-calibre cannon for use in anti-submarine vessels and ground fortifications. Sixty thousand workers were employed at Toyokawa. They turned out machine guns, optical instruments and ammunition in a large, low-lying complex of smoky buildings which robbed 6,000 acres from the rich and beautiful farming country in Aichi Prefecture, just a few miles from Japan's historic coastal road, the *Tokaido*.

The reports of ship sinkings which reached the admiral's office now confirmed his suspicions that the war was lost. Unlike his counterparts, the Becks and the Stauffenbergs in the German armed forces, however, this conviction did not lead him to attempt a change of government, or even to advise a negotiated peace. Once the Emperor had committed the nation, there could be no turning back. With admirals, as with farmers or second-class privates, "it was our duty to do our best until the end." The whole nation resembled the monster cast of a new Greek tragedy, a House of Atreus with 80 million inhabitants, foredoomed and knowing it, but going on tirelessly towards its end.

One thing the admiral did protest in his dispatches to Tokyo. This was the resolve of the military leaders, taking shape in 1944, to arm the entire population with every weapon that could be scraped together—swords, rusty rifles and bamboo spears—for a last-ditch suicidal fight against an American invasion. Shimizu thought that the "bamboo spear strategy" was a reflection on the mentality of the stupid army leaders. No bamboo spears were ever issued to workers at the Toyokawa Arsenal.

* * * * *

It was in this atmosphere of desperation that Tadao Yamazaki finally realized his boyhood wish to become a soldier. In September, 1943, Tojo finally abolished the conscription law allowing college students in liberal arts courses to put off their military examination until graduation.* Yamazaki was able easily to pass the relaxed wartime physical requirements. This time he elected to join the Navy.

After a rough period of boot training as a seaman second class, he passed an examination for officers' candidate school. There he went through five months of basic reserve officers' training, before transferring to the navy radar school at Fujisawa. At Fujisawa, for the first time since entering the Navy, he was able to sleep in a double-decker bed. (The Japanese Navy believed in sleeping its recruits and lower ratings in hammocks.)

Yamazaki was commissioned a *shoi* (ensign) in the Imperial Japanese Navy in December, 1944, five months after the fall of Saipan and two months after the American landings in the Philippines. He could hardly be called a member of Japan's military caste. Like thousands of other reserve officers, he had little faith in the grandiloquent statements of twentieth-century *Bushido,* found navy discipline unnecessarily harsh and resented the "maltreatment" of seamen by their officers. But as he put on his new blue uniform, after polishing the brass buttons with the anchor and cherry blossom insignia of the Navy, there was still something in him of the boy in Saga who had wanted to be a *samurai* soldier. He was proud of the uniform. His first obligatory duty as an officer was to get himself a long military sword. He had not inherited one from any ancestors, as others in his class had, so he went out to buy one at a swordmaker's. He got a cheap but serviceable model for a little under $10.

---

* College students in the United States, since the passage of the 1941 Selective Service Act, did not enjoy such a dispensation. The Japanese —even Japanese militarists—always had a very high regard for a liberal arts education.

Yamazaki was glad to be in the war as an active participant, but he had scant hope of coming out of it. He told himself that his commission meant only that he was "one step nearer the end." By this time the pessimism of the admirals and a few intellectuals had seeped down to the nation at large. Defeats could no longer be disguised. The word *"gyokusai"*—literally, "glorious defeat," had begun to appear on the newspaper pages in stories about the annihilation of Japanese garrisons in the Pacific. When Yamazaki received his orders as a radar officer, assigned to the First Transport Fleet, a unit of twenty-odd troop transports, he flew from Tokyo to Formosa with a sense of complete foreboding. It was "a flight to death."

The rest of Yamazaki's frustrated navy career was a tragi-comical epitome of the defeat of the world's second largest Navy—the story of a new sailor vainly trying to find a ship. Reporting in to the navy base at Takao, in southern Formosa, he found out that the entire Combined Fleet, including the ship to which he had been assigned, had been disastrously beaten at the Battle of Leyte Gulf two months before. The *Sho* Operation, code name for the Japanese Navy's all-or-nothing attempt to arrest the American landings on Leyte, had ended in failure, after narrowly missing a considerable victory. Ensign Yamazaki was temporarily put on the watch list as an assistant operations officer in the Philippine Operations section of Takao Navy headquarters. In February, 1945, he was reassigned to duty with the fleet in China waters.

He headed for Shanghai aboard a 1,500-ton assault transport, through waters now teeming with American submarines. During the trip, the ship accompanying Yamazaki's was torpedoed. It sank almost immediately. The submarine was able to escape.

In Shanghai, he was again assigned to shore duty. But he fell ill—probably with malaria, shortly after arriving, and spent the next three weeks in the hospital. There, for the first time since he had left college, the ex-student was able to do a little reading. He had taken three books with him in his seabag: some of the famous epigrams of the Japanese poet, Basho, the teachings of Shinran Shoin, Japan's great Buddhist saint, and a copy of Goethe's *Faust*.

What he had seen in his brief navy service left Yamazaki doubly convinced that Japan had lost the war irrevocably. In the long nights in the Shanghai naval hospital, trying to sleep away his fever, he had some long and disturbing thoughts. "The situation," he remembers, "was one where an individual's effort, no matter how frantic or how desperate, could not contribute to turning the tide. We could never win. Our homeland would now be isolated like the garrison on Rabaul. There were only two courses open—a fight to the bloody end, or surrender, so that there wouldn't be any more bloodshed."

After he recovered, Yamazaki was careful to keep these thoughts quiet. A few other reserve officers, former college students like himself, felt the same way. But they were chary of hinting at these ideas in front of their superiors. It would have meant a court martial for "dangerous thoughts."

Unknown to Yamazaki and his friends, some very highly placed men in the Navy Ministry had been thinking the same thing. As early as the winter of 1943-44, Rear Admiral Soichi Takagi of the Navy General Staff had prepared a detailed study of the war situation, concluding that victory was impossible. He advised an immediate peace, even at the cost of sacrificing Japan's overseas possessions. Civilian leaders in the Japanese government and intimates of the Imperial Household joined the admirals in following this line of thinking. But, although they were able to force the resignation of the Tojo government in July, 1944, after the fall of Saipan, surrender was put off until a year later. At home, Tojo's followers in the stubborn ruling clique of the Army were still too strong to be ousted, and the "unconditional surrender" policy adopted by Roosevelt and Churchill, although it made good reading in the American press, played completely into the hands of the "all-or-nothing" militarists.

* * * * *

Navy headquarters in Shanghai finally gave Yamazaki orders to join a ship, the new 3,500-ton destroyer *Suzutsuki*. Since no one in Shanghai knew where *Suzutsuki* was, he was given air travel orders to return to Japan. The best thing to do, his superior advised, was to check the ship's position with headquarters in Sasebo.

For three days Yamazaki tried to leave Shanghai, but U.S. Air Force bombings closed down all the fields. He was given new travel orders, to sail aboard the *Conte Verde*, an Italian liner which the Japanese hoped to convert into a carrier. Unfortunately the *Conte Verde*, recently refloated after her sinking early in the war, was not very seaworthy and capsized in the Whangpo River. Yamazaki got a dunking. Four days later he finally managed to get on a flight to Japan.

Sasebo, the sooty, brawling town surrounded by rocky hills and facing a magnificent fjord-like harbor, was traditionally one of the four home bases of the Japanese fleet. By April, 1945, when he got there, it had become a frontline outpost in the last struggle of the Japanese Navy to defend its home waters. There his bad luck—or rather his good luck—continued. A few days before he arrived, *Suzutsuki* had left port, part of the destroyer screen accompanying the battleship *Yamato* on her last sortie, an abortive effort to attack the American transports now pastured off the Okinawa beaches. Once more Yamazaki was stranded on dry land.

Next, Ensign Yamazaki was assigned to the destroyer *Natsutsuki*, *Suzutsuki's* sister ship, then about to be launched. He was made radar officer on this ship, one of the first and last Japanese ships of World War II to install modern radar search equipment. Late in April, 1945, *Natsutsuki* steamed past the humpbacked hills of Sasebo Bay, with two other destroyers, and headed north for the Inland Sea. *Natsutsuki* saw no surface action. The little squadron was ordered to disperse in June, to cut losses from the almost daily American air attacks. After surviving a punishing series of bombings, while in drydock at Sasebo, *Natsutsuki* sailed northward to the small port of Senzaki, at the tip of the island of Honshu, where she was when the war ended.

* * * * *

On April 7th, *Yamato* herself, without air cover, was detected by American search planes on her hopeless mission. Hit by the bombs and torpedoes of four waves of carrier planes, the pride of the Japanese Navy sank at 2:30 in the afternoon, northwest of the Amami Islands, in the East China Sea, just 100 miles from her objective. Ironically, Admiral Shimizu's 18-inch guns, which outranged those of every battleship in the world, had never been used in a line of battle action. *Yamato* was sunk the same way H.M.S. *Repulse* had been sunk in 1942. Far more than the British in Malaya, the Japanese admirals, who had used air power to such advantage themselves, sent the pride of their Navy on this mission, knowing well that the odds were overwhelmingly against her return. But they had no carriers left to send with her.

For four months after, the soldiers of the Japanese Army, forced by their generals to act out their tragedy to the last minute, fought on hopelessly but without complaint in the jungles of Burma, the caves of northern Luzon and on the dull slate cliffs of southern Okinawa. The twentieth-century Americans who fought them called them "fanatics." By their own standards they were doing the only possible deed of honorable men, dying in a loyal effort to hold together the web of emperor, nation and family that had bound them since they were born. Judged by any standards, they were brave almost beyond belief.

The last weapon of the modern Japanese militarists was the traditional defiant suicide of the *samurai* facing defeat. Too late to affect the war's outcome (though in time to do great damage to the American fleet off

Okinawa), the half-trained pilots of the Special Attack Air Corps—the Kamikaze—took off singly and in pairs from their airfields in Kyushu on the long, one-way flight southward.* Relentlessly, if crudely—many had barely 100 hours total flying time—they flew their tiny fighters in to Okinawa, generally from the west, over the blotched green of the Kerama Islands. As they reached the air above their targets, the pilots would begin their dives, one hand welded to the control stick, the other often religiously grasping the long sword awkwardly jammed inside the cockpit.

The last Kamikaze pilot, as nearly as records can tell, must have flown out of Kanoya Navy Airbase on Kyushu, two days before the surrender. His identity is unknown. As he came into view, off Okinawa, a small, wavering speck, the gun crews running to battle stations on the ships scattered below him had no way of knowing that his was to be the last attack. For a second, his plane, like the others which had come before it, hung precariously over the rising white puffs of the anti-aircraft guns. Then, jerkily, it dove, shearing its way down through the fire, as the puffs became clouds and the rattle of the twenty and forty millimeter anti-aircraft guns from fifty ships spread their noise across the sky.

Nearer the water, spectators aboard ship and on shore could see first the wings, then the fuselage. Finally the bright-red ball insignia of the rising sun came clear in their binoculars. As the aircraft dove through the smoking sky, one or more of the puffs smothered it. There was a flash of orange fire. Then a few fragments of wing and fuselage fell into the sea, not far from one of the ships.

Small pieces of wreckage scattered on the sea's surface,

---

* The Kamikaze attack was a navy innovation, first used by land-based aircraft of the navy's First Air Fleet against U.S. carriers at the Battle of Leyte Gulf. Explaining the effectiveness of this tactic after the war, Captain Rikibei Inoguchi of the First Air Fleet remarked, ". . . if you start out on a mission with the idea of coming back, you won't proceed to carry it out with 100 percent efficiency."

tossed by the gusts of a strong northeast wind. The wind came from Japan, from the Grand Shrine of Ise, from the rubble of the bombed navy arsenal at Toyokawa, from the bomb-pocked runways of Kanoya, carrying the ashes of the last Kamikaze pilot farther out to sea. In another century the same northeast wind had blown against Japan's Mongol invaders a vengeance so turbulent that it seemed divine. It was called Kamikaze then—the "Divine Wind." Then, the wind—and the gods of the nation—had seemed to serve their purpose. Now, in 1945, the Kanoya pilot and his comrades had failed in theirs. The steady wind remained. But the gods were gone forever.

THE EMPTY SHRINE

> "Among the bamboo and the flowering dates
> Buddha has long been sleeping;
>
> And with the withered fig by the wayside
> Christ, it would seem, is also dead.
>
> But we, the actors, must rest—
> Even on-stage, in front of the scenery."
>
> *Poem from "Kappa" by Ryunosuke Akutagawa*

Behind the camouflage of an American artillery observation post, a Japanese army officer, holding a pair of binoculars with his muddied white gloves, took a professional look at the chalky hills to the south. Satisfied, he turned and put his finger on a target square near the center of the observer's map. The observer telephoned. They waited. Within 100 seconds the spiral of outgoing 105 millimeter shells whirred overhead and black smoke crashed around the place he had indicated. The Japanese officer was watching the destruction of his own unit's headquarters, where the remnants of his artillery battalion, their guns wrecked or without ammunition, had withdrawn for a last stand. He had left the headquarters himself only a few hours before. Shortly afterward an American patrol had captured him.

Several thousand miles away, during another last-ditch battle, U.S. troops captured an officer from a Japanese front-line headquarters. When language officers guardedly began to interrogate him about the disposition of the Japanese garrison, he smilingly asked for maps, pencil and paper. He was given a desk in a corps G-2, where he spent the next week sketching out the complete order of battle of the Japanese—their positions, commanders and equipment. As the battle had not yet been won, his information was the kind that military reports refer to with sincere cliches like "of inestimable value."

After a surface attack on some Japanese small craft, not far off the shores of Honshu, an American submarine picked up a Japanese navy prisoner. He was a petty officer, an affable, unusually intelligent man who had worked, it turned out, in the headquarters of the Japanese anti-submarine command. The Japanese sailor lived comfortably with the submariners throughout their patrol. He steered them through the web of minefields that had lately been sown around the approaches to the Japanese home islands. The information he had, which he readily put down on charts, greatly simplified the activities of this and other submarines in sinking more Japanese ships.*

These three men were not renegades. Although their stories make better telling than most, they were representative of the great majority of Japanese prisoners of war taken during World War II, docile, ingratiating and harmless. Mysteriously, in a few days or hours following capture, the frenzy and élan of the Japanese fighting man seemed to drain out of him. Given a minimum of competent handling, no Japanese prisoner would ever try to escape. Very few would consistently try to withhold military information, even when what they told was of the most damaging sort. There is one recorded case where a prisoner attempted suicide, because of the tacit snub administered, when American intelligence officers did *not* interrogate him, where they had interrogated all of his companions.

---

* I have purposely juggled and slightly falsified the circumstances of these three incidents, to avoid giving embarrassment to any of the men involved, all of them loyal and useful citizens of Japan.

There were some good circumstantial reasons for this odd behavior. The Japanese had been fed atrocity stories about the Americans just as lurid—and, in some cases, just as well-founded—as the atrocity stories which the Americans had heard about the Japanese. Prisoners who fell into the hands of the Japanese had a grim future ahead of them. The average Japanese prisoner, having no other yardstick than his own standards and his own experience, expected a similar fate. The dirty, wounded Japanese machine-gunner, brought into the presence of some Japanese-speaking Americans, would ask, "When are you going to kill me?" in the matter-of-fact tone of a man long prepared for the inevitable. A few days of decent treatment in an American prison camp left him amazed and grateful to his captors.

Japanese troops had no indoctrination in security, since the army command trusted all to the "spiritual training" which taught that any good Japanese soldier would die rather than allow himself to be captured. No intelligence officers had briefed them on giving only their names, ranks, and serial numbers to enemy interrogators. In all innocence, therefore, the Japanese soldier would often talk expansively of his comrades back in their cave positions, or the ammunition factory near his home village in Japan, without realizing that the least scrap of information would have some value to his enemies.

More sophisticated soldiers would tell everything they knew on the premise that the war was already lost. They understood that little they did or said could affect the outcome. This was certainly true during the last year of the Pacific fighting, when prisoners for the first time were taken in large numbers. When Japanese junior officers led some of their men into the American lines to surrender, it was good evidence that the war was nearing its end. This happened in the last stages of the Okinawa campaign.

There were also a few idealists in the Japanese Army who deeply opposed the war. These gave themselves up out of patriotism or a feeling for humanity that was seldom seen in the Japanese Army. In late 1944, the Marines manning a perimeter around the skillful and desperate defenders of a Japanese-held island, were amazed to find a tiny man with thick glasses, apparently kept within the earth's gravitational field only by an oversized steel helmet and a huge dispatch case, come walking out of a cave waving a white flag. "They are monomaniacs," the little officer sputtered in English, pointing back towards the Japanese lines, "They do not understand man of science." He was the regimental surgeon, who gave himself up after vainly begging his colonel to surrender. In another campaign, a serious law graduate of one of the universities and his friend, a former policeman, surrendered themselves and volunteered to bring back more of their friends. Over several weeks time, they coaxed upwards of 100 Japanese troops out of their hiding places, after they had convinced them that further fighting was futile.

Men like this were exceptions. And, for the mass of others, neither good treatment nor bad security indoctrination could explain their conduct. The primary reason for the prisoners' behavior reached back to the roots of the Japanese web system. The perspective of years has sharpened the realization that the prisoners were more than men who had failed in their mission or disobeyed standing orders. In differing degrees, each of them was by his own standards a weightless question mark, floating in a spiritual void, cut off from the life-giving bonds of a social relationship that served him for religion, morality and self-respect.

There were no instructions in the Japanese military manuals warning soldiers to avoid capture. This was not necessary. The idea that capture in battle was the ultimate disgrace had been resurrected from Japan's *samurai* past by the modern militarists and ruthlessly drilled into the generation that grew up in the thirties. It was stimulated not only by evoking the ghosts of medieval heroes, but by the examples of men like Yamazaki's childhood model, Major Kuga, who killed themselves, true to the belief that only suicide could wipe out the disgrace of capture. In the extreme of Japanese society which the militarists constructed, the recruit was taught that any deviation from this rule was an irreparable breach of faith with the Emperor, the Army and his comrades, with his ancestors and his immediate family. It was not the trust—the *shinyo*—that fathers like Sanada taught their sons. It was not a man's individual disgrace, but a larger shame which he visited on all his loved ones by his act.

When a Japanese soldier was captured, whether voluntarily or after great resistance, the weight of this disgrace lay heavily upon him. It was the totality of excommunication added to the bitterness of treason. He frequently attempted suicide, but he seldom tried to do harm to any of his captors at the same time—he was not concerned with them. *"Haji desu,"* he would say. "It is a great disgrace." No translation could do justice to the terrible word *"haji,"* no description could convey the resigned eyes and the quiet tone of speech, the painful face and the twisting hands of the man who said it.

Through the blur of his *haji*, the soldier saw all his old loyalties cracking and falling away. He said goodbye to his family, because it was not thinkable that he see them again. Not one out of a hundred Japanese soldiers ever availed himself of the machinery of the International Red Cross for notifying his family that he was safe. The question would be asked: "Do you want your name sent back home?" They chanted the reply like a tragic chorus: "I don't want my name made known." The web had broken. There was nowhere to go.

But if the act of becoming a prisoner jarred and shattered the formal ties of the Japanese to his particular web society, it did not at one stroke remove his instincts to attach himself to something similar. After the shock of captivity had passed, the prisoner began groping for new loyalties. The obvious objects of new loyalties were his captors—in World War II the Allied officers with whom he came into contact. In a curious way he tried to fit himself into their pattern. What he actually did was attempt to fit them into his. Japanese prisoners often developed a lively sense of personal loyalty to one or more of their principal captors. The ties of respect and subordination which a man had felt for his old company commander Captain Yamamoto, he might easily transfer, or try to transfer to the prison camp commander, Captain Smith.

The prisoners who expressed a hope that they be given some farming land in California did not say this in jest. Members of a clan society, they hoped to join another society by adoption, just as young men of one clan had often been adopted by childless *samurai* of another. They personalized the new society through those of its members whom they encountered and especially respected. They were anxious to learn its laws and customs, so that they might again take up residence in a web of *shinyo*. There is no doubt that most of them, if given the farms in California which they requested, would have made good citizens.*

---

* That is, if they could have endured the race prejudice which has thrived there. There are few meaner pages in modern American history than the record of Pacific Coast hostility to Japanese immigrants. The real cause for the anti-Japanese feeling was the fear that Japanese workers and farmers, used to working for far lower returns, would drive "native" Americans out of their jobs. This was disguised by all sorts of social, medical and political reasons. From 1900 to the start of World War II, the state of California led in enacting a sequence of restrictive measures against the Japanese immigrants, including segregation in the schools, and restrictions on ownership, or even the leasing of land by the Japanese. After the 1906 earthquake in San Francisco—when Japan contributed more to the city's relief than all other foreign countries totaled—visiting Japanese scientists were stoned in the streets. In 1924 Congress passed the infamous Exclusion Act, to the satisfaction of California's civic groups.

The effect of this hostility on Japan was not lost. The existence of the Exclusion Act and stories of Japanese "second-class" citizenship on the Pacific Coast of the United States made it an easy job for the militarists to stir up anti-American feeling in the thirties. There is no doubt that California's attitude played its part in making the outbreak of war in the Pacific far easier than it might have been. Japanese-Americans who remained loyal to the United States during World War II were rewarded for their loyalty by being indiscrimi-

This is the reason why Japanese prisoners were so bafflingly cooperative. Swamped in the wreckage of their own beliefs, they looked for something new. Their hearts and their habits were still the shrine of old gods, its walls covered by old ivy and its beams stained black by the incense of centuries. But the shrine was empty.

Until the 15th of August, 1945, these prisoners of war were cut off from their nation, for all time, it seemed to them, by this desertion of old values. On that day, at a turning point of Japanese history, they were pointed in their misery and their perplexity by the whole Japanese people. The Divine Empire, that had stood victorious for 2,000 years, was beaten. The Divine Mission could not be achieved. For the first time in history the web society looked in upon itself to see what was left at its core.

* * * * *

Despite the despair of Japan's condition in the spring of 1945, surrender was not easy. In April, the Army *Kempeitai* arrested Shigeru Yoshida (the present Premier), a leading advocate of an immediate peace, and several hundred others—although they were soon released. After the fall of Okinawa the army and navy chiefs of staff intensified the fortification of the homeland. The home armies were put on a tactical footing and all the military stores available were set at their disposal. The naval and air defense program called for a concentrated attack against the invasion forces by Kamikaze pilots and suicide torpedo boats. Although Admiral Shimizu could prevent the issuance of bamboo spears to his workers at Toyokawa, the "bamboo spear strategy" of a last-ditch civilian fight against the in-

---

nately placed in desert jails, euphemistically called "relocation centers."

Happily, one effect of the war was to scatter the Japanese population throughout the country. They have in this way been better able to assimilate themselves to the larger American community.

vading armies was being preached and prepared for throughout Japan.

In the crisis time, Hirohito at last prepared to use his authority against the military. On June 18, 1945, at a conference of the military staff chiefs and the civilian cabinet leaders, he said: "The situation is such that the war has gradually lengthened. Although it is natural for the military to wish to attain the objective of the war, it is however a matter of question whether the war should be continued any longer, without some thought for its ending. Have the government and the chiefs of staff thought about this?" Foreign Minister Shigenori Togo, supplying the greatest understatement of World War II, answered, "At present the situation has not reached the point we had wished for." In the context of the deviously worded system of communication between the Emperor and his subjects, this was a flat and a blunt exchange.

On July 27, the Emperor advised accepting the Potsdam Declaration of unconditional surrender. The military chiefs demanded that Japan hold out to the end. By August 10, the two atom bombs had been dropped on Japan and the Russians had jumped on the Allied bandwagon, by announcing their entry into the war. Still, the staff chiefs, in particular General Korechika Anami, the War Minister, asserted that a fight to the death was Japan's only honorable course.

On August 10, Hirohito called an Imperial Conference. After a discussion *à outrance* between the civilians and the soldiers present, the Emperor spoke again: "I agree with Foreign Minister Togo about the acceptance of the Potsdam Declaration. Since the beginning of the Pacific war, there has been a tremendous disparity between our calculations and the realities. Now I hear that both the Army and the Navy are preparing for a battle in the homeland. I feel the same way about this. One of the important places to defend is Kujukuri-hama [a long stretch of beach land north of Tokyo]. But there is a great deal of difference between what the Chief of Staff had to say about the defense of Kujukuri-hama and the observations of my chamberlains. They tell me that the defense of Kujukuri-hama is only one-tenth completed. Also, the production of airplanes is far from adequate.*

"With things in this condition, how can we win, even if we have a battle in the homeland? If all the citizens should die, we would hardly be able to perpetuate the nation. I think that we must decide at this time to terminate the war, although it is an unbearable thing. Were we to terminate the war in this way, it would mean losing the Army, which we have had since the time of the Emperor Meiji. However, when I think upon all the men who have died, and the families of the dead, I feel as if my heart were broken [in Japanese idiom, "as if my belly were cut open"]. In order to open the way to future peace, we must bear what is unbearable. It is needless to worry about the royal family or myself."

There was complete silence in the chamber except for the sound of weeping. On the following day, the Japanese government transmitted its acceptance of the Potsdam surrender terms to the Allies.

There was at the last an effort by younger army officers to forestall surrender. But their attempt to take over the Imperial Palace was quickly frustrated. To disseminate the news of surrender to his people, Hirohito recorded a broadcast speech shortly before midnight, on the eve of the formal surrender. General Anami committed suicide the next day.

* * * * *

On the morning of August 15th, Sakaji Sanada and his family were busy gathering in the last of their rice harvest, putting the grain into rough straw sacks for delivery to the

---

* Japanese aircraft production for the month of June, 1944, its peak, was 2,541 planes; by June 1945, it had dropped to 1,340; by July, to 1,131. This was at a time when operational losses exceeded the total factory output.

town offices. As usual, they were barely able to meet their assigned quota. When the announcement came that the Emperor would broadcast an important message, Sanada looked again at his disappearing granary and resigned himself to an Imperial Rescript, ordering the nation to fight to the finish.

An hour before the broadcast, neighbors began to gather at his house. They all concurred in Sanada's supposition. But they waited for the message as one waits for an extraordinary event. It was the first time that a Japanese emperor had spoken so directly to his people.

At noon, the speech which Hirohito had painfully recorded the night before was broadcast over every radio in Japan. It was, for all the imperial delicacies of phrase, as forthright a statement as a Japanese ruler had ever made:

"After pondering deeply the general trends of the world and the actual conditions obtaining in our empire today, we have decided to effect a settlement of the present situation by resorting to an extraordinary measure.

"We have ordered our government to communicate to the governments of the United States, Great Britain and the Soviet Union that our empire accepts the provisions of their joint declaration...

"Despite the best that has been done by everyone—the gallant fighting of the military and naval forces, the diligence and assiduity of our servants of the state and the devoted service of our 100 million people, the war situation has developed not necessarily to Japan's advantage, while the general trends of the world have all turned against her interest.

"Moreover the enemy has begun to employ a new and most cruel bomb, the power of which to do damage is, indeed, incalculable, taking the toll of many innocent lives. Should we continue to fight, it would not only result in an ultimate collapse and obliteration of the Japanese nation, but it would also lead to the total extinction of human civilization.

"Such being the case, how are we to save the millions of

our subjects, or to atone ourselves before the hallowed spirits of our imperial ancestors? This is the reason why we have ordered the acceptance of the provisions of the joint declaration of the powers. . . .

"We are keenly aware of the inmost feelings of all of you, our subjects. However, it is according to the dictates of time and fate that we have resolved to pave the way for a grand peace for all the generations to come by enduring the unavoidable and suffering what is unsufferable. . . ."

The impact of the high, nervous voice hit Sanada and his neighbors like a hard physical blow. "We were so dumfounded," he recalls, "That we must have resembled a bunch of staring *ningyo* (puppets). We all walked around in a daze. And for three days no one did anything."

* * * * *

Admiral Shimizu sat in his temporary office in the navy officers' quarters of the arsenal at Toyokawa. It was one of the few buildings which escaped damage in the B-29 raid just a week before. The shrubbery around the building and the quiet pool and fountain beneath the portico, untouched in the fire, gave little relief from the piles of ruptured steel and concrete that stretched in all directions around the house. Shimizu was lonely and depressed. The deaths of his workers hung on his shoulders like an incubus.

When the Emperor's broadcast came, he heard it with only a slight sense of shock. He had known defeat was certain. This was the final thankful acknowledgment of a dwarfing reality. He dismissed it as that. The blackened wreckage that he saw from his window did not leave him time for reflection.

* * * * *

Hideya Kisei did not hear the Emperor's broadcast. His unit, pushed back deep into Burma by the British and Indian armies, was barely able to keep up wireless communication with its rear headquarters. He was tired, hungry. So were they all. Every man knew that Japan, by this time, had been beaten badly. But, as Kisei says, "Deep in our hearts we hoped that some miracle would turn up."

When the officers told their men of the surrender, they cried. It was a world ago that the same men had stood up in their quarters in the transport off Shanghai, cheering the news of Pearl Harbor.

Kisei reacted to the news just as Sanada had—with shock and bewilderment. It seemed neither an end nor a beginning. It was like something taken out of time and experience. Several days passed before the shock lessened and Kisei found himself "feeling much lighter in mind." He began to think now of going home. In his dreams he saw his wife, his mother and his children. The other men, when he talked with them, turned out to have the same feeling themselves. They talked quietly of home—unashamedly for the first time in the past year—and wondered what damage had been done to their farms and cities. They also wondered how the occupation troops were treating their people, especially their women. On this score, many of them had guilty consciences, from their own experiences in occupied countries.

* * * * *

Tadao Yamazaki heard the Emperor's broadcast in the small harbor of Senzaki, where his ship *Natsutsuki* was still moored. On his uniform collar he now wore the two stars of a lieutenant (j.g.). He had been promoted just a few days before, almost on the same day as the terms of the Potsdam Declaration was announced in Japan. This made him what he and his fellow-officers jokingly called a *"Potsdam chui."*

His first reaction was sheer relief. Characteristically, almost as soon as the news sank in, he began analyzing what the war had been all about. For the first time since he entered the Navy, he felt perfectly free to do so. "It was a foolish, foolhardy war," he thought. He tried to understand how the Japanese had ever gotten themselves into such a predicament. "Our archaic thinking," he remembers discussing, "was all wrong. So was our egotism—the egotism that we were right." He decided at that moment that the military men who led the war, as well as the ultra-nationalists, should be expelled.

A few young military men aboard *Natsutsuki* wanted to continue the fight. For about a day there were bitter arguments in the wardroom. Discipline won out in the end, as it did in almost every other naval and military installation in Japan. *Natsutsuki's* captain obediently headed her towards Kure. Before tney got under way Yamazaki gave a short talk to the men of his division: "We have lost the war, but we need not lose our pride. Our work has just begun. We must return home to our loved ones and start the reconstruction of our country. We must not attempt anything rash. We must cooperate and give our best, so that there will be peace for everyone." When he finished, he wondered whether he had been too optimistic.

Lieutenant Yamazaki's last orders were to report in at Kure naval headquarters, for assignment to one of the ships doing repatriation work, a depressing shuttle between Kure, or Sasebo and the remnants of Japanese colonies and garrisons overseas. At the last moment, however, it was decided to leave this work to regular officers and enlisted men. In mid-October, after giving him this last lesson in military confusion, the Navy formally demobilized Yamazaki. Wearing his uniform of undress green, with heavy boots and the blue raglan overcoat which the Japanese Navy had borrowed once from the British, he started the trek northward to see his family.

His parents now lived in the village of Yokogoshi, his mother's birthplace, a farming community deep in the mountains of Niigata, the snowy northern prefecture on the coast of the Japan Sea. Until May, 1945, they had dwelt in Shizuoka, a small manufacturing city on the plain below Fuji, almost midway between Nagoya and Tokyo. His father had resigned his last teaching post, in the Shizuoka Commercial School, to join the Foundation of Cost Accountants' Association, one of the government-sponsored organizations thrown together to plug the leaks in Japan's wartime financial structure—in this case, by auditing the books of the new wartime cartels and munitions corporations. When the association lost its purpose on the 15th of August, Hachiro Yamazaki wearily took the train trip up to Niigata, to join his family.

It took Tadao a day and a half longer to make the journey to Niigata than it did his father. It was a trip he never wants to repeat. Kure itself was wretched enough—the rats running wild through the scorched warehouses, the debris of the torn docks, the big black bottom of the battleship *Hyuga*, sunk months before, sticking out like an oversized buoy in the middle of the channel. But during his late flirtation with war, he had grown used to the mess of bombed naval bases. He was not prepared for the mess of ruined houses and ruined people that he now saw.

The third-class train—there were no better coaches for the use of the civilian population—rocked northward along the patched-up tracks. The locomotive was small and tired, the cars had no windows left, some of them no seats. The outsides were dust drab or black, depending on whether the coach had been pulled out from some abandoned country siding, or scorched in a city air raid. The only heat was the stale warmth of hundreds of bodies pressed together. The only food was the rice or barley, packed in old army mess-kits which most of the travelers carried, or an exorbitant piece of fruit bought from a shivering woman on a station platform.

* * * * *

The route of the train was the Jeremiad of Japan's defeat. Four years ago there was the Way of the Gods, the Way of the Emperor, girding the nation in tinsel glory; now there was just the way of the train, a trip which its takers gratefully concentrated on, for few knew what was at the end of the line, nor even what there had been at the beginning. A society bared its teeth at itself in a cracked mirror on a glass-strewn station platform, where the very old and the very young were trampled in the headlong rushes to and from the trains, each man who rushed thinking only of the immediate—the journey that he must take.

Most of the stations were damaged in some way. Okayama was skeletal. Kobe was a relic—the green hills of Hyogo which Shimizu had watched from his ship 20 years before were black and disordered. Below them almost nothing but a tangle of untidy flatness was left of the booming port city that had hustled its way into the narrow space between the hills and the sea. Only Kyoto was intact—the one major city which the Americans had designedly spared. But the swarm of ruined people spreading out over the Kyoto station gave to the scene by the railroad tracks a look of destruction as real as if it had been bombed.

The limping progress of the train bound Japan together in its wretchedness. Nagoya's grand new station, too, had escaped damage—one of the few buildings to survive the most devastating punishment visited on any city of Japan except Nagasaki and Hiroshima. But the square marble arches echoed to the phthysic cough of hundreds of homeless, sleeping under scraps of mustard-colored Army blankets in the gathering October cold. When a train came in, they rose and shambled up the cold stone stairs, packs on their backs, babies on their backs, scraps of furniture and kitchen utensils on their backs. As one line got on the train, another got off it. The clink of hobnailed boots drummed down the stairs as the men came home, unshaven and uncombed, muffled in torn army overcoats. These were the survivors of the Greater East Asia Co-Prosperity

Sphere—some from Rabaul, some from Peking, some from Truk, a few tired ones from Wake.

In Tokyo, Yamazaki got off the train. He walked through the shell of the Central Station, rain pouring inside through the gape of the gutted Victorian roof. He took a streetcar to Ueno, on the other side of town. The few buildings around the station were intact; Tokyo's modest, but well-built approaches to skyscrapers still challenged the higher level of the Palace walls. But everywhere else, there were patches of blankness where other buildings had stood. Of the buildings a few stones and water-filled foundations remained. Of the houses there was nothing—just charred spots in the ground where some family had once had its wood and paper dwelling. At Ueno station he elbowed his way through more crowds of homeless and aimless. After waiting several hours, he got himself on another train heading north and west over the mountains.

The sights along the way of the train never left Tadao Yamazaki. "Everything around me seemed lost, wrapped in misery and desolation," he remembers, "everyone looked haggard. It implanted deeply on my mind what war does to a nation and to the human race." As he looked at the faces of others in army or navy uniform, he wondered what had happened to his friends and classmates, with whom he had marched in the military training classes at the beginning of the war. He later found out that one-fourth of them had been killed. Two of them had died as Kamikaze suicide pilots in the Special Attack Air Corps. It was more and more of a shock to him, just to realize that he was alive.

Nearing home, Yamazaki noticed the mark of war on the countryside. The mountains still reared themselves modestly up to the sky, the paddyfields still gave off their burdens of grain, but the forests were thin and bare. There were only desperate little piles of brushwood, where he once remembered ancient stands of trees. In Yokogoshi he found his family safe, but hardly well. They had shrunk to "skin and bones." At the dinner table they ate bits of soybean refuse. Rice was gone. His father was smoking cigarette butts made of *yomogi* (sagebrush). It was a life that beggared anything he had heard of. He realized that the military had lived in a special society, with all the privileges—and most of the food.

"My emotions," said Yamazaki, thinking back, "were topsy-turvy. My feelings were loaded down with apathy. I now realized that war deprives one of his life and his destiny. A war does not only take human life, it also destroys culture, morals, livelihood and civilization."

* * * * *

In 1945, and throughout past history, men of other nations had thought the same. But in the West or in China, military defeat had seldom meant the total defeat of a national ethic and philosophy. There was always, for the defeated, a refuge which had not been involved in the catastrophe. Generally, this was a religious belief or an interior cultural sense which either was not directly connected to the nation's policy or stood outside it. The German Christian, in 1945, could turn to his old Christian faith and ponder on the aberrations which had taken him from it in the first place. Or, failing this, he could still fall back on the traditions of nineteenth-century humanism which had existed in his country. The Chinese could maintain his version of the Confucian ethic without disturbance. The observance of the Five Relationships, in their Chinese context, did not depend on any particular political system to keep them alive.

In modern Japan, however, what Tadao Yamazaki said was almost literally true. A political system which pretended to omnipotence, traded in the supernatural and confirmed its appeal by its historical success, had failed. With it, a national religion and a national ethic had failed, also. For a time, it was impossible to separate them. Politics and religion had never been forcibly disentangled in

Japan, as they had in the West. The Meiji reformers, in founding their modern state, had so rewelded the two together that the one was fatally involved in the collapse of the other.

The mechanics of government in the web society of Japan had never separated itself from the belief in the Divine Mission of the god-inspired nation. The first word for "government" in Japanese was *"matsurigoto"*—which meant, literally—"the business of rites." However complicated the functions of government became, there was always at least the suggestion that it was more than a man-made social institution, that it was somehow bound with the notion of the Sun-Goddess and the reverence owed to the divine *kami* of the Japanese ancestors.

It was in the fourteenth century that the historian *Kitabatake Chikafusa* wrote, "Great Japan is the land of the Gods. Here the deity of the Sun has handed on her eternal rule. This is true only of our country and there is nothing like it in any other land." The modern revivers of state Shinto had taken this same idea and written it into the laws of Meiji Japan, where it remained. Twentieth-century Japanese like Yamazaki, Shimizu and Kisei, could disavow any real belief in this politico-religious unity. But it was a part of their culture which continued to exercise a subtle influence on their thinking, whatever their protestations. The modern American may smile at Puritanism, or attack its stern pulpits and its whipping posts, but he cannot honestly disown it; Puritanism has laid its hand heavily on his environment and, to a certain extent, has formed him. Far more heavily than this, the more ancient island tradition that insisted on the unit of politics and religion pressed on the Japanese.

It was the mixture of religion and patriotism that gave fuel to the banzai charges and the last-ditch stands of the Japanese military. During the war, the Japanese Army had been a study in the extremes to which loyalty could contort the human will. After the war, by the same token, Japan became the extreme projection of the defeated country.

Every force in the national ethos had been engaged in the war. Because all was engaged, all was defeated.

When the B-29s smashed Tokyo with fire bombs and tore out the heart of Hiroshima with the atomic bomb, almost every Japanese realized that, logically, his country was beaten. But there was a gap between the understanding of defeat and the sensation. In the case of Shimoyoshida, for instance, it was the three days when Sanada relates that "nobody did anything"—just after meeting the shock of the Emperor's surrender announcement. To some the sensation of defeat came swiftly. It grew slowly in others. It was never felt without the dawning of a deeper realization—a consciousness that Japan had been wrong —practically, if not morally—and the fear, further, that the faith in Japan and of Japan which a man held must be seriously wanting.

The idea of the divine mission and the divine country promised a successful country, which had never been beaten—and could not be. When Japan was defeated, where was the faith in Japan's invincibility? Where was the faith in Japanese spiritual values, which had been represented as superior to all others? Where, by extension, was the faith in Japanese mechanical efficiency, in Japanese art, in Japanese scholarship? The values of Japan had been highly relative ones, not easy to transplant outside the rarefied air of the victorious and superior Shinto state. In strengthening these values and codifying them, the Meiji reformers may not have realized how heavily their structure depended on success—especially on military success. Success was the linchpin. When Japan was defeated, the linchpin fell out, and the whole mechanism tottered slowly and uneasily on its foundations.

Outwardly the national society remained the same as it had been. The web of contracts still existed. The shrines had their worshipers. Pilgrims prayed for peace and atonement at Ise and bent women in black *kimono* filed through the gateway of Yasukuni Jinja in Tokyo to pray for their vanished sons. But there were traces of a deep inner uncertainty. The local policeman was slightly less decisive in his manner. The neighborhood association was less sure of its social pressure. The son was a trifle less ready to obey his father's wish.

The whole structure of authority had been undermined by defeat. It was in this way that the entire country, stunned and hurt, felt as rootless as the prisoners of war on Saipan or Okinawa. There was resignation to whatever came. The worst had already happened. But there was also a sense of dissatisfaction with the system that had led the nation into a disastrous war. The bonds of the web were not broken, but they were limp. The purpose had gone out of them. There was an almost voiceless wish to replace them with new ones, or to destroy them altogether.

The Emperor was the one rallying point which the web society had left to it. His leadership was not enough to infuse new life into the web society, but it had saved it from annihilation and, this done, it then kept it from disintegrating. The myths grew weak and withered. But the man remained. He was somehow exculpated from a share in the debacle. His people could rationalize—with some cause and ample precedent—that he had been misled by bad advisors. Perhaps they did this with something less than conviction. But, aside from a few of Japan's Communists, there was no one who voiced the suspicion that the Emperor, too, had been wrong. The hold of the Emperor on Japan was too great. There has never been a debacle from which something could not be retrieved, and the cord that bound the Emperor and the Japanese was too strong and too old in its strength to be broken by this one. It was weakened. But it stayed in place.

The militarists did not escape so easily. They had failed very conspicuously. Having led the nation up the garden path and off the precipice, they enjoyed little popularity among the shaken survivors at the bottom of the cliff. The voices which were raised against Admiral Shimizu in Toyokawa were echoed throughout Japan. A more realistic people than the Germans, the Japanese, when they began to recover from the first shock of defeat, had less trouble finding valid scapegoats. For the first time since the very early thirties, Japanese began to use the word "*gumbatsu*—the military clique" freely and with bitter derrogation. Tojo was not a popular man in Tokyo.

The reaction against the militarists was often angry, but it was not noisy. There were almost no demonstrations and, compared to defeated peoples elsewhere, the Japanese made little outcry. The war had implicated everyone too deeply to permit of overmuch recrimination. Catastrophe had brought despair, but it was resigned and quiet. In their worst hour, the Japanese showed a touch of greatness. In their heyday in East Asia, released deliberately by their commanders from the morality they kept within their own society, they had beaten, plundered and killed in other countries with a disgusting lack of restraint. Now, back within their own society, they awaited retribution calmly. There was no self-pity. There was no pretense that they had been beaten accidentally, no spurious excuses that victory could have been won, if only this commander had not abandoned his position, or that general staff had not miscalculated. They were licked and they knew it—in contrast to their erstwhile allies, the followers of Adolph Hitler.

* * * * *

Yamazaki, after he had thought a good deal about the defeat, said very succinctly what a whole generation of young Japanese felt, as they clumped through the streets of Osaka, Fukuoka or Hakodate in their muddied Army boots, looking for the wood and the tools with which to build their new house: "I learned that our generation was too honest. We were too simple at heart, too naive in our thought. We did what we were told to do, without asking why, because it seemed the right thing to do. Our generation went to war. Our generation took a beating. Our generation lost. And now it is our generation which has to work to restore humanity to our country."

In their work of "restoring humanity," the Japanese of 1945 were more receptive to new ideas than at any point in their history. Undoubtedly they would recover from their shock. In time, if left to themselves, historians could find plausible reasons for the defeat and their own priests and sociologists could explain their feeling of frustration and bewilderment. But this would require years. At one particular moment in history, they were as docile as a wild animal, stunned by the hunter. At the hunter's discretion, it seemed, it could be turned loose, or led away into captivity, taught new habits and ultimately returned, changed, to its haunts.

They were amenable to almost any change. The reservations they had always held against wholeheartedly swallowing the civilization of the West were, for a moment, withdrawn. They had come from pride of nation— and there was no pride of nation left. The empty shrine stood waiting for something new to fill it. Communism, democracy, Christianity, socialism, baseball, French movies, jazz and *laissez-faire* capitalism—all of them had once held strong appeals for the Japanese. All of them, in varying degrees, had been repressed or stamped out in the decade and a half of militarism. All of them—or some of them—were fated to return. Confusing, but welcome, the gods of the West waited outside the doors.

8
ADVANCING GARRISON ARMY

"The frog in the well knows nothing of the ocean."

Japanese proverb

Shortly before the first American occupation troops arrived in Shimoyoshida, a few of the local leaders, whom Sakaji Sanada remembers as "fanatics," circulated scare stories about them. The Americans, they said, were truly *"mono osoroshii*—fearful creatures," who were capable of the vilest atrocities, especially towards women. Sanada and his friends were afraid that these stories might be true. There was talk of sending the women and children, at least, further up into the mountains for safety. But, at the last, this advice was rejected. Obeying the Emperor's command, the people of Shimoyoshida fought down their misgivings and waited timidly for their conquerors. Most of them, outside of their movie experiences, had never seen an American before.

When the occupation troops came, they were friendly and apparently easy-going, quite unlike the caricature of the enemy which the war leaders had encouraged. Sanada found them "gentlemanly." He started to ponder why and how his leaders had ever taken the notion to wage war against a nation so civilized.

His good feelings were reinforced by the first personal contact he had with the Americans. A month after the surrender, two soldiers drove into town in a jeep, to investigate a local munitions plant. They stopped Sanada, who was walking down the road, and asked directions. One of them spoke a little Japanese. Speaking simply and with gestures, Sanada offered to take them where they wanted to go. He climbed awkwardly into the back seat and the jeep chugged off down the main street. As it passed his neighbors, they looked on with misgivings, wondering, as Sanada recalls, "what wrong I had committed and where the soldiers were taking me." Possibly to their disappointment, since Sanada was regarded as too bossy by some of the townspeople, nothing of this sort happened. When they reached their destination, the soldiers grinned and nodded their thanks. The one who spoke Japanese said something resembling "*arigato*—thank you."

In the same month that he met the gentlemanly soldiers, Sanada received an official letter from the town office telling him that Sergeant Mitsu Sanada had been killed in action in northern Luzon on June 15, 1945. The place of his death and the circumstances were unknown. It was a deep blow. He could not believe it. Whenever the family heard the sound of shoes outside the doors, they would start, wondering whether Mitsu had not, after all, returned. ("There were not very many," Sanada remembers, "who wore shoes shortly after the surrender.") Sorrow and pity for Mitsu were the only emotions the Sanadas had left. "It doesn't seem fair," Sakaji growled at his weeping wife, "There are some families here who have had as many as six sons taken in the Army and all of them have returned. We had one and he is gone."

Surprisingly, the Sanadas made little connection between Mitsu's death and the smiling young Americans in jeeps. There was no rage at the conquerors. The relatives of the dead seldom wept with this sort of anger. Seemingly, it was some almost personified force called "war" that had taken them away. "War," at least in conversation, was not identified usually with those who had waged it— the victorious Americans. In the way the Japanese regarded it, it seemed less like a condition of affairs than a felt presence, that by itself had mysteriously burned houses, destroyed cities and killed only sons. Expecting the frustrated rage of the defeated, the first Americans to land in Japan were startled to find smiling guides spring up from shacks huddled in the waste of bombed Tokyo. Even touring marines in Nagasaki reddened when Japanese offered in threadbare English "to show interesting places of atom ruin."

In Japan after the surrender there was, in the accepted Western sense, very little bitterness of the defeated towards their conquerors. On the contrary, once the occupation army had proved itself "gentlemanly," it became the subject of an all-out effort on the part of the Japanese to make friends with the conqueror. There were a few who held back from this effort—mostly the military men who had projected the war in the first place. But all military men by no means made up a united front. The first American navy officer to arrive for duty in Nagoya, a wide-eyed lieutenant (j.g.), suddenly found himself the guest of honor at a banquet which Admiral Shimizu and his staff (he had been placed in charge of the Nagoya area after the surrender) put on at their own expense at a large restaurant outside the city.

In the cities of Japan, freshly taught taxi dancers foxtrotted with G.I.s in made-over Japanese officers' clubs. City shops sprouted "Welcome Allied Troop" signs and at first refused to accept payment from their new customers. Booklets called "How to make English conversation with Occupation Force" were selling fast in Japanese book shops. As fast as they mastered their English lessons, Japanese put them into practice. At Tokyo, it was the age of the "Sincere Clothes Shop," "The G.I. Laundry" and the "Forgive and Forget Electrical Company."

The occupiers had a weird sense of being adopted. Within a few months toy manufacturers were producing jeeps and model airplanes with U.S. markings. The G.I. became the idol of Japanese schoolboys who had only six months before been issued bamboo spears for a fight to the death against the Americans. Japanese newspapers, referring to the occupation forces, made use of a revealing adjective. The epithet "advancing" which had always prefixed any mention of the Japanese armed forces, was transferred to the American. *"Shinchugun,"* the occupation army was called, "The Advancing Garrison Army."

It is still sometimes said that this turnabout was calculated, a characteristic Japanese device to float with the tide while it is strong, only to breast it once it ebbs. But such mass deception is almost an impossible thing to manage. An entire nation could hardly have begun to live such a complicated lie in unison, still less continue it through six years of peaceful occupation. Nor was the desperate friendliness of the Japanese prompted by a sense of "war guilt." There was very little consciousness, in the Japan of 1945, that the Japanese had sinned against "the moral law of nations" by invading China and bombing Pearl Harbor. The lightning change in the Japanese attitude was, on the contrary, a normal and honest reaction of the people in the web society, when confronted with national crisis.

The roots of this attitude could be found in an old and often quoted Japanese proverb. *"Kateba kangun; makereba zokugun,"* it runs, "The Emperor's army—if you win; the rebel army—if you lose." Nothing could better epitomize the Japanese ethical system; its pragmatic worship of pure success, its substitution of a maze of contractual obligations for a definite notion of good and evil. Since the early Middle Ages, the politics of *kateba kangun* had operated like an unwritten law settling the internal troubles of Japanese society.

It was paradoxical that this be so, in a society that set so much store on the virtues of loyalty. But Japanese ideas of loyalty were limited at their origins. The feudal loyalty —which lay at the base of later Japanese morality—was founded solely on the contract; and the contract depended on personal ties between the liege and the vassal and, in the last sense, on the power of the feudal lord to take care of his dependents. It was a power relationship. The incentive to be loyal for the sake of loyalty, i.e., because it was virtuous or Christ-like, which existed in European feudalism, did not often obtain here.

There were outstanding examples of loyalty to the powerless, the dethroned, or the dead, like the case of the Forty-Seven Ronin. But these were almost always questions of immediate personal loyalty, generally confined to single acts of bravery, retribution or revenge. They represented only the basic loyalties of clansmen, which did not go beyond the clan chiefs for their objects. They were not abstract. By the very nature of this system, the Japanese were capable of transferring their higher loyalties easily and without strain of conscience. Above this immediate pattern of personal clan loyalty, there was little idea of moral allegiance based on principles rather than people. There are very few national histories which contain so many battlefield defections and switches of political fealty.

All these shifts of loyalty, however, were made within the context of the emperor system. The emperor had always been the prize of the strongest. Once a de facto rule of the country had been set up, the victorious shogun or regent could instantly legitimize his power by issuing his commands in the name of the emperor, the descendant of the Sun-Goddess who remained the nearest thing the Japanese system had to a moral absolute value. (That is to say, if the emperor was on your side, you were "good.") When Saigo Takamori rebelled in 1877, he intended, if successful, to take on the government in the emperor's name—despite the fact that the Emperor Meiji had sent one of his relatives to take the field against Saigo. If Saigo had won, his army would have become the *Kangun*, the Army of the Emperor. In the same spirit, the young army officers who attempted *coups d'état* during the 1930s always did so in the emperor's name, although they generally tried to assassinate the emperor's closest friends and advisors. On the Japanese chessboard, pawns or stronger pieces were expendable. Get the king and the game was won.

The rude and rough changes of power sanctioned by the code of *kateba kangun* at once indicated and strengthened a warped ideal of justice. Those Japanese who were aware of this defect were disillusioned or icily cynical about it. A well-known modern legal scholar once admitted to an American acquaintance, "Justice for us is not immutable. In our society it has meant merely the rules adopted by the strong to govern the weak." Almost three centuries before him, Arai Hakuseki, the mordantly brilliant philosopher of the Tokugawa era, wrote to a friend, "In our country, those who have won are invariably in the right and those who have lost are in the wrong."

The bulk of the Japanese, like the citizens of any other nation, were not so introspective about the national vices and virtues. The idea that power sanctions any rule had infused itself into their lives in too many ways to be discussed or easily disentangled. It helped strengthen a national preoccupation with the workability of things, rather than with their worth. If something worked, if it was powerful, if it succeeded, it had a right to be accepted. The same pragmatic philosophy has made great headway in the West. But despite its success, Americans and Europeans retain from their ultimate Christian and Greek heritage a body of moral standards, whether they are called "moral absolutes," "eternal verities" or "socially accepted values." The Japanese have not been so lucky.

As a result, the American army of occupation walked into Japan with a peculiar moral advantage guaranteed it by its strength. Its power and efficiency were impressive. Sanada and his friends gaped at the streams of new jeeps and trucks that chewed their roads into flying clouds of dust; Shimizu, in his turn, watching the lavish electronic equipment of the Americans, wearily conceded that his own technicians had been further behind the times than he had thought. The Americans were winners. Their most casual actions had the weight of self-confidence, from their nonchalant donations of candy and Coca-Cola to the flippant ease with which they repaired motorcar engines. It was obvious to the average Japanese that the way of life which produced this American workability was worthy of adoption. As eagerly as they had swallowed Chinese ethics and a Prussian-style constitution, the Japanese braced themselves to gulp down whatever the Americans had to offer.

And so *Shinchugun* became *Kangun*. The Advancing Garrison Army was the Emperor's Army as well.* As desperately and as blatantly as the wartime Japanese prisoners, the nation tried alternately to fit itself into the American pattern, or to fit the American occupiers into its own.

With other occupation armies of history, obsessed with the idea of retribution and tribute, this naive effort would have failed. As it happened, the army which stepped into the void left by Japan's military collapse was dedicated to an equally naive objective—the peaceful and cooperative rehabilitation of an enemy country and its transformation into a stable member of international society.

To call the objective "naive" is not to belittle it. It was founded on the implicit American conviction that the form of government and the way of life evolved within the 48 states is God-blessed and superior to any other in existence. An attitude that finds its vice in international priggishness, in its best form it represents a Christian opti-

---

* There were at least a few Japanese who took this identification literally. In one of the most famous apocryphal stories of the early occupation, a U.S. army military government colonel, taking a public opinion poll, asked an old farmer what he thought of General MacArthur. The man answered quickly, "The Emperor couldn't have picked a better man."

mism which the existential societies of Europe often seem to have forgotten. There was more of the virtue than the vice in its application to Japan. No other people but Americans—optimistic, expansive, equally confident of their political institutions and their machines—would have so attempted to remake another nation, a former enemy, in their own likeness. With no other people but the Japanese—pragmatic, assimilative, conditioned by their morality to accept winning ideals as well as a winning army, could this attempt have had so good a chance of success.

The basic instructions for the effort to make Japan over into a stable world citizen came from Washington. But the course of the U.S. occupation, through its most formative years, was determined by General Douglas MacArthur, its Supreme Commander. A classic American idealist, his native feeling that men could master history was reinforced by the confidence of long years of command in the U.S. Army. "Politically," he once remarked, "the Japanese are young and plastic enough to copy anything." There was no question in his mind of their ability to copy the form of government he knew best—his own.

This optimism of MacArthur's, watered by an aversion to unpleasant facts, and a highly immodest conception of his own place in history, in time was responsible for some of the occupation's great defects. It made, however, the original difference between success and failure. MacArthur put flesh, muscle and heart into the skeletal directives that came out of Washington. With a political imagination that only one other American of his time, Franklin D. Roosevelt, has shared, he sensed the peculiar opportunity for democratizing the one people in the postwar world who were eager to be taught something.

Outwardly his personality was as precious an insulation against the shock of new ideas as the web society of the Japanese. As a people which stress group consciousness at the expense of the individual, the Japanese have always been oddly vulnerable to hero-worship. When a man is great enough to set himself apart from their society, he has generally been able to order the society to his own ends. The great American military man who spoke with Japanese grandiloquence stepped into the tradition of Oda, Hideyoshi and the other great men of Japan—a democrat right out of the Sun-Goddess' heaven. Like General Nogi, the victor of Port Arthur, he was simple and soldierly in his tastes. Like Admiral Togo, he used the stirring phrase at the right moment. His loyalty and his single-minded dedication to duty struck responsive chords in the people he had set out to change. They were valuable stabilizers for his work.

* * * * *

The first months of occupation were enough to give the people of Japan a growing actual confidence in General MacArthur's army—to strengthen their wishful expectations. In Sanada's case, the confidence was so great that, in December, 1945, through no fault of the Americans, it cost him and his fellow-farmers 240,000 yen. Early that month a smooth-talking city man arrived in Shimoyoshida, posing as a Japanese employee of the occupation. He told the farmers that the occupation authorities were releasing some fertilizer at cost to farm communities. The farmers of Shimoyoshida, desperately in want of soy-bean waste and other standard fertilizers, commissioned Sanada to purchase the fertilizer in Tokyo. They gave him all the money which could be scraped together—240,000 yen.

The city slicker had told Sanada that the occupation forces had a liaison office in the Shiba district of Tokyo, which he could reach through the offices of a newspaper called *Nogei Shimbun*. Sanada took the train down to the capital the very next day. He found the *Nogei Shimbun* office, whose proprietors suavely accepted his money in the name of General MacArthur. They assured him that Shimoyoshida would get the extra fertilizer in a matter of days. He thought it odd at the time that no American soldiers were present at the transaction, but he said nothing about his suspicions. When he came back several days later to check on the fertilizer, the *Nogei Shimbun* and the confidence men who edited it had disappeared. He tried to return what he could to his neighbors, but he has never lived the incident down.

* * * * *

Hideya Kisei got back to Japan in February, 1946. He found his wife Kiyoko weary, but safe, still hard at her job in the company store at Yahata. The men in the family had not been so lucky. Two of his brothers and his brother-in-law had been killed in action in the South Pacific.

Shimoyoshida, a small farming community, had been able to adjust rather easily to the changes of war, peace and occupation. Yahata was still hard-hit. The wartime bombings had not damaged the plant so extensively as Kisei had expected. Most of the bombed buildings were warehouses and dormitories. The furnaces themselves had come through the war intact, but they were badly run down, the result of the last desperate struggle to produce more steel for the Japanese Army. Most of the equipment had aged through hard use to the point of inefficiency or actual breakdown. There was no material for making repairs. More basic than this, there was no iron for the furnaces, and only a little coal.

Kisei found that his neighbors still had a real fear of the occupation army—but it was quickly fading. Of all the scare stories he had heard in Burma and on the trip home, none had come true. The greatest enemy of the steel workers was their own discouragement and fatigue. The shock of the defeat, after the long days and nights of frenzied production for the war, had had a delayed action effect. There was little food. In a silent rebuke to the breakdown of the economic system that had first drawn them into the narrow cities, the farmers' sons in Yahata had trudged out the way they had come, to buy and beg some extra rice in the green fields beyond the city, then free for a time from the clouding smoke of the furnaces.

About the time of Kisei's return, thin funnels of smoke began to rise once more. Back in his job at the Kukioka plant, he pitched in with his old companions on a limited, but slowly increasing work schedule. The American military government authorities began to visit the plant, busily taking notes and asking questions. They did all they could with their available resources to get a token production going. What it would develop into was being decided, in Washington and Tokyo, by new sets of economists trying a fresh hand at the old problems of Japanese industry. For the time, the smoke stayed thin. But, as the Americans imported food, the workers gradually began their return from the fields into the city, to pick up the old tempo of their life.

* * * * *

The next month Admiral Shimizu walked out of his office at the Toyokawa Arsenal for the last time. After six months of cataloguing and sorting, the assets of his bombed factories had been either destroyed or turned over for use in the civilian economy. His part of the inventory had been tiring and depressing—endless conferences with local occupation commanders, civilian government authorities and traveling U.S. army or navy intelligence teams, sweeping up the last bits of information about the Japanese war effort, before its traces were destroyed. There was very little left of his old dignities. The small black Packard which he had used, was now in use as the staff car of a local U.S. army colonel. Of the rest of his establishment—furniture, papers and decorations, he took nothing. When he presented a young American officer with a small vase from the base officers' club, he scrupulously paid out to the Japanese government the exact amount he thought it was worth—a moral nicety observed by few officers, Japanese or American, during these hectic days.

Late in March, Shimizu began to look for a job. Some old friends who ran the Shonan Manufacturing Company asked him to join them. He took his family with him up to Odawara, 50 miles south of Tokyo, where Shonan engaged in the manufacture of oxygen generators.

* * * * *

Hirohito, for his part, was growing used to some spectacular changes in his way of life. At the beginning of the occupation, he drove to the American Embassy, where General MacArthur had taken up residence, to pay his respects to the chief occupier. It was the first time since his European tour as Crown Prince that he had gone calling. The old Imperial Household Ministry, which had run the affairs of the throne since the days of Meiji—without interference from any outside authority—was quickly marked for dissolution; and the number of palace retainers was severely cut. Marquis Kido, since before the war the Emperor's closest advisor, was scheduled to be prosecuted as a war criminal. This was a good gauge of the sentiment toward Hirohito himself then prevailing in the victor's camp.

On the first of January, 1946, Hirohito, by order of the U.S. occupation, sent down to his people an Imperial Rescript the like of which no Japanese emperor had ever written. "The ties between us and our people," he wrote, "have always stood upon mutual trust and affection. They do not depend on mere legends and myths. They are not predicated on the false conception that the Emperor is divine and that the Japanese people are superior to other races and fated to rule the world." It was, all things being considered, a graceful adjustment of the imperial position.

* * * * *

Yamazaki took a longer time to recover from the war than the others. He had no job to return to, and no family of his own to supply the goad for finding one. He had no ideas to turn back on—tragically, since he of all the others lived by ideas and needed them. He was sophisticated enough to reject joining the hasty efforts of his countrymen to assimilate the new occupation army into their own pattern. He was not perceptive enough to sense the dramatic attempt at re-education which the same occupation army, haltingly but bravely, was about to make.

As winter came, the winds and the snows pinned Niigata in its yearly imprisonment between the blizzards of the Japan Alps and the cold gales from the Sea of Japan to the west. Through the days and nights he sat shivering in the farm hut his family had rented in Yokogoshi, worrying over the direction of his future. At first he decided to give up school. Education seemed pointless when there was so much obvious work to be done in Japan. But he sensed at the same time that he must re-educate himself before he could be of much use. He was still, he felt, "saturated with anti-humanism," the legacy of his war service and the old confused college days under the militarists.

No Americans came to Yokogoshi and Yamazaki read only fragments of what was happening in the newspapers. But painfully and alone, he began to work out for himself a rough parallel to the re-education program which men in Tokyo and Washington had sprucely outlined for Japan. At first it was not successful; he was still too puzzled and confused by the collapse of the old values, although he did not, like others, regret this. He read every book he could get his hands on—books on philosophy, religion, history and economics. But he never finished more than two or three chapters. Nothing really interested him.

After two months of listless reading, his mind began to clear. Times had grown worse. He had no money left. The government, by an occupation directive, had recalled the 2000 yen (then worth less than $50) which he had received as a veteran's allowance. Inflation had begun to spiral, stimulated rather than checked by the didoes of an inept finance minister and diffident occupation economists. The longer he waited, the more difficult it would be to make a living. He decided that further education was, after all, only possible by returning to the university. In December, 1945, he took the long train ride over the mountains back to Ueno Station, in Tokyo.

Yamazaki spent nine months at the university before getting his degree. In ordinary times he would have had two years to finish, but the Japanese educational authorities had decided that veterans who could pass the proper examinations and submit a thesis would be allowed to graduate within nine months. This was the only G.I. Bill of Rights which returning veterans in Japan could enjoy. It was, however, a considerable concession from a stiff-necked university tradition.

In Tokyo, Yamazaki shared a room with his younger brother Masao, who had graduated from commercial art school in December. Through Masao, who had found a job with the Toho motion picture studios, he was able to pick up some extra work drawing cinema posters.*

Outside of this extra employment, he spent most of his time either shuffling to classes at the university, or scribbling out his thesis at home. The subject of Yamazaki's thesis was *A Historical Outlook on Marxism and Max Weber*, an ambitious project for someone who had not been able to finish two consecutive chapters of a book just a few months before. He finished it satisfactorily and got his degree in September, 1946.

The thesis theme is a faithful index of his interests at the time. Japanese history no longer interested him. Like the young men of the Meiji Restoration—and he was very conscious of this—he rejected most of his own country's past as valueless and an unprofitable object, even of

---

* Japanese students working their way through the university called this part-time employment *"arubaito,"* after the German *Arbeit*. It is a good example of the odd way foreign words turn up in Japanese. Yamazaki's generation and the one following it, in dating themselves from the war, often call themselves the *"apure geru,"* after the French *après la guerre*.

research. Japanese history, he and his friends of that day agreed, was too "absolutist," too much a study of extremes. To Yamazaki's mind Japanese culture and civilization "were not for every citizen, but only for a limited few." Accordingly he plunged into the history of Western civilization—particularly the period covering the eighteenth and nineteenth centuries, which interested him vastly as "the beginning of democracy and individualism."

American history did not interest him so much, if at all. "The United States," he argued, "had the flower of western civilization transplanted to its shores from Europe. This flower, first cultivated in Europe, is now blooming in the United States. I do not belittle America's frontier spirit, or her power and might, or her literature and culture. But was not all this inherited from Europe? Thus to me it seems only fitting and proper that we retrace the advancement of western civilization to Europe for the basic foundation which makes a nation great." His reason, if oversimplified, had some logic to it. Unfortunately he did not follow out his logic by tracing European history itself back beyond the eighteenth century.

* * * * *

Although Yamazaki did not study American history, he was not uninfluenced by American ideas, as conveyed by the Advancing Garrison Army. He could hardly have written a thesis about Marx—or even about Max Weber, in the guarded university life of prewar Japan. For the first time in his life as a student, he had free and open access to any books he wanted. The discussions in his classes, and the roistering editorials in the big Tokyo dailies (which, pendulum-like, swung hard to the left, once the militarists had been ousted) would not have been possible without the permission and encouragement of the occupation. In the first few months after their arrival, the Americans had abruptly taken the lid off the ferment beneath the surface of Japanese society. Thin clouds of ideas long-suppressed and discussions long whispered billowed formlessly into the open air.

It was not the plan of the occupation simply to perform this negative service. MacArthur had pledged his command to attempt a mass indoctrination in democracy. It took him a few months to fulfill first the coercive tasks of the Occupation: demilitarizing the Japanese armed forces, hunting down fugitive war criminals and removing the obvious restrictions on human freedom which had developed in the Japanese political structure through the past 15 years. As preliminary insurance that his orders would not be subverted, he drew up a vast purge list including all former government officials, regular military officers, the leaders of patriotic organizations, newspaper editors and major executives of banks and corporations connected with the government, who had held their offices between 1937 and 1945. About 186,000 people were thus excluded from participating in public life. Then he began the positive work of democratizing.

In its plan to destroy the old web society of Japan (whether or not the Americans recognized it as such) and to implant a native democracy on an American model, the occupation army worked along two parallel lines: edict and example. Much of the example was unconscious—although in the long run it may prove to have had a more lasting influence than the laws and directives. It was the impact of Americans and the way of life they represented, on the Japanese. Watching the Americans in Japan, the Japanese could observe that here was another people, far more relaxed and individualistic than they, whose way of life had quite evidently brought them at least as much satisfaction and certainly more success.

Since his first encounter, Sanada met many Americans on the roads near Shimoyoshida. Generally, they were G.I. tourists carrying cameras; generally they asked him to pose beside his horse, with Mt. Fuji in the background. They always thanked him and gave him a few cigarettes as a present before they left.

The comparison of this easy-going conduct with the tense, unpredictable activities of their own troops in foreign countries was not overlooked—either by Sanada, or by the millions of other Japanese who had similar casual contacts with their occupiers. In the old web society geniality was never one of the virtues. Japanese could be kind and they could display a sense of humor. But to display informal geniality, as the Americans do, was too risky a business for a man fettered by complicated and codified moral contracts.

The spontaneous kindness of Americans, whether it came in the form of a bottle of Coca-Cola or in the form of mass grain shipments to prevent starvation, was also noted and admired. The mass of the Japanese have not forgotten it. There were (and are) petulant intellectuals in Japan, as there are in France and Britain, to whom *coca-coloniser*, the verb coined by the Communist daily *L'Humanité* is an accurate description as well as a dirty word, symbolizing a vulgar American effort to impose "materialism" or "dollar imperialism" on the peoples of the world. But men like Sanada and Kisei were well aware that, in the early bitter months of the occupation, it was dollars which kept Japan from starving. With American "materialism" coming in the form of food and clothing, it was hardly the unmixed evil which its enemies painted.

There were rapes and robberies committed by Americans in the occupation of Japan, as well as many of the frictions which normally occur between victorious troops and the people of an occupied country. But they were surprisingly few. On the whole the Japanese got along well with the soldiers of the occupation. An American soldier would run across the street in Tokyo to pick up a Japanese boy who had fallen from his bicycle. He would do this naturally, without fear of the *sekinin*—the responsibility—he was assuming. The same man could be genial, kind, yet sincere in performing his duty. Watching conduct like this was an impressive lesson to the people of the web society.

The casual force of example was not left to shape the

new Japan by itself. MacArthur and his staff drew up their edicts from his headquarters in Tokyo, a new, square-pillared building—formerly the home offices of the Dai Ichi Insurance Company and the most antiseptic structure in the city. These edicts, taken together, made up a tremendous blueprint, designed to transplant the expansive government philosophy of America's wheat country to the narrow, rice-growing valleys of Japan.

In the beginning the changes which the officers of SCAP (for Supreme Commander for the Allied Powers) planned were not so sweeping as they turned out to be. But it was discovered that insuring a democratic future was no easy job, even legally. Not to speak of the actual anti-democratic ordinances which Japanese governments enacted in the thirties, the flaws of Meiji democracy which permitted evil to flourish were deeply imbedded in the national system, and only a sweeping reform would clear them away. One revision of law or practice led like a link in a chain to another. Try to destroy the cartels, then something must be done to the investment laws; reform the investment laws and this leads to overhauling the stock market; overhaul the stock market and the effect is no good unless a large-scale propaganda campaign is pushed to encourage new investors.

* * * * *

At the start of the occupation the Japanese themselves gave witness that any drastic reform of their political philosophy must come from the outside. For four months a committee composed of Japan's most eminent legal scholars worked over the draft of a new constitution. What they produced differed only in degree from the constitution of Prince Ito. They had missed the whole point of "democratization" by leaving intact the same imperial powers which Japan's militarists had so easily exploited. Their plan was rejected—and lights burned on into the night from the American offices in the Dai Ichi building—mocking the darkened palace grounds across the moat, as MacArthur and his staff tried to create an abiding rule of law for another nation. The result of their efforts, the Japanese Constitution of 1946, was to be the basis and the safeguard of American political reforms in Japan.

The Hamiltons, Jeffersons and Madisons of the new Constitution all wore uniforms. Their ranks ranged from that of a five star general to a navy lieutenant (j.g.). MacArthur, alone at his desk, wrote out a number of significant phrases in his clear, old fashioned hand: "The emperor is the head of the state . . . his duties and powers will be exercised in accordance with the new constitution and responsible to the basic will of the people as provided therein. . . . War as a sovereign right of the nation is abolished. Japan renounces it as an instrumentality for settling its disputes and even for preserving its own security. It relies on the higher ideals which are now stirring the world for its defense and its protection. . . . The feudal system of Japan will cease. . . . No patent of nobility will from this time forth embody within itself any national or civic power of government. . . ." Elsewhere on the sixth floor of the Dai Ichi building, the officers of SCAP'S Government Section took these basic ideas of the General's, wove them into sound Anglo-Saxon legal language and enlarged on them with hundreds of specific guarantees of individual liberties and prohibitions of old abuses.

The finished product wore a prominent "Made in 1789" tag tied around its middle. "Sovereign power," it declared in its Preamble, "resides with the people." In simple Jeffersonian terms Article 13 proclaimed that "all of the people shall be respected as individuals. Their right to life, liberty and the pursuit of happiness shall to the extent that it does not interfere with the public welfare, be the *supreme consideration* [italics mine] in legislation and other governmental affairs." It was with some difficulty that Japanese translators rendered the philosophy of eighteenth-century America into the language of twentieth-century Japan.

The Constitution was MacArthur's way out of his dilemma: how to "educate" a people to democracy, when there is no native tradition of democracy (or any stable alternative thereof) sound enough to build upon. Its idealism, its democracy, its naivete and its untactful concreteness—these were the virtues and faults of General MacArthur's occupation. The virtues of the Constitution, however, were considerable. It provided guarantees for basic democratic freedoms which Japanese may have glimpsed in the past, but had never in security enjoyed. Some of its provisions were elementary—the legal prohibition against unlawful search, and double jeopardy, the guarantee that an accused man would not have to testify against himself. But if Japanese democracy was to grow at all, it needed elementary safeguards.

The new Constitution bluntly attacked the philosophy behind the old one, which began with the Emperor Meiji's statement that "The rights of sovereignty of the state we have inherited from our Ancestors. . . ." Prince Ito and the Meiji reformers had flirted with the idea of popular sovereignty. The great liberal Itagaki Taisuke had once said in a public speech that "The freedom to which we so earnestly aspire is the principal which pervades Heaven and Earth. . . ." But they had never pursued their glimpse of freedom to its logical conclusion—and popular sovereignty in the Japan of 1946, was a deep and revolutionary break with tradition.

Most of the Japanese did not understand the concept of popular sovereignty, with its delicate balance between rights and duties and its barely justifiable dependence on an educated electorate. But many, like Yamazaki and his fellow-students in Tokyo, were trying to understand it. The Constitution, with all its unfamiliar wording, was a desperately needed instrument to safeguard their liberties while learning them. At the same time it was an example of the liberties that one should strive for, and the pitfalls that one should shun. If a native democracy or a reasonable alternative succeeds in Japan, MacArthur's Constitution can claim a great share of the credit. Temporarily it has functioned like a vital bit of foreign matter—a silver plate or a piece of platinum—which surgeons sometimes insert in the body of their patient, until nature's slow but surer processes can attend to the business of healing.

The faults of the Constitution were obvious from its wording. It was written, largely, by a group of people with little more than a superficial knowledge of Japan; in their document they made almost no concessions to the traditions, the environment or the tastes of the people they wrote the document for. Not all Japanese traditions are bad, nor all American traditions good. The Constitution was difficult enough in itself for the Japanese to swallow, without the spice of foreign notions that were probably indigestible. Ideas of government like the "pursuit of happiness" spring out of a purely American background. The pursuit is Jeffersonian, the product of a philosophical system derived from the eighteenth-century French Deists. Many Americans, especially those who are pious Christians, do not share all of Jefferson's optimistic philosophy. Most Japanese have difficulty even in comprehending its premises. It is difficult to explain to a people schooled in the value of sacrifice why the idea of pursuing "happiness" as an end in itself must be a fine and laudable thing.

Article 23 of the Constitution said "Academic freedom will be guaranteed." Americans in the postwar years have had difficulty defining "academic freedom" themselves, as witness incidents like the loyalty oath controversy at the University of California in 1950. What were the Japanese to make of it? To begin with, the Japanese student studies in a different atmosphere from the American; like students in universities, he and his professors share a strong tradition of overt political action. When police later broke up rallies of Communist students and professors, were they not transgressing Article 23 of the Constitution?

General MacArthur's famous anti-war clause, at one with his prediction that Japan could become "the Switzerland of the Pacific," was understandable in the air of hopeful idealism that warmed the world at the close of World War II, just before the coming of the Cold War. But constitutions are supposedly written for the centuries. Scarcely three years after it became law, the "anti-war" clause had become also a rallying point for Japanese neutralists, Communists, anti-Americans and all who for political reasons or from a genuine horror of war refused to face the fact of Russia's aggressions and Japan's alignment with the West. Hideya Kisei still quotes it hopefully in his talks with friends at Yahata. In 1948 Fumio Shimizu said sympathetically to an American friend, "I think General MacArthur must be having a tougher time mentally than I or any other Japanese, because of that clause. The people of Japan are most fortunate because of it—but, with changing conditions in Asia, it must be hard on the General."

With the Constitution as their charter and starting point, the *Shinchugun* began in earnest to democratize Japan. In Tokyo, one occupation directive after another rolled off SCAP'S mimeograph machines, expanding, clarifying and adding to the list of basic freedoms. Land reform destroyed the bondage of the tenant farmers.* The 8-hour day became a law in Japanese factories. Women received the franchise. New textbooks were written for the schools—a sorely needed project. The coercive powers of the police were shorn. Freedom of the press was certified and explained.

The winds of an unruly change rattled the structure of Japanese society as neither the Great Change of the seventh century nor the Meiji upheaval of the nineteenth century had. They tore through the roofs of newly impoverished temples, where Shinto priests, for the first time in centuries, had to subsist without government contributions. They rustled the trees in Tokyo parks where the newly emancipated women in their ill-fitting print dresses walked self-consciously hand in hand with their boy friends. They rattled the windows at village meetings, where earnest military government officers talked about

* See Chapter 10.

"local responsibilities" to rows of polite but puzzled farmers. They blew past street corners, where candidates for the Diet yelled out new political slogans to the new free electorate.

There was no corner of Japanese life where the ideas of the "democracy" of the Americans did not reach, however imperfectly. Chic Young's "Blondie" became overnight the most popular Japanese comic strip. The owners of Japan's nine million radios adjusted to a new diet of variety shows, soap operas and quiz programs—and some good documentary programs explaining what democracy was. A wave of elopements rolled over Japan after the occupation authorities had denounced arranged marriages as "feudalistic."

Unsure of just what democracy is, the Japanese, in their enthusiasm for the new, easily confused its accidents with its essence. Women in one city organized an American-style box social; a luckless man was elected "most democratic" male in the city by the same feminine group. In Nagasaki, school children were crowded into makeshift auditoriums to learn square dancing, because an overenthusiastic military government officer thought it "democratic." Coeducation received an unexpected revival in Japan, since this form of instruction was held to be "democratic," too.

On a higher level, the occupation's policy-makers showed the same confusion of democratic trappings with democratic spirit which they had implied in their Constitution. A supreme court modeled on that of the United States gave needed direction to Japan's Byzantine legal system. But it hardly seemed necessary to dress the Japanese justices in black legal robes (imported from the United States) instead of their traditional red. The Tokyo police department needed improvement, but this was scarcely effected by outfitting patrolmen with the same night-sticks used by the force in New York. The American polity had grown great through political federalism, with a maximum of autonomy given to states and municipalities. This did not demand that the occupation authorities force a similar system of local autonomy on Japan, a smaller and more ethnically centralized country. Democracy had previously proved itself workable in the more centralized government systems of British and France.

For all the sins committed in its name, democracy, in one way or another, was leaving its mark on the lives of the Japanese. Hirohito, Shimizu, Sanada, Kisei and Yamazaki—all of them were somehow affected by it.

* * * * *

On a February morning in 1946, Hirohito drove across the palace moat in his black Mercedes Benz sedan, on his way to meet the people of Japan. He took an 18-mile journey to Kawasaki, south of Tokyo, which before the war and the bombings had been one of the leading industrial cities of Japan. The familiar route led through a cold desert of crushed smokestacks and girders blackened by fire, desolate acres made more striking by the wooden hovels which people had built in the ruins of steel and concrete. The purpose of the visit was to establish a new kind of personal bond between the citizens of the ruins and a shy personality which for almost 20 years had been sealed up in the role of an immanent Presence.

Hirohito's first attempts to "democratize" the throne were of such an awkwardness as to make foreign spectators physically uncomfortable. There were few traces left of the earnest and well-schooled young Crown Prince who in 1921 had known just the right things to say to Lloyd George, the President of the French Republic, or a Scottish gamekeeper. Visiting the workers of the Kawasaki factory of the Showa Electrical Works, Hirohito now asked questions perfunctorily and with great nervousness, a tense, shuffling figure in a gray overcoat and a crumpled pearl-gray hat. His unfailing comment on the answers *"ah, so*—is that so?" was scarcely inspiring. Foreign newspapermen present were indifferent, pitying or contemptuous. In their perspective, it was difficult to see how this imperial popularizing could have much of an effect.

The pain of these early visits did not deter Hirohito or his advisors, who realized that under the pressure of new democratic ideas it was essential to the imperial prestige to assume the role of a popular constitutional monarch which had been planned for him in the twenties. Driving by car or by train on carefully planned trips throughout Japan, the Emperor grew accustomed again to mass contacts with people. From a reluctant player in a walk-on part, he became a competent, if not a poised performer. This is not to infer that his new role was an actor's pose. It was, after all, something very near to the function for which his Westernized advisors had educated him. And few kings have been so sincere in a desire to help their people prosper, so remorseful for a war which left their people poor and dispirited.

The crumpled gray hat became in time the badge of a successful political campaigner. The monosyllables in which Hirohito had conducted his early interviews with the common folk grew into coherent questions and intelligent replies. The shy man waved his hat in the air to acknowledge greetings. He smiled. Slowly the sense of a personality behind the walled moat of the Imperial Palace communicated itself to the people of Japan.

When Hirohito visited Nagasaki in 1949, in the course of a tour of Kyushu, it was clear that his new role of the constitutional Emperor was well established. As in the old days, the residents of areas where he would pass spent hours before his arrival decorating their houses, sweeping the streets and filling in the smallest holes in the pavement. When the Emperor appeared, they were rewarded by the sight of a self-possessed man, still more obviously nervous than the average, but no longer afraid of personal contacts. He spoke simply and directly. He said to a group of union leaders, "Thank you for your cooperation. I hope you will work for a healthy labor union." He said to some coal miners at Tagawa, "I should like to ask you to produce some more." He told the children of a Catholic orphanage, "Work hard, pray to Jesus Christ and grow to be good men."

In moments of relaxation on the trip, he never forgot his scientific hobby. On a walk through the hills of Unzen, a beautiful mountain spa, he noticed an odd type of moss growth in a pond. He began to wade in after it, but his chamberlain held him back, suggesting that this might be "too dangerous." By this time a small army of Japanese photographers had already jumped into the pond to take pictures of the Emperor. "If it isn't dangerous for them," Hirohito protested, "why is it dangerous for me?"

To record any conversation like this—or to bring photographers to such an occasion, would have been impossible before 1945. Although there were traditionalists to deplore such relaxations of protocol, the Japanese in general responded to it. The crowds who greeted Hirohito at Nagasaki were respectful, but they were loud and smiling. People cheered and clapped, shaking their paper flags. The banzais thundered through the streets, as the Emperor's party drove through shipyards, past reconstructed houses and the thin white pillar that marks the center of the atom bomb's explosion. There was obviously deep respect; there was also curiosity and varying degrees of patriotism, approval and joy. But the silent awe of the prewar years was present only in a few. It was clear that, by 1949, the Emperor of Japan held his position firmly, but on a slightly different premise than before.

* * * * *

In May, 1946 Hideya Kisei joined a union. With the help of the local military government officials, a few workers drew on their hazy memories of prewar labor organizations to form a new one. It was the first independent trade union at Yahata, since the old one was smothered after the strike of 1919. Kisei was among the first men at the Kukioka plant to organize. Like the others, he was vague and uncertain about what a union could and should do—many years had passed since his early eager studies in industrial economics. To fill the void in their experience, the occupation supplied a great deal of material on the workings of trade unions, well illustrated with examples from those in the United States. Unions in other industries, who had already organized, sent more information and encouragement. So did the Japanese Communist party.

For the first half year of its existence the union organized itself slowly and smoothly. There was no opposition from the management of the plant, which itself was undergoing a drastic shake-up; and SCAP's benediction guaranteed that the group would be respected by the local police and other government authorities. But tensions began to pull from the inside, once the union began to grow strong. They were familiar tensions. The rank and file howled suspiciously at the announcement declaring that a union chairman would be elected by the central committee. A rumor went through the plant that management had a tacit understanding with the committee members. Kisei for one believed it—and he took the lead in some of the angry meetings where the rank and file denounced their representatives. Bending to the pressure, the union officials resigned. When a new slate of officers was elected by popular vote, Kisei was one of them.

Between the new union and the pressure of the new laws that came down from Tokyo, the lives of the Yahata workers saw what Kisei proudly admits was a "terrific improvement." Wages rose steadily—although they barely kept ahead of the spiraling prices of rice and clothing. Safety rules were enforced as they never had been—and there were far fewer burns and broken limbs to be attended to at the company dispensary. Rest periods and overtime pay became standard—a new development for Japanese industry. Ultimately, under the new stock arrangement, workers were able to buy shares, as individuals, in their company (see Chapter 10). As the industry recovered itself, business boomed.

The improvement transcended a rise of physical living conditions. In the prewar days Kisei had thought of himself and his fellow workers as "robots," fearful even to exchange opinions on political conditions, unprotected from the punishments and the prying of the company management and the police. In the budding democracy of the occupation era, the air had cleared. Without understanding the "popular sovereignty" clauses in the new Constitution, the steelmen had begun to think of their lives as something more than a web of duties. They worked. They had rights. They had power.

In 1948 they tested their new rights in a series of strikes. In relays the plants at Yahata went idle—each for a period of three hours. Kisei at first supported the idea of the strike as a straight protest for better working conditions. But as further strike agitation developed, he found his young union in the grip of the same inner struggle which, all over Japan, was weakening the new labor movement. Communists had joined the union at the beginning. Mechanically filling out their pattern, they at first brought the inexperienced workers good service and invaluable enthusiasm. Then, in the meetings, they gradually introduced proposals for more violent action against management. They held that the workers' goal was to gain total control of the factory. In the confusion of the 1948 strike, they tried with some success to turn a legitimate workingman's protest into a political campaign for Communist party objectives.

Kisei reacted strongly against the Communists. After the 1948 strike, he insisted that the union use negotiation and arbitration as its primary weapon. He saw more clearly than most of his friends at the mill the danger of confusing politics with trade unionism. Deeper than this, there was something about a strike which bothered his Satsuma conscience. "As workers," he once said to a union meeting, "we have no right to leave our places of work. Once we leave them, we are workers no longer." It was not an unusual attitude; in fact, his speech was very popular. The new trade unionists were willy-nilly the products of the old web society, where the bonds of a mutual contract bit hard and deep. To strike was to sever those bonds, an ultimate course of action which was never taken without a great many earnest misgivings.

In this case, as in others, one influence of the web society was not so bad after all. Kisei is justly proud that he and his followers in the Kukioka plant never once left their place of work. Their furnaces were never allowed to stop operating. This attitude, Kisei once explained, "did not mean that I was lukewarm towards the labor movement. My idea was that we should fight strongly for a contract; but that, once the contract was obtained, we should respect all its provisions. If we became dissatisfied with it, then it was up to us to negotiate again for a new one."

Kisei kept stubbornly to this attitude, through all the waves of pro-Communism, anti-Communism and plain bewilderment that passed over the liberated Japanese labor movement. The Communists called him a hidebound socialist and worse; management termed him a radical. He was becoming a good democrat.

* * * * *

While Kisei fired the furnaces of the new labor movement, Tadao Yamazaki was watching the struggle of democracy from another direction. On his graduation from Tokyo Commercial University, he began looking for a job where he could use his brain, without being tied to the monotony of a daily fixed routine. He decided on journalism. Both the newspaper *Asahi* and the Japan Broadcasting Company were at the time holding examinations for recent college graduates—the standard method for entering most Japanese businesses. He applied for the *Asahi* job first, passed the examinations, and got it. His starting salary was about 600 yen a month—at the 1946 rate of exchange, equal to about $40. It was better than average. The *Asahi*, a 75-year-old landmark of the Japanese press, is a good, though exacting employer. It publishes three national editions of what is basically the same newspaper in Tokyo, Osaka and Kokura, in Kyushu, with one of the largest circulations in the world (the combined circulation is 6,000,000).

"The press," he said quoting an old editorial room maxim, "leads the public. Journalism meant that I would be realistically and at the same time ideologically working to better our society. Now I had a chance to see, hear and write for myself. I would be contributing my share in reconstructing a humanistic and democratic Japan."

Yamazaki's humanistic crusade got off to a slow start. He spent eight nervous months as a cub reporter in the Tokyo office, a vast but fast-moving mechanism that oddly combines the austerity of the New York *Times* with the hustle of a big-city tabloid. It was a busy time for the newspaper business, which for a while resolved itself into a hopscotch of keeping editorials and news coverage in focus with the stream of occupation directives, and the sudden complication of world news outside. But there were many hands to do the job: well-manicured foreign correspondents—temporarily denied permission to resume their international coverage—swelled a staff already ridiculously large for the job of putting out a paper rationed by newsprint shortages to four pages. Yamazaki was unhappily shifted from one desk to another. His one break was the chance to cover the Tone River flood, the biggest disaster to hit Japan after the surrender.

In the late summer of 1947 Yamazaki was assigned to the *Asahi* bureau in Urawa, a fair-sized town 30 miles north of Tokyo. A few months after arriving there, he went up with several other reporters to the town of Honjo to check on a peculiar disturbance involving a town official and one of *Asahi's* own correspondents. What he found there was an unusually neat microcosm of the forces for and against the new democracy in Japan.

Honjo is a drowsy, run-down town of 22,000 squatting

just off the broad Nakasendo highway running northward from Tokyo. It is noted for its silk and the good quality of the rice sold there. Its food surpluses are not surprising. The envy of hard-pressed mountain towns like Shimoyoshida, Honjo is surrounded by the gently rolling rice country of Saitama Prefecture, the "rice-bowl of Tokyo," a pure sea of productive green that reaches for 60 miles north of the capital.

The drowsiness of Honjo was deceptive, its quiet dearly bought. Like many Japanese towns, it had been run for generations by a tight coterie of local bosses, known as *oyabun,* who had managed to make a very good thing for themselves out of the old web traditions of loyalty and sacred commitments. On a small scale, the *oyabun* of Honjo and thousands of other places had duplicated the trick of Tojo and the militarists—unscrupulous and heedless of observing social commitments themselves, they had taken a stranglehold on their local society at its weakest point, the tendency of the average Japanese to put blind faith in the integrity of anyone with whom they have a standing relationship or even a solitary commitment. Helped to power by the defects in the web society, they had used the web to cement their hold on their fellow townsmen.

The first citizen of Honjo—and its most efficient *oyabun*—was a man named Kazuichiro Oishi. He and a few friends ran the town. Just as they had grown fat on war industries, they now in the occupation era had run up a profitable trade in black-marketeering, gambling and blackmail. No one in Honjo cared or dared to challenge their rule, and the townspeople gratefully accepted the donations which Oishi made out of his profits to local welfare projects. The local U.S. military government officers, although they disapproved of Oishi's activities, found it next to impossible to get evidence warranting them to take action against him. As long as he continued in power, the preachments on the "new democracy" which came to Honjo were rather cynically regarded.

One sultry evening, during a town banquet, a local newspaperman who worked part-time for *Asahi* got into an argument with Oishi. Before the discussion reached the point of blows, it was patched up. But Oishi was not satisfied. Shortly afterward, he called in the local press and told them that, in the future, he would dictate what they were to report. As long as he was running the town, Oishi said sharply, they should have no illusions about what would happen to anyone who disagreed with him. Later, the *Asahi* newspaperman was beaten by some Honjo hoodlums.

When this news reached the third-floor editorial offices in Tokyo, the editors of *Asahi* decided to make a fight of it. Yamazaki found himself in Honjo as part of a quickly dispatched task force, with the mission of exposing corruption inside Oishi's headquarters. They worked in Honjo for weeks, running down leads and pleading with close-mouthed citizens to give them more. As far as it could—without interfering directly in a local Japanese matter—the occupation gave them its full support.

Oishi made a fight out of it, as well. *Asahi* got no help from the town officials and ran into open hostility at the local police station (Oishi was, officially, chairman of the Honjo Citizens and Police Society). But the reporters won. The Honjo *oyabun* and most of his henchmen were tried, convicted and given jail sentences.

The Honjo incident became famous. A book was written about it and a successful semi-documentary film, *"The Pen Does Not Lie,"* describing the Oishi case appeared a year later in Tokyo's theaters. It was evidence that the new ideals had taken some root below their surface of box socials, university debating societies and black judicial robes. A few old-time liberals left on the *Asahi* staff measured it with surprise and satisfaction against the days, barely ten years before, when the soldiers had stomped into the *Asahi* building unmolested to smash the presses with their bayonets.

Yamazaki was elated. "The incident," he could say with justice, "was undoubtedly the first genuine test for democracy and a free press in Japan. If we had lost, it would have been a clear indication that the seeds of democracy had not taken root. The crusade was successful and it instilled new life and hope in the people of Honjo. They know now what it means to fight for fundamental rights."

He came back from Honjo with a new sense of the importance of his job. He had also had an object lesson in another essential of democracy—the importance of the citizen's participating in community politics. Nor did he deceive himself into thinking that he and his fellow reporters had done the job alone. "The might of the occupation impressed itself upon me then," he remembers, "we would have failed, if we had not had the occupation's blessing."

* * * * *

Honjo was not an isolated incident. There was the stubborn fight of a teacher named Minoru Uchida, who had lived through the bloody debacle of the capture of Saipan and Tinian, to teach "democracy" in a schoolhouse on the slopes of Mt. Akagi, deep in north-central Japan, to children who had never seen a modern motor-car, against equally stubborn local farmers who preferred the old way. There was the struggle of Moriji Yamaga, once a navy captain, who had learned democracy in an American prison-camp and who spent his life savings traveling through towns and villages in the countryside, trying to teach what he knew.

These people and hundreds of thousands of others, in varying ways, had caught sight of a new society which could replace their old one. Few of them were as literate as Tadao Yamazaki in describing what they wanted. Many of them completely mistook democracy for something else. Some, like Shimizu and Sanada, were content to remain as observers of the new changes. But many tried very hard to understand them. There was almost no community in Japan where the conflict between the old and new did not blaze into the open, after the first realization that the Americans demanded something more than a reshuffling of the national standards, something more than a readjustment of the web.

The catechumens of democracy were often intolerant, Americans as well as Japanese. Like the first reformers of Meiji, who wanted their shocked Buddhist countrymen to switch to eating meat dishes immediately, as a sign of their good faith, they often dogmatically insisted that the symbols as well as the system of democracy be scrupulously observed. There was a wide tendency in the late nineteen forties, as there had been during the eighteen seventies, to heap abuse on native institutions. This missed the point. The web society, after all, was not intrinsically an evil thing. It was a dangerous thing, because it had proved its extreme vulnerability to dictatorship and the enshrining of false and relative values in the heart of the nation.

It was a vastly more difficult job than the occupiers imagined to convey the sense and spirit of democracy to the Japanese. For centuries they had had their lives ordered by the laws of one national politico-religious society. The idea of a secular democracy embracing many ideals and religions within it has been difficult for most Japanese to grasp. The Japanese are at heart a religious people, as every Christian missionary from Xavier to the present had found out (once he penetrated their reserves of suspicion and misunderstanding). They have often felt a little naked, clad only in the sober democratic rationalism of Jefferson and John Locke. And the Americans who brought them the democratic message were generally too diffident and unsure of their own ideals, or too forgetful of the premises of their own democracy, to present to the Japanese its revolutionary message and its Christian idealism, as well as the mechanics of how to run a public health service and operate voting machines.*

MacArthur in this respect did a great service. His faith in his own institutions was moving and it was highly communicable. But there were not many in his immediate staff with the same faith and competence. There were military government officers and men, as well as some among the personnel of the Tokyo headquarters, who had come to Japan with a clear sense of mission; unfortunately their abilities frequently did not match their zeal. There was also a disproportionate number of Americans who had come to Japan for the ride: they boondoggled with great success.

In any assessment of the American occupation of Japan, the failings of personnel should be remembered. What the occupation did, it did on short rations. Hastily manned and equipped, its departments were constantly dwarfed by the vast task they had set themselves. It was often physically impossible to do a job adequately. Until the damage was past repairing, Washington and the American public did not realize the staggering task which they, indirectly, were attempting in Japan, and on which they all, as Americans, would be judged by the world. Perhaps this lack of understanding grew out of General MacArthur's aversion for taking Washington into his confidence, or his

---

* There were some spectacular examples of how the Japanese reacted to this deficiency. In 1949, when several Communist votes turned up in their local elections, the village elders of Saga, a small farming community in Kyoto prefecture, were horrified. The threat of revolution had never come so close to them. To fight this new ideology—evidently in their midst, the town fathers resorted, neither to their Buddhist priest nor to American occupation officials. With remarkable feeling for the religious appeal of Communism, and their own religious deficiencies, they sent a delegation to Roman Catholic priests in the city of Kyoto, asking them to teach Saga Christianity. The priests were at first skeptical, but the villagers proved to be sincere. Some 1500 of them, the great majority of Saga's population, are now baptized Catholics.

overenthusiastic press releases. Perhaps it was impossible that the American people, then stubbing their toes on the threshold of international responsibility, should have realized what issues were at stake.

For all these reservations, the occupation sowed its message. It did not democratize Japan, but it made a democratization of Japan possible. It did not transform Japanese society into something else, but it would take generations of determined reaction to wipe out the totality of its achievement. The externals of the old web society remain. It may tighten in new ways or assume new forms, but its old mold is permanently shattered.

9

THE COMMUNIST ATTACK

Comrades! Japan's "1917" is rapidly drawing near! Indeed, will we not by our efforts hasten that day!

Sanzo Nozaka

In the world of the laboratory, formulae can always be reasoned through, the lines on a graph prove something, figures never lie and human impulses are always predictable. In its beginnings the occupation of Japan resembled laboratory work under optimum conditions. American democracy, the active ingredient of Japan's transformation, was a constant. The old order of the web society, which democracy planned to replace, was a constant, also. Both the Americans who ran the occupation and the Japanese who accepted it were easily handled variables, guided with equal efficiency by occupation directives.

By the beginning of 1948, however, it was clear that an unexpected factor, explosively variable, had crept into the original equation. The march of postwar Communism was felt in Japan with peculiar distinctness. As an international force, it drummed home to the Japanese and to General MacArthur that the world was not so soon destined to be a brotherly place. Japanese war prisoners languished in illegal Russian prison camps and Soviet gunboats ruthlessly patrolled the northern waters off Hokkaido. Mao Tse Tung reached out from Yenan to dominate the land mass of China. Faintly but clearly, the echoes of the Berlin blockade and the Communist infiltration of Europe sounded in Toyko.

Inside Japan a native Communist party made a strong revival. It got a respectable toe hold in the new parliament. It successfully recruited the familiar shock brigades of dissatisfied intellectuals and students doped on Marx and revolution, of labor agitators and the unionists whom they duped. There was soon the familiar spectrum of deep reds, red-tinted fringes, parlor pinks and fellow-travelers shaded neutral. The party at first withheld attacking the American democratization plan directly. But, working indirectly, it became a thorn in the side of some occupation projects.

The first open Communist attacks on the occupation did not occur until the period of the Korean war. Long before they started, both Japanese and Americans were alerted—in varying ways—to the fight they faced in the middle of the experiment. The rear area laboratory found itself ever closer to the front lines, the target of heavy enemy fire.

Under the circumstances, the technicians inside had to revise their project. The whole design of the laboratory had to be altered. Glass walls became bunkers and test-tube racks were made into a firing step. Almost no corner of the occupation escaped this remodeling. The education program had stressed a peaceful, positive approach to democracy; now part of its energies were diverted to spreading a militant anti-Communism. An economic plan that started out as a leisurely redistribution of the nation's wealth switched to a hurried effort to get the nation producing and independent of foreign aid or foreign intimidation. The occupation leader who had held out to the Japanese a promise of unending peace and neutrality had to discuss questions of military bases and rearmament.

Most tragically of all, an occupation authority pledged to inculcate free speech and democratic habits found itself forced to abridge free speech and curtail democracy, when the Communists threatened their abuse. The trouble admittedly, was not wholly brought on by the Communists. There is a basic paradox involved in a military occupation which sets out to teach democratic habits to the occupied. The United States Army, during its occupation of Japan, did not solve it. With a military concern for keeping order as an end in itself, the lawmakers of SCAP were often blind to the fact that the revolutionary ideas they themselves had injected into Japan could hardly be carried into fact without some disturbances and disorder. But they would never have throttled strikes, or cropped newspaper criticism to the extent they did, if the active attacks of the Communists had not thrown them on the defensive.

It was difficult to regard a strike as a normal spasm of labor's growing pains, when Communist union leaders had fatally intertwined their political propaganda with the statement of the workers' honest economic complaints. It was hard to receive criticism, knowing that it would be exploited for no constructive purpose. Whether or not each suspected case of what the occupation authorities liked to call "Red agitation" was so in fact is not essential to the question. The important thing is that the Communists, inside Japan and outside it, by 1948 had created an atmosphere of conflict and suspicion that badly damaged the laboratory experiment.

The occupation was not only forced to renege on some of its own promises; Communist agitation inside Japan and the threat of Communist invasion from the outside forced the United States to continue its occupation as a military endeavor long after its discontinuance had been decided on. Like the Meiji reformers in their day, the American democratizers were forced to compromise their reforms in the face of attack. Possibly, if the Meiji state had not been threatened by European imperialism, the Japan that evolved from it would have been built on a sounder basis

Certainly the American reformers could have done their work better, if Communist imperialism had not threatened it so drastically.

* * * * *

There were some special reasons why Communism might appeal to the Japanese. In its preachments and lip service to democracy, it at first seemed like a more dynamic version of the democracy taught by General MacArthur. The Japanese are not overfond of philosophy, and the web society, as has been seen, is out of its depth in the currents of absolute values. There was never, except among a very few Japanese, any sensitiveness to the fact that Marxist materialism is essentially different, in its approach to life, from either Jeffersonian democracy, Fabian socialism or other forms of government which spring from a belief that man is something more than part of a materialist movement in history. Tadao Yamazaki, who has spent considerable time studying Marx, still feels that classic Marxism—as distinguished from the Stalinist adaptation—is "good and humanistic," a system devised for the betterment of man.

With typical pragmatism, the Japanese attitude towards Communism was shaped by the way Communism behaved, not in the least by what it taught as principles. Fumio Shimizu and Sakaji Sanada are at one in abhorring the Communist system because of what it does, not what it is. Shimizu, who has studied Marx himself, has no quarrel with the theory of Communism, but detests Communists as people who "have no manners, discipline or feeling of humanism." Sanada's view of Communism, similarly, is shaped by its penchant for causing disorder. Kisei, until the Communists showed themselves to be a disruptive force in the Yahata union, was quite happy to work along with them; he welcomed their help.

With no opposition to Communism on principle, the Japanese at first were attracted by its activity and its workability. It fitted comfortably into the old web society. The extreme appeal of Communism, its liturgy of slogans, its sacramental sense of mission, its hierarchy of leaders—all struck a warm response in a people who had traditionally confused and blended politics with religion. The diffident, rationalistic attitude of the Americans was a weak contrast to the forest of waving red flags at Communist rallies and the sense of dedication that the party insisted on. There was no place in a democracy for the suicidal loyalty of Kamikaze pilots or the Forty-Seven Ronin; but this quality would make good Communists. A transfer of allegiance along these lines actually happened. As in Germany, the Communists could draw on a core of ex-militarists and extreme nationalists, who found little trouble shifting their basic loyalty from the Sun-Goddess Amaterasu to Stalin.

Democracy's insistence on individualism was puzzling to the people of the web society. The Communist view of the individual, however, was a comforting reaffirmation of the group life in Japan. The new family of the Internationale again offered the puzzled survivor of the web society a handy package of loyalties, contracts, duties and obligations, minus the confusions of notions like "the pursuit of happiness" or the "sovereignty of the people."

The revolutionary urges of Communism, also, seized the imagination of Japanese intellectuals who felt the impulse of new ideas after the war, but were frustrated in their zeal by the iron wish of the occupation to limit demonstrations of any revolutionary activities.

* * * * *

After the war the Communists shrewdly began to capitalize on these appeals to the Japanese, without doing anything to jar old traditions or trespass on old taboos prematurely. Although a few party enthusiasts had made speeches demanding that the Emperor should, at the least, abdicate, headquarters quickly changed its tune and went back into a discreet silence about the monarchy. Party strategy was directed from a plain-looking three-story building in the Yoyogi district of Tokyo by Sanzo Nozaka, a well-traveled Cominform man whose last address had been Yenan, China. Nozaka, a Japanese Maurice Thorez, preferred Trojan horses to splintered wooden barricades as a revolutionary technique. He made the party look like the forward echelon in the fight for democracy, seldom directly attacked the occupation, and relied for the moment on parliamentary methods to get his ends. The technique for a while was most successful. In the elections of 1949, the Communists sent 35 representatives to the Diet and got 3,000,000 popular votes.

As the Cold War of the late forties hardened, the party's tactics changed. Nozaka's planning gradually gave way to the rough approach of the party militants like Yoshio Shiga, the young editor of *Akahata* ("Red Flag"), the Communist newspaper. Having gone perhaps as far as Communists can go as a legal political party, the Japanese Politburo developed a campaign of sabotage and open acts of violence, not only against Japanese political opponents, but, finally, directly against the American occupation. In July, 1949, Sadamori Shimoyama, the president of the national railway systems, was found decapitated on the tracks near Tokyo, at the height of a stormy strike, led by Communists, against the railroad management. A month later, during another transport strike, a streetcar was deliberately released from its barn in the Mitaka district of Tokyo and sent careening down a hill. It jumped the tracks and killed six bystanders. Tadao Yamazaki rushed up to Mitaka in an *Asahi* car to cover the story, shortly after the deaths had occurred.

Acts of violence like this, coming at a time of especially noisy Communist agitation, were premature. They forced the people of Japan to a decision about Communism which they might not otherwise have made for a long time. In exploiting the urge of the web society to put itself under discipline, the party generals had forgotten that its instincts for good citizenship and preserving the established order are equally strong. Sanada and his friends in Shimoyoshida literally recoiled when they saw the headlines of latest labor disturbances. Communists were condemned as "extremists" of the worst sort. Several years before the same sort of thing happened in the United States. Japanese businessmen began to scrutinize the records of college graduates looking for employment: Communist sympathizers need not apply. Ironically, in the three-cornered struggle between Communism, democracy and the web, it was the old web society which resisted Communism most strongly, after the Communists prematurely attacked it. The cause of democracy was oddly benefited by the system it set out to liquidate.

In the summer of 1949 the Communists made their most spectacular gesture, and committed their most spectacular error. The Soviet Union, after four years delay, agreed to send back to Japan a portion of the some 450,000 Japanese war prisoners still held in Russian prison camps since the collapse of the Japanese Manchurian armies. It had been suspected in American quarters that the prisoners returned would show the effects of Russian indoctrination. The fact proved worse than any fears. As the former Japanese hospital ship *Takasago Maru* sailed into the fjord-like harbor of Maizuru, on the west coast of Japan, the harsh choruses of the first wave of returning repatriates, singing new Communist songs to the tunes of old militarist ones,* opened the curtain on as chilling a preview of life under Communism as any free nation has thus far received.

The repatriates were tough, disciplined and well fed. Outside of new Russian boots and Soviet Army forage caps, they wore their old Japanese army uniforms. The rigidness of their behavior, their strict obedience to the orders

---

* This was literally true. *"Akahata*—The Red Flag," one of the principal Communist songs in Japanese, has been fitted to the music of *"Bando no Sakura,"* one of the standard marching songs of Japanese soldiers during and before World War II.

of the Communist cadres among them and their first hostility towards their own people showed at a glance that the Russians had been able to superimpose their brand of regimentation on the web society of the Japanese Army—by simple switches of slogans and simple changes in the emphasis of their instruction and the objects of their duties.

To clinch their hold on the returned soldiers and, possibly, to intimidate the country with a convincing show of strength, the Japanese Communist party decided on a mass campaign of rallies and trainside demonstrations to welcome the repatriates, as soon as they left their reception centers. The demonstrations themselves were a part of the Communist preview. Well-disciplined party organizers confused stationmasters, and rerouted trains to deceive official civilian welcoming committees. They called up every available supporter and sympathizer in their areas, equipped with flags, loudspeakers, to fill the streets and plazas in front of the railroad terminals. The repatriates, getting their first look at Japan since the war, understandably got a distorted view of Communist strength. Following orders as they had done for years past, they filed into the rallies and signed membership applications for the Communist party. They made speeches about the good life in Russia (from prepared texts supplied by local Communists). Parents and relatives who had come to meet them were brushed aside.

At the first demonstrations both American military government officers and Japanese police, taken by surprise, had no clear program for handling these rallies. Here, again, was a touchy case involving "free speech." It was legal to demonstrate in public. But was it legal to demonstrate for the purpose of a public double deception (i.e., deceiving the repatriates about the strength of Japanese Communists and deceiving the Japanese public about the political feelings of the repatriates)?

The rallies boomeranged. The ultimate damage which they did to Japanese Communism was directly proportional to their first great success. Years later, in harder times, or after long propaganda build-ups by the Communists—Russian and Japanese—they might have helped Sovietize Japan. In 1949 they alerted the Japanese to the danger of this possibility. Rudeness shocks Japanese as nothing else does (that is, rudeness out of their pattern). The compassion for the war prisoners detained in Siberia was felt, in the web society, as a family compassion. The tragedy of separated families is deeper in Japan than in most nations. When the well-organized local Communists dragooned the repatriates into political rallies, rudely ignoring their families and the officials from the national family who had come to welcome them, it made a lasting bad impression.

The military discipline of the Communist rallies, with massed red flags waving and Communist slogans shouted in unison, brought back the echoes of 1937 and 1941, as forcibly as the repatriates' marching songs. In 1949 the memories of those days were fresh enough to make the new flag-waving distasteful and suspicious. It made a great many Japanese realize that the Communists were something more than a legitimate political party, or labor agitators, or a more active type of democrat.

As the repatriates went home to their families, the effect of their tight Communist indoctrination began to wear off. Lies that were called truth were seen to be lies. The definiteness of their goal dissolved—like their brothers and fathers, they had to look for a new one, but they could look for it themselves. Only a hard core of the repatriates—less than 10%—remained Communists or strong Communist sympathizers. They were popularly called "tomatoes" ("red outside and in"). But the government officials assigned to deal with the repatriates found that the great majority of them were "radishes" ("red outside, but white inside"), whose Communist outer layer wore off through exposure to a freer society.

None of the five gentlemen of Japan had any intimate contact with the repatriates. Only Kisei, through his union work, ran into a few (who universally denounced the idea of the Soviet "workers' paradise"). So the story of the repatriates must be told completely outside of the experience of Shimizu, Sanada or Hirohito. It is worth telling, if for no other reason than to acknowledge that the web society of Japan and its products are no more immune from Communism than the societies of China, Europe, or the United States. Kunisuke Yamada was not a Central European intellectual like Klaus Fuchs, a disgruntled American like Paul Robeson, or an opportunistic Menshevik Russian like Andrei Vyshinsky. But for a year or so, he felt their community.

* * * * *

When Kunisuke Yamada was twenty-two, the Japanese crossed the Marco Polo Bridge at Peking to begin the 1937 invasion of China. Yamada went with them. A conscript with two years of training service, he served as a gunner in the Kwantung Army's artillery. For three years he marched through China behind the victorious Japanese infantry, shouting himself hoarse with banzais, waving flags and enjoying the stares of beaten people. Like most of his countrymen, he liked the going, when it was good.

Yamada left the Army in 1940 to go to Manchuria as a civilian. He worked in the city of Hunchun for five years as an army civilian employee—one of the few Japanese, despite their country's overcrowding, who was contented to stay overseas and live the life of a colonist. At the time of Pearl Harbor, he was running a small canteen near an army post. Like the soldiers around him, he was buoyed up in the enthusiasm of the first Japanese victories against the Allies. Business in Manchuria boomed, and hopes were high. But as the temper of the war changed, Manchuria seemed more like an icy backwater than a base channeling new munitions and material to the victorious Japanese troops. By 1944, the heavily censored war news from the Pacific was enough to convince any old soldier that Japan was no longer winning battles. If further proof was needed, there was the steady departure of the best troops of the Kwantung Army from their Manchurian barracks, hastily reformed into brigades and special expeditionary forces, to fight against the advancing Americans.

In July, 1945, Yamada was called up. He had only one bad week before it was all over. That was during the few days of fighting after the Russians made their late and painless entry into the Pacific war. Massed tanks and artillery coming down from the north gave the Japanese a slight taste of what the Germans had experienced in their long retreat from Moscow. On August 15, Yamada was a Russian prisoner.

Yamada's first experience of Russian captivity was surprising in its bitterness even to a product of another, if less vicious, absolutist system. The Russians speedily killed the rumors that the prisoners would be repatriated immediately to Japan. Yamada and his fellow artillerists were packed into boxcars and carried deep into Siberia. For two weeks they were penned inside the cars, without once being let out. They arrived, "more like animals than men," as he remembers at Camp 38, a clearing with log huts well beyond the Amur River.

For a year and a half at Camp 38 and, later, at Camp 115, the prisoners in Yamada's contingent lived as laborers, working on lumber projects at a bare subsistence level. The prisoners were left under the command of their own officers. There was scarcely any contact with the Russians —although Russian guards occasionally beat the Japanese officers if they found anyone slacking on the job. The officers, in their old army tradition, passed the beatings along to their men. Sick cases were sent to "reconditioning" camps, where they were fattened up, then returned to the work details. "The Russians had a great eye for excess fat," Yamada recalls, "they could tell at an instant how necessary the muscle is on you. Their muscle-testing techniques were very advanced."

One day early in 1947 Yamada noticed a newspaper lying in one of the barracks at his camp. It was the first piece of reading material he had seen in a year and a half. Titled *"Nippon Shimbun"* (*The Japan News*), it looked like a tabloid version of the papers he had known before the war. There was very little current news to read in it. In general, the contents were strange and new to Yamada—stories about the Soviet five-year plan, long references to a man named Marx and liberal quotations from people named Stalin, Lenin and Molotov. There was much talk in the paper about "democracy"—"a word which before the war I had hardly ever heard."

The copies of *Nippon Shimbun* multiplied. Similar publications, mostly books and fresh-printed periodicals, began to appear. By the middle of 1947, a few newcomers, prisoners from other camps, had arrived to explain some of the unfamiliar words. They ostentatiously called one another *"doshi*—comrades" and insisted on being known as "progressives." They sang odd new songs called "struggle songs" during the rest periods. They began to make speeches. They distributed more pamphlets explaining a new "democratic movement."

It was about this time that the food rations in the camp began to improve. For the first time since their arrival, the men in Camp 115 could eat some nourishing meals.

Most of the "comrades," Yamada later found out, had come from a large Soviet indoctrination camp at Nahodka. Others were from prison camps where the "democratic movement" had already been started. Whether they had been in training since early 1946 with this end in view,[*] or whether the Russians, after virtually ignoring the prisoners, suddenly awoke to the large-scale possibilities of their use in post-war Japan is a moot question. Yamada and the other repatriates never found out the answer.

In 1947 the men in Camp 115 were still under the commands of their own officers, who grew steadily more

---

[*] The *Nippon Shimbun,* at any rate, began publication in September, 1945.

oppressive as their confinement continued. Resentment against the officers was the big grievance inside the camp. The recently arrived comrades were well aware of this. With the instinct of Communism for finding and exploiting the big grievance, to make way for the big lie, they began to discipline this resentment against the officers' rule. In arguments and discussions (which they generated) they quoted Russian pamphlets talking of the class struggle and the abolition of class distinctions. "Throw out the officers" became a camp slogan. Within a few months it was acted upon. Led by the comrades, the prisoners staged a rally and, in a "spontaneous demonstration" demanded that the officers be withdrawn from the camp. The Russians obligingly took the officers away, leaving the grateful rank and file free to elect the "comrades" to run the camp in their place. Oddly enough, spontaneous demonstrations of the same sort, Yamada later found out, occurred at the same time in prison camps throughout Siberia.

Yamada, like others elsewhere in the world, had no notion of Communist dialectic or methods, but he was grateful to the Communists for satisfying his grievance. He said later, "The theory of this new 'democracy' was over my head, but even the simple fellows like me could understand the value of kicking out the bad officers."

On the nominations of the comrades, certain of the more intelligent participants in the "anti-officer" discussions were sent away for a two-months schooling period in "perspective." When these local representatives returned from their tutoring in Communism, the "democratic movement" in Camp 115 began in earnest. The life of the camp was divided into three sections—work, housekeeping and "instruction of the ignorant." Leaders for the sections were scrupulously chosen by secret ballot. On the analogy of Russian democratic procedure, however, each ballot had only one set of candidates. It was invariably made clear to the electorate by balloting time who was, in every case, the "best man." Discussion groups on world affairs and Japanese politics sprang up as spontaneously as the elections. Unobtrusively, the camp authorities made them compulsory.

By 1948 the temporary Communization of the camp had been completed. Indoctrination sessions stretched through the day from seven-thirty A.M. to "lights out" at ten—always featuring either Marxist theory or a Marxist-eye view of world events. Through articles copied from *Akahata*, the Japanese Communist newspaper, Yamada read that the Communist party alone could save Japan from lapsing into the reaction pattern of former days. Further afield, he learned why the "lazy West Berliners" had to be constantly supplied with food by the Americans, while the "progressive East Berliners," under Russian leadership, were on the road to prosperity. This was Camp 115's explanation of the Berlin blockade.

The discussions turned on a suave mixture of Communist propaganda and local camp problems, the former generally—or at least at the first—riding on the latter's coattails. The one obvious local grievance which the prisoners had left—the very fact that they had been detained so long—was attributed to an American refusal to grant enough shipping for the move. The Americans, it was hinted, were characteristically doing a bad job in this respect, as well as in their occupation of Japan.

Yamada, who is shrewd but not well educated, grew to understand some of the theories behind Communism—in the most favorable light. His first apathy to the discussions gave way to interest. As he rationalized, "If one has to attend group discussions long enough, he can't help but take an interest in them."

The indoctrination which the comrades and their pamphlets riveted on the men in Camp 115 was almost all positive. There was little actual denunciation of the United States or other "capitalist" countries, aside from some harsh things said about the "reactionary" government of Japan. Rather, the vision of the workers' paradise was painted in bright and winning shades, as a collectivist utopia where every worker, in return for his industry, was taken care of by the state. Slowly and smoothly, the prisoners found themselves being transferred to their new web of contracts, again one with a strong ideology to steady it. Once the rules were made, they could be counted on, by every instinct of their past training, to obey.

Some of the rules were unwritten. If a discussion, for example, floundered or got out of hand, it was customary to ask the camp's Propaganda and Education Department, or one of the "comrades," how to end it. Most of the rules, however, were minutely written out and minutely obeyed. "Criticism meetings" were held periodically, at which all those present examined the feelings of those who had flouted the system in any way. "We learned," Yamada said, "to microscopically examine the feelings of anyone who had gone against the rules."

The new "rules" tied a taut string to every detail of the prisoners' lives. A man could break the rules by not attending a propaganda lecture, or by forgetting to close a screen door. Minor rule-breakers, as well as the few who opposed the Communists for ideological reasons, were lumped together as "reactionaries." The only way for a reactionary to escape punishment was by prompt confession and a classically complete recital of his guilt. If he refused to confess, the next step was arraignment before the local "people's court" of the camp, which in the logical progression of people's court administration, immediately declared him guilty. Punishment was called the *kampa*. Prisoners stood in a circle, arms locked, with the culprit in the middle. Shouting slogans while they did it, they kicked him from side to side. ("After 1948," Yamada said after his return to Japan, "as our organization became better understood and more thorough, we had less and less necessity to beat anyone. . . . To force anyone is undemocratic anyhow.")

The peoples' courts, the criticism sessions and the system of unostentatious leadership by trained cadres, expert at organizing spontaneous demonstrations—they have all become familiar as part of the Soviet Communist pattern. The "reactionaries" of Camp 115 found themselves kicked and beaten by the same rules and the same techniques that had beaten and would beat other helpless men in China, Bulgaria, or elsewhere in Siberia. The genius of the Russian system, as it worked on the Japanese repatriates, lay in the skillful unobtrusiveness with which the Russians managed it. They worked on the analogy of the fabled majority stockholder in a large capitalist holding company, who can control hundreds of subsidiaries without divulging his identity at a single board meeting.

The Russians first trained a small group of Japanese Communists, certainly with the assistance of old-time Japanese party members, then operated solely through their agency. Most of the prisoners, as, at first, did Yamada, believed that their spontaneous demonstrations were really spontaneous. The few whom the Russians trained, by their aggressiveness and their unity of purpose, were able easily to get an almost moral ascendancy over the others. When they succeeded in eliminating the officers—the major popular grievance, their prestige got a solid foundation of achievement. After that the passage became very smooth. The cadres guided the others through the intricacies of the Communist scriptures and the chants of Lenin's litanies. The tools that helped them—better food, suddenly released reading material, carefully timed rest periods, all appeared so naturally that the coincidence of their arrival and the indoctrination effort went unnoticed.

The Russians kept their attitude kindly, but aloof, after their propaganda began to work. No Russians addressed the meetings, or participated openly in any of the Communist activities. The impression which they gave was one of warm friendliness and, if anything, surprised pleasure that their late enemies were discovering for themselves the virtue of "democracy." Their aloofness and apparent impartiality fostered the vision of the workers' paradise. "Yamada and his friends thought of the Soviet Union as a noble classless society, where "a member of the

Supreme Soviet is no better and receives no better treatment than a common worker." There was no red tape. "In the Soviet Union," they agreed, "one single document is usually sufficient for accomplishing anything." They were unconscious of the irony.

In February, 1949, Yamada and his group were moved to Voroshilov, where they all received a new issue of clothing—heavy blue denim trousers, quilted jackets, and thick Russian boots of imitation leather. The Russians explained, as they had before, that the delay in repatriation was due to the refusal of the Americans to supply the ships.* Four months later, they were sent to Nahodka, where they boarded the *Takasago Maru* for the trip back to Japan.

When Yamada's train rolled up beside the Victorian station at Kyoto, he found the platform already a sea of Communist banners. Numbed from the shock of his return, he marched obediently into the Communist rally on the station plaza, led by the same Communist cadre members who had run his life in the Siberian camps. He sang the same "struggle" songs they had sung in the prison camps and signed a membership application in the Japanese Communist party as part of a mass demonstration. In the melee of flags and slogans, he was barely able to see his father Toyoji, his mother and his wife, who ran desperately through the crowd holding high a cardboard placard with "Yamada" written on it in large characters.

His first weeks in Japan were a shock. He found out that the Communists, far from running the new Japan, were an unpopular and decreasing minority. He found out that the Russians, not the Americans, had delayed his return for four years. He discovered that Japan was orderly and, by comparison with what the Russians had pictured, very

---

* In Japan, of course, this excuse could hardly be made. When the Russians blamed delays in repatriation on bad weather conditions, the Americans offered to send ice-breakers. The offer was refused. Japanese Communists quickly explained that the ice-breakers were in bad condition.

prosperous. In talking with his father and their neighbors he filled in a more exact account of what had been happening in Japan and in the world since 1945. He discovered a great many facts which had either not appeared or emerged in sadly twisted form in the columns of the *Japan News*. He never went around to Communist party headquarters to make his membership application official. Like most of his fellow repatriates, Yamada proved himself to be a "radish."

He found a job not long after his return, in the Hamamura Dry Goods Store, a small shop near the Nijo station in Kyoto. His ambition is to become a small businessman himself—a minor capitalist—and he saves as much as he can towards the day when he might buy into a business or get one of his own. His salary, however, is small: 10,000 yen a month, although he is the chief clerk and buyer for the store. His father Toyoji smiles when his son complains about his struggle to get ahead. He nods and smiles at Kunisuke's two-year-old girl. *"Kodomo dake moketa sakai* —if you've profited only by a child, you have made a success," he says, quoting an old Japanese proverb.

In the fall of 1951, Communist students and their friends swarmed around the Emperor's car, during an official visit to Kyoto, demanding that Hirohito speak out against rearmament. Yamada was as shocked at their rudeness and disrespect as his parents had been two and a half years before, at the rude singing of his group of repatriates. "If I were a Communist," he told friends, "I'd be ashamed of what happened. An incident like that was entirely uncalled for." He has seen through the obvious Communist lies and the clumsy attempts to provoke disorder in Japan.

This is not to say that the work of the Russian propaganda experts who supervised Yamada's indoctrination has been altogether wiped out. The seeds sown in Siberia were hardy and sank deep. They sometimes blossom unexpectedly. Some of the results are harmless and superficial. Yamada, for example—like a great many other Japanese, and despite his own Siberian experience—greatly enjoyed the Russian film "Tales of Siberia," a technicolor musical which was shown throughout Japan in 1950. He likes Russian films because they are "simple and realistic," not dwelling in the realm of fantasy—"like living in a castle or flying to the moon." He can still remember individual Russians whom he thought very highly of.

Other scraps of his old indoctrination came back to him when he worries about his individual problems of struggle and success in a capitalist society. Sometimes he thinks of his society as "a truly vicious capitalistic world." Its lack of security has impressed him deeply. He rightfully points out that there is no social security in Japan, no plan for succoring the aged when they have finished their life's work. In an earlier day this was done by sons and fathers, bound to support their families by the rigid laws of the web society. In the world of 1953, with the web society weakened and new ideas of individuality and democracy coming in, the state has not yet taken up the slack by replacing family welfare programs with at least the limited government welfare schemes found in the United States. "There is no *shinyo*" Yamada laments, "no trust." The world of *shinyo* may still exist in farmer Sanada's village, but in cities like Kyoto it is in some ways passing too quickly to be immediately replaced.

Yamada has described his lot (in his more pessimistic moments) in this way: "We are living in Japan like a bunch of bamboo shoots. We all push our heads above the earth. We grow, but as we grow, we are enclosed and in time cut off. There is no hope for the future. The only hope I have is to see that my children get the chance to rise above my world." He broods about the impossibility of getting money for a small business of his own. There is no credit available to him. To save the half-million yen he needs would take him at least ten years. At times like this the vision of the workers paradise comes back to him from the pages of *Nippon Shimbun* and the cheerful sound tracks of the old Soviet propaganda movies. He repeats phrases which he learned and still almost believes—"In

Soviet Russia the State looks after one's welfare. This inequality would never happen there, because everyone is treated equally. If a man passes the work norm, he is rewarded. He doesn't have to worry about illness or old age."

But he does not dwell overmuch on these thoughts. He is a mercurial character, perfectly willing to admit that his grousing is in large part just that. He has never ceased being glad to be home. He likes his work. He likes Japan. He has no nostalgia for the people's courts of the repatriates or the *kampa*, the vision of locked arms and kicking feet visiting the punishment of the "reactionary" on someone who could not conform, inside a low hut deep in the Siberian forest.

* * * * *

The mass of Yamada's countrymen fortunately have not had to live down the effects of a two-and-a-half-year Communist indoctrination. Judging both their native Communists and the Russians by their acts—and the interconnection between their acts, their picture of contemporary Communism has grown into a monochrome, distasteful to look at. There is real resentment against the enemy that crept into the laboratory of democracy. It is in some cases based on fear or annoyance, in others built from the wreckage of hopes in the goodness of Communism itself, which rose too high.

Yamazaki, who wrote his college thesis on Marx, has been disillusioned—not about Marx, but about his current disciples. He feels that the Russian Revolution was the greatest event of the twentieth century, which "struck at the core of imperialism, absolutism and capitalism." But he is angry at how Leninism and Stalinism have perverted the Revolution's spirit: "The Machiavellian Communism of the U.S.S.R. is a far cry from the Communism laid down by Karl Marx." He has seen many more Soviet movies than "Tales of Siberia" and has been thoroughly repelled. He caught the suffocating insistence that the Russian Communists are "the absolute, the supreme people, who are trying to cram their superiority propaganda down everyone's throat." He has been particularly disgusted by the technique of twisting the facts of the lives and times of great Russians—Pushkin, Glinka and Tolstoy, for callous political purposes.

Initially, at least, he believes that the Japanese Communist party did some good. Communists fought for land reform, female rights and the organization of the new labor unions. "They used wrong methods," he concedes, "but they did fight the return of feudalism. I think we owe it to the Communists for keeping us reminded not to fall back into our prewar society." To some extent he is right. The occupation's first task was destructive—to destroy the old web of Japanese society as thoroughly as it destroyed the guns and tanks which that society had produced. In a work of destruction, Communists are generally useful. The Communists helped greatly, just as they helped greatly in the European resistance to the Nazis throughout World War II—and for the same purpose.

Yamazaki has seen the Japanese Communist party for what it is. "Every move made by the Japanese Communists," he concedes, "has smacked of Russian influence. Most of them have regarded Moscow as their motherland: they wanted to instigate a revolution, one that was inspired in the Kremlin." Yamazaki has known a good number of Communists. For a period ending in 1946 the journalists' union at *Asahi* was dominated by them. In the university and after graduating from it, he has had long talks with others whose ideas of Marx were warped and restricted as his was not. He has been pained by this. He found that the Communist attitude towards the occupation forces, as well as their domestic propaganda, was "not in keeping" with the spirit of the Potsdam Declaration, the noble-sounding charter that struck an oddly responsive note among Japanese liberals. In summation, he feels, "the Japanese Communist party failed and I am dissatisfied and disappointed."

* * * * *

Sakaji Sanada had no hopes for Marxism to live down. From first to last he has found Communism a suspicious foreign idea, rude, noisy and dangerous; and in this sentiment he is joined by the majority of the Japanese. He believes that the Communists are far worse than the *"oyabun-kobun"* system, the old-fashioned Japanese bossism that Yamazaki helped extirpate at Honjo. "At least," he argues, "the *oya-ko* were Japanese. They had a code which called for mutual duties and responsibility. The Communists simply destroy."

There are very few Communists in Shimoyoshida and these, Sanada is proud to say, have all come from the outside. As he and his neighbors agree, "No one who was born and raised on Shimoyoshida soil would ever think of becoming a Communist." For all his confidence, Sanada well realized the great effort which the Communists made to win support in farming communities. He never worried about this, since he feels that the local people sense the incongruity of Communist promises as well as he. "They take everything," he sputtered, "and claim they are going to distribute it equally. Do they ever consider the time and labor, the sweat and money a man puts into what belongs to him? If what a man owns did not belong to him in the first place, if he didn't earn it, then the Communists could be justified in their deeds and beliefs."

* * * * *

After the repatriates' riots in 1949, the course of Japanese Communism ran ever more violently. It is doubtful whether the two Communist bosses, Sanzo Nozaka and his friend Kyuichi Tokuda, the old-time revolutionary jailbird, were overly happy at the change developing in the tactics of their party members. Although the young intellectuals of the party argued for frankly revolutionary attacks against the government and the occupation, Nozaka had misgivings about abandoning the pretense of legality, which the party had kept up during the four years past. The Cominform, however, decided that further operations as a legal political party would be unhealthy for the Japanese Communists. Titoism was in the air and Nozaka and Tokuda, who had run their party in an original fashion, were slightly suspect. The Korean invasion was being planned, a military operation which needed active Communist support from all the Asiatic countries. Furthermore, it seemed probable that legal Communist tactics had gone as far as they could efficiently go. The occupation, through its reforms, had taken the sting out of the same Communist social criticisms which had attracted so much non-Communist support in China.

In January, 1950, the Cominform openly censured Comrade Nozaka for his unrevolutionary tactics and his nationalism—"the naturalization of Marxism—Leninism under Japanese conditions." Nozaka rolled with the punch and kept his leadership in the party, but the handwriting on the wall was heeded. All play at legality and the quest for a Communist-run Popular Front was at last abandoned. What the party lost in breadth, it tried to compensate for in depth. The rallies grew smaller, they grew noisier and more destructive. As the number of supporters dwindled, those who were left became more aggressive. On May 30, 1950, Communist students demonstrated near the Imperial Plaza in Tokyo against the use of the Plaza by Americans for Memorial Day services. Some of the crowd attacked and beat several American soldiers who were watching. It was the first act of violence committed against an American soldier since the occupation began.

The Memorial Day incident, and the pattern of violence of which it was a part, forced the occupation to take action. The party was not outlawed, but, shrewdly, General

MacArthur placed the Communist leaders on the same purge list as the old militarists, barring them from political activity. If this forced the Communists underground, it only completed a process which they had themselves already begun. The party cadres split up and went into hiding, keeping up their communications and planning a program of open revolutionary action, should the situation arise where this might have a chance of success.

By the time the Korean war had begun, the Communists were organized underground, on a military basis, throughout Japan. They rarely appeared in strength above the surface, but then it was to strike with all their force at a specified objective. On May Day, 1952, they demonstrated how well their discipline worked. A militant core of a few thousand Communists, by heckling and planned interruptions, first turned a peaceful labor demonstration at Hibiya Park, in Tokyo, into a confused shambles. This done, the Communists set out for the Imperial Plaza, their favorite target for demonstrations, sweeping along with them many confused and leaderless non-Communist May Day celebrants, who had not planned on being part of a Red *putsch* against the Tokyo police. The Communists—and some of their dupes—battled the police for hours in one of the bloodiest riots Tokyo has ever seen. Before they were subdued, they had burned several American cars and roughly handled the few Americans whom they encountered. In the actual fighting, 1,434 people were injured. (That only one demonstrator was killed—accidentally—is a tribute to the control and forbearance of the Tokyo police.)

In this and the subsequent demonstrations they organized, the Communists had a double aim. They wished as far as possible to disrupt the normal life of the country, while giving an exaggerated impression of their strength. Their secondary purpose was to provoke the Japanese government or, better still, the American Army in Japan to rash acts of retaliation. The Communists want martyrs— Horst Wessels are almost indispensable to the success of any immoral revolutionary movement. These objectives are of course dangerous. The Japanese Communists have demonstrated their competence at attempting them. But the harm this group of under 100,000 can do as outlaws is far less than the damage they might have done to the future of Japan, at a critical moment in its history, as partners or leaders of a popular front political movement, playing on the natural Japanese reluctance to re-arm and the deep desire for peace.

In their later agitation, the Communists drew their most obvious supporters from among Japan's university students. The Japanese student continues to put into political action much of the energy American students expend on football and fraternity initiations. The white shirts and red flags of every riot and demonstration were shaded by the blue caps and uniforms of students from the big Japanese universities, some of them convinced Communists, but a greater number vague sympathizers or restless souls who enjoyed a riot in the Imperial Plaza *per se*.

Shimizu's son Toyotaro graduated from Keio University, Fukuzawa Yukichi's old school, in 1950, at a time when this student political ferment was bubbling hottest. He deprecates the seriousness of student Communism, however. As a former engineering student, Toyotaro is anxious to stress that almost all of the trouble was caused by students in the faculties of Law and Literature (traditionally the grazing grounds of young university radicals). Some of his friends went along on the strikes or attended the mass meetings, but most of them—from his description—impelled by the same curious fun-loving spirit that provokes Yale boys to derail New Haven streetcars after football rallies.

The reaction of the Japanese public has gone far towards separating the sympathizers from the real Communists. Traditionally, Japanese business firms offer students job opportunities in the December before they graduate. The March 1951 graduates ran into a grim set of personnel managers who had been reading about student political activity in the newspapers. Many for a time were unable to get jobs—certainly the Communists among them could not. Heeding this cool wind, they trimmed their sails. Since then, the incidence of university Communism has decreased, although the student mind still explores the possibilities of bringing Marx to life outside the textbooks. The really convinced student Communists have gone underground with their older friends.

* * * * *

The clamor of the student rallies was not permanent. The disruptive acts of sabotage which the Communists have instigated since their political eclipse, by the end of 1952, had achieved a negligible result. But Communism, indirectly, has laid its hand heavily on Japan. In the confusion of the obvious Communist attacks, not many Japanese have realized how Communism crimped the brave laboratory experiment in democracy, which was begun in 1945. There was a direct connection between the attacks of Communism, foreign as well as Japanese, and the cautious retreat of the American occupation from its original drastic reforms; bold and sweeping in their nature at first, the armed spearheads of democracy turned back on themselves somewhat, to avoid the danger of being outflanked.

* * * * *

Hideya Kisei had a good chance to observe this sequence, in his work with the labor union at Yahata. After the short strike in 1948, Kisei and others like him in the union openly broke with the Communist element there. By the middle of 1949 a socialist faction, the Democratic League, in Yahata and elsewhere in Japan, was cutting into the strength of the Communist dominated unions. Workers were as shocked as farmers or city merchants at the Communists' graduation to violence. The popular frontism of 1947 and 1948 was almost over.

In October, 1950, with the example of Korea at its doorstep, the Japanese government ordered a purge of Communists from industry as well as public life. Since Communists in many cases were also officials of important unions, this amounted to an attack on segments of organized labor. The temptation was strong among company managers to get rid of the most troublesome (to them) and the most honest and effective (to the workers) trade unionists, on the pretext that they were Communists. The temptation in many cases was not resisted. Even if all concerned had been Communists, the fact was that fellow-travelers and assorted Red sympathizers were so mingled with honest trade unionists that the downfall of one faction implied the embarrassment, if not the crippling, of the other. The Communists at Yahata demanded a protest strike against the purge. Kisei voted against them. Worried by the murk of suspicion that surrounded the situation in the union, he decided "that conditions were still not ripe for the labor movement's advance." He resigned from his office in the union.

Kisei is defensive about his resignation. He has argued that the stepped-up shifts of the Korean war era left him little time for union activity. He again complained about the effect which working near the constant heat of the furnaces had on his memory. But beneath his obvious, and partly valid excuses, there was disillusionment and near despair. The Democratic Leaguers had not been active enough or quickly enough on the scene to take the leadership from the Communists and continue it vigorously. The clear-cut call for the workers to better their lot had been overlaid and confused by the tremulo of charges and counter-charges, Communist plots and anti-Communist witch hunts. The Communists may not have sabotaged machines in the factories, but their ultimate damage was greater: they had sabotaged the free Japanese trade union movement.

The prospect of being fired as a Communist did not force Kisei out of the union. His anti-Communist record was too obvious for him to be considered as a purge case—this company officials later told him. But he felt the discouragement and uncertainty of the rank and file over the purge operation. His own case, Kisei feels, "would appear to be good evidence that only Reds were fired." But he was not utterly convinced. "The Red propaganda that anyone active in labor unionism could be fired on the pretext of being a Communist did more to discourage the rank and file than anything else. There is no denying the psychological effect on them. Many of the men were reluctant to assume any union position for fear of being thought a Red. On the other hand, there were some men fired in the purge whom I still find hard to believe were Communists. The company assured me that they were secret party members, but I had known them for a long time—and it was hard to swallow."

The union at Yahata has not recovered. Kisei occasionally counsels the present leaders, who are Democratic Leaguers, but there is no pressure on them from the rank and file to move more actively. A wiser management and a wiser government than Japan now possesses might have realized that a strong democratic labor movement in any country is the best possible insurance against Communism. Instead the government has shown a tendency to weaken the purged unions with the same tools and on the same pretexts as those that were justly used against the Communists.

In the process of abdicating control of Japan the occupation, for its part, did little to protect the new unions, to strengthen them against an imbalanced situation where management is closely allied to a conservative government. The fingers of SCAP's labor organizers had been burned once by the Communists. By the time the Communists were ejected, the climate of their experiment had changed. Korea was being fought, and the closed air inside the laboratory fortress was not the atmosphere to permit the tensions of new labor disputes. This is not to say that the Japanese union movement, in which Kisei and others held such high hopes, has been beaten down or suppressed. It has at least been purged of Communism—an achievement that other national labor movements can envy. But the purge has left it weak.

* * * * *

In its preliminary encounter with postwar Stalinist Communism, Japan fared differently from the rest of Asia. Where Communism has succeeded, it has come to power in a classic, if not a primitive manner. First, an intelligent revolutionary elite has organized itself, then set out on a planned conquest of its society. It has capitalized on certain monolithic grievances of that society—poverty, and official corruption in China, French colonialism in Viet Nam—to secure mass support. It has gained control, or partial control, by ousting another small autocratic group which controlled the society from above. It has installed its own members in positions of power, then set out to canalize the wave of popular revolution which it exploited. It has often kept popular support by creating at least the appearance of minimal reforms—which are welcomed as an improvement on old times. The sense of a struggle for new reforms is injected into the populace, then Communism is ready for its old power game with its subjects, guiding the mass with the classic small carrot and the classic big stick.

It was not possible for Communism to come to power by these methods in Japan. Barring a truly apocalyptic disaster, it will not be. The Japanese are a literate people; the basic literacy rate of 97% is higher than that of some American states. They are also a cohesive and inbound people; one end of the islands knows what the other end is doing, and so with the classes of society. However imperfect it is, they do have a tradition of parliamentary government shared by no other Asian country. They freed themselves from Western colonialism 75 years ago. The slogan "Drive out the white man" is not unknown in

Japan—the Japanese, after all, invented the phrase "Asia for the Asiatics"—but there is not the explosive connotation that the phrase has in India, Viet Nam or Indonesia. The Japanese standard of living is the highest in Asia. A Chinese farmer's lot might be bettered by life on a Soviet collective farm, but not the Japanese farmer's—he has an electric light in his house and, in many cases, a radio. More recently, he has watched an American occupation remove many of the actual grievances he had remaining.

In a word, the Japanese as a people are politically sophisticated in a way that other Asians and many Europeans are not. The methods which successfully Communized colonial countries or backward sovereign states could not and did not work in Japan. The original leadership of the Japanese Communist party knew this. That is why they tried to gain power by parliamentary methods with exactly the same operating procedure as the Communist parties of Italy and France. Happily they had their plan aborted by higher Communist authority. Temporarily, Communism in Japan has been defeated—more signally than anywhere else in Asia—and more crushingly than in any large nation on the European continent.

But Communism strikes a nation with a double-edge sword. On the one hand, as Kunisuke Yamada and his friends can witness, it showed itself capable of retying the threads of the Japanese web society in a tighter and simplified knot, bound by a totalitarianism harsher than the Japanese had ever known before. With this obvious, direct menace exposed and checked, the danger remains that militant reaction to Communism will itself draw the web tight in something resembling the old-fashioned pattern. Hot and cold, some philosophers feel, are logical identities, and the sins of Communism—or the threat of those sins—can produce equal excesses of reaction. Hideya Kisei and his friends stand in the middle, the loosening of their old society a constant temptation to extremists at either end to make it tighter again.

10

RICE, MOUNTAINS AND MACHINES

Hana yori dango—
Dumplings are better than flowers

Japanese proverb

The train of the Kyuko Kabushiki Kaisha in which Tadao Yamazaki rides to work each morning is almost a reproduction of the economic society in which he and his countrymen live. It is badly overcrowded, but more passengers get on at every stop. The equipment, although serviceable, needs repair; but since Yamazaki and his fellow-passengers have no other way of getting to their destination, there is no possibility of taking the train out of service for an overhaul. Like all electric trains, the cars get their power supplied from distant generators. If the current from this far-off source of power is cut, they cannot move.

Japan met the industrial world of the eighteen eighties head on, with no historical brakes or shock absorbers to cushion the impact. Japan in the nineteen fifties is nearer than any world power—possibly excepting Great Britain—to a head-on reckoning with the complexities of modern industrial society. There is no camouflage about this reckoning in Japan. Yamazaki, Kisei and Shimizu all know that whether there is enough wool and cotton on their backs and enough rice and vegetables on their tables depends intimately on whether there is coking coal in China, iron in Malaya, or cotton in Pakistan—and whether the people in those places are willing to sell these materials, in return for what Japan can offer them.

The population of Japan is increasing at the rate of over a million people a year. In 1920 the Japanese census showed a figure of 55,391,000. Ten years later it was 63,872,000. In 1946 there were 76,155,000 Japanese—the losses in war had been more than balanced by the repatriation of colonists from China and the Pacific. In 1952 the population was, roughly, 85 million. Before 1970, barring catastrophe, this number will grow to 100 million. The increase is geometrical and inexorable. In the short run, even the widest application of birth control methods can not do more than arrest this progression slightly.

The islands on which these people live cover 142,270 miles of land, a slightly larger area than the British Isles and a slightly smaller area than the state of California. They are mountainous. The evocative word "mountainous," translated into scientific language, here means that 65% of the land in Japan has a slope of 15% or more. Where mountains, or the nearness of mountains do not make farming impossible, bad soil, erosion or poor drainage often does. Only about 17% of Japan's soil is fit for any type of cultivation.

The Japanese are good farmers. A moist climate, but not excessively rainy, gives them the luxury of considerable double-cropping. Besides rice and other staple grains, they can grow a sweeping variety of foods. The broad wheat lands of Hokkaido are not unlike the fields of Minnesota and the southern soil of Kyushu favors tropical citruses. The Japanese are good fishermen. In normal times they account for one-fourth of the world's fish products— from offshore octopus and herring to whale meat from the Antarctic. But by any reckoning, the farmers and fishermen of modern Japan have not and will not be able to produce more than 80% of their food supply. This figure, in itself, is optimistic and based on a bare level of subsistence.

Japan is thickly forested. But until a better reforestation program can show its results, Japanese forests can meet little more than 60% of the nation's demand for wood—not only for the wood to build houses, but wood for paper, fuel and the thousand other uses for timber which the Japanese, chronically poor in metal resources, have improvised. Without stripping the forests bare—completing the damage caused by the war economy of World War II—wood must be imported. There are some fiber materials in Japan, but wool and cotton must also be imported, if the Japanese are to have anything like an adequate clothing supply.

In industrial raw materials, Japan's deficiencies are more profound. The short but turbulent rivers are a fortunate source of electric power—Japan has one of the largest hydroelectric power systems in the world. There are narrow veins of coal under the ground of Kyushu and Hokkaido, almost all that the Japanese need for low-grade uses. There is much sulphur, and copper in some quantity. Here the list of assets almost comes to an end. Although Japan has 22 of the 33 industrial minerals in one form or another, the supply of most is very scanty. At the lowest production levels, the Japanese must bring in over 2,000,000 tons of ore each year, 80% of the iron needed for their steel mills. Their coal is not suitable for coking. Lead, tin, copper and other lesser metals must be imported. They desperately need potash and phosphate for their chemical fertilizers. They have no land sources of salt. There is scarcely any oil.

These handicaps have far from crushed the Japanese. Like other island nations, they have worked hard and traded hard. They have fought for their own bread and taken the bread from the mouths of others. They have known days of great prosperity. During World War I Japan was a booming creditor nation, with most of the European Allies in its debt. Even today the Japanese, as a people, enjoy the highest living standard in Asia.

But poverty of resources is the unvoiced threat over the life of modern Japan. Shimizu, Sanada, Yamazaki, Kisei and Hirohito—they all in different ways live the economy of scarcity, in a country where there is never quite enough. Scarcity has made them suspicious of the outside and envious. It has helped drive them to war. It appears in the austerity of their art and the simplicity of their houses. It has its echo in their solidarity and their urge for cooperation, their fascination for the collective.

There is very little waste in Japan. Small children pick up carpenters' shavings and take them home to their parents. Unburned bits of coal are snatched from factory cinderpiles. Tree stumps are scarcely visible, because Japanese woodsmen painstakingly cut so close to the roots. Newspapers are seldom thrown away. Paper and string from packages are saved—not by especially frugal people, but by all the people—because all Japanese are frugal. Frugality is in fact a bond among them. It has shaped their tastes to an inclusive degree. The rich man may have beautiful wood in his house or ancient and expensive scrolls in his alcove, but there is very little difference between the kind of house he has and the houses of the middling well-off or of the very poor.

In 1936, in an issue of *Fortune* magazine devoted to Japan, Archibald MacLeish gave an awed American description of this scarcity:

"There are the roads always narrow and mostly at the wood's edge or the river's. There is the straw piled on brushwood bridges off the loam and the trees only growing at the god's house, never in the fields. There are the whole plains empty of roofs, squared into flats of water, no inch for walking but the dike backs, not so much as a green weed at the foot of the telegraph poles or a corner patch gone wild.

"There are the fields empty of crows after harvest: thin picking for black wings after cloth ones.

"There are the men under moonlight in the mountain villages breaking the winter snowdrifts on the paddies to save days of spring.

"There are the forest floors swept clean and the sweepings bundled in careful, valuable piles.

"There are the houses without dogs, the farms without grass-eating cattle. There are the millet fields at the sea's edge following the sweet water to the brackish beginning of the salt, the salt sand not the thickness of a stake beyond.

"There are the rivers diked and ditched and straightened to recover a napkin's breadth of land and the hill valleys terraced till the steepest slope turns flatwise to the sun.

"There are the mountains eroded to the limestone where the axes and the mattocks have grubbed roots.

". . . Japan is the country where the stones show human fingerprints: where the pressure of
has worn through to the iron rock. . . .'

* * * * *

By the standards of the American's description Sakaji Sanada has left his fingerprints on more stones than he would care to remember. Yamazaki or Kisei can easily feel deceived about their country's power and material stability, watching the new concrete office buildings spilling over Tokyo's business section, or wrapped in the smoke from the busy furnaces of Yahata, which now pour out nearly their capacity load of finished steel. But Sanada can never escape a reality as hard as those rocks in his fields: too many men on too little land.

In Japan Sanada is a prosperous farmer. Before the war he had twelve acres of field and paddy land; although land reform has cut his holdings to less than six, this is still far above the average size of a Japanese farm. He plants rice, wheat, barley, white potatoes and vegetables— beans, corn, pumpkin, squash and gourds. The rice he sells. Each October he averages a harvest of 120 bales which he currently sells at 3,720 yen per bale,* a better price than he has realized for a long time. The wheat, barley and vegetables he grows for the use of his own family and relatives. Some is used as feed for his one horse. Inside his house his looms are kept working from six to twelve hours a day—except during harvest and planting time. The two machines currently in use will make about 600 yards of silk material per month (which he sells in Tokyo at 600 yen a yard).

This division of Sanada's interests is the result of necessity, not of choice. The looms provide the margin between a bare subsistence level and a few small luxuries for the Sanada family, as they do for most of the population of Shimoyoshida. The crops they grow insure, generally, that there will be food** on the table and some clothing on their backs. But even this minimum of security is bought only with constant struggle. The upland fields are not rich. In other, more spacious countries, they would be used for pasturage. To bring forth any kind of a crop, Sanada must use large amounts of fertilizer—both chemicals and the night soil which gives Japanese fields their familiar odor. He is barely able to harvest one crop a year. The fields are used without rest. Sanada plants potatoes or vegetables between the rows of wheat.

Each day of his life Sanada can look up from his work to see the summit of Mt. Fuji serenely watching the hills around him. It is the symbol of Japan that is universally known and admired. Many Japanese climb Fuji almost in the manner of pilgrims going to a religious shrine. Foreigners are seldom content to leave Japan without at least looking at it from close by. But, although appreciative of

---

* One bale equals 60 kilograms.
** Only once have the crops failed. Shortly after World War I, a cold north wind swept down on Shimoyoshida in late August. The rice would not ripen. Sanada remembers that the rice kernels looked like tiny silver bells, just empty. The farmers raised funds to purchase rice from the outside, the only time in Sanada's memory that Shimoyoshida had to import its staple food.

the slight tourist business which Shimoyoshida, somewhat off the beaten track, gets from the Fuji visitors, the struggles of his daily life have given Sanada a practical grudge against the sacred mountain. "It is beautiful to watch," he concedes, "but we can't eat or live from it. Fuji stops the warm ocean breezes that would otherwise come in on us from the Pacific. We'd be a much happier, much wealthier farming community if we could enjoy the climate which they have on the southern side of Fuji. We'd be happier, in fact, if something blew Fuji away—perhaps an atom bomb."

Sanada's fields lie over a mile from his house. Instead of one broad patch of land they are a hodgepodge of diked squares, looking almost ornamental in the symmetry of their borders. They do not border one another; it is impossible for anyone who is not a resident of Shimoyoshida to tell which field belongs to Sanada and which to his neighbors. The fields of all the households in the *buraku* are tangled together in a way that would make neighborly cooperation a pressing need, if it were not already practiced. At the times of planting and harvesting, Sanada's entire family, down to his grandchildren, are out in the fields with the neighbor families working over the crops. It is the same at home, where daily work is broken down and distributed among members of the family with the regularity of a military operations plan. Except for the very young and the very old, everyone has his job, duly assigned and performed, which takes precedence over all else. The Japanese have found out that the only way to compensate for overpopulation is distributive work.

Sakaji Sanada inherited the economy of scarcity from his father and his grandfather, who in their time owned even smaller plots of land. His standard of living is better than theirs. If he were to go even further towards the roots of his family tree, he would not be envious of the bare scrabbling for existence of his peasant ancestors. Sanada, with his radio, his ballot box and the two daily newspapers he gets from Tokyo, could no more be called a "peasant" than a farmer in Iowa. Yet Sanada's generation lives face to face with a far harder set of realities than their ancestors of a century or two ago.

In the olden time Japan was a rich country. In 1697 the agriculturalist Miyazaki Yasusada could write with justice:

"Apart from China and Korea, it is said that nowhere can such a fortunate country be found. . . . All kinds of cereals, vegetables, plants and herbs, in fact all varieties of agricultural products for food, clothing, habitation and other human wants can be raised in our country, if proper knowledge and appropriate methods are applied and suitable seed is used. . . . With the exception of certain trees and plants, it may be said that everything could be supplied without relying on imports from abroad."

The population of Japan was then about 26 million. It remained about the same for over a century, until the resumption of foreign trade in the eighteen seventies. Poverty kept it from rising. If not by actual famine, the numbers of new Japanese were kept down by large-scale abortions and the killing of new-born children, in houses which could not support them. This poverty, however, was the result of unfair distribution of wealth, rather than a lack of it. In Tokugawa Japan, the farmers were exploited to fatten the stomachs and purses of a parasite class of *samurai* and officials. It was an adage that "the farmer should neither live nor die." But if land and the products of the land could have been distributed fairly, something approaching the good life could have been enjoyed by all Japanese.

Sanada cannot console himself with any similar plans. In his time the land, for practical purposes, has been distributed fairly. There is no real parasite class in Japan. Almost all Japanese work hard and work together. But the fact is inescapable that a rich country of 25 million population has become a poor country of 85 million population. The rise of science, trade and industry in the late nineteenth century encouraged the sensational rise of births. And birth begat its own problems.

* * * * *

Modern Japan is a creature of modern industry and trade. It stands or falls by them. Almost one-half of the working population is engaged in tilling the soil, but their labor is not decisive. The finished goods from Japanese factories and the maintenance of a profitable stream of commerce with the outside decide Japan's survival, as well as its prosperity. Even Sanada, in his upland farmhouse, is vitally affected by changes in the world textile market, or the appearance of new fibers discovered thousands of miles away from him.

The structure of business and finance which the Japanese have raised to meet this challenge is a peculiar one. Like the structure of prewar Japanese political government, it was built on quickly laid foundations, and, necessarily, from materials on hand. Additions and superstructure were of increasingly modern design, but always altered by the singular nature of the foundations. The result was the usual tantalizing mixture of old and new. The selling methods of a Japanese firm, or its scientific testing laboratory, might be as modern as the rakish, swept-back stacks of a *Mogami* class cruiser or a new NYK liner. But the ownership set-up, with all the postwar reforms, is generally as traditional as the high poop-deck of a Japanese fishing sampan.

The web society shows its traces clearly in any contrast of Japanese business practices with those of other nations. Competition exists in Japanese life, just as it does everywhere else. No one who has seen the variety of shops or individual peddlers who somehow sprouted out of the ruins of Tokyo in 1946, selling a weird and amazing variety of merchandise for a bombed-out capital, could doubt that in one sense the Japanese are a nation of free enterprisers.

But free enterprise, pronounced in Japanese, has a sound and a meaning all its own. In a country where waste can be fatal, not just annoying, large-scale competition, to begin with, has very stern limits. Historically, it has also been hedged with rules, under-the-counter agreements and trade organizations on a low level, and with cartels and labyrinthine holding companies on a higher level.

The instinct for the collective that brings Sakaji Sanada to help his neighbor at harvest time or creates a reluctance in Hideya Kisei to impede production by a strike is more, however, than economic determinism, the result of Japan's pinched natural geography. The Chinese, after all, have lived in a similarly crowded economy, hedged by famine and bitter economic injustice; but their form of competition is free to the point of being destructive. The differences in Chinese and Japanese definitions of competition have been dramatized in their contacts throughout Asia. Put five Chinese businessmen and five Japanese businessmen on a strange island. For a while, man for man, the Chinese will outsell the Japanese. After six months, however, the Chinese will have begun a destructive competition against each other, as well as the Japanese. But the five Japanese businessmen will have organized a workable cartel, which will then use its combined assets to crowd the Chinese, singly, out of the running. (If the cartel somehow failed to do the job, the Japanese, in the old days, would call in a cruiser to complete the ruin of the competition.)

Besides this island instinct for group action—and related to it—is the determined effort to share work. Japan's poorness of resources has given the Japanese an idea of manpower totally the opposite of the American. In America, where resources and machines abound, they do the work of men. In Japan, where resources are scarce, men do the work of machines. Labor is cheap in Japan. This is not so much a passing survival of a feudal outlook on life or a reflection of a backward technology, as it is recognition of some cruel but basic economic facts. American reporters in Tokyo were amused to see Yamazaki and his fellow-reporters on

Asahi covering their stories "by platoons." But this did not necessarily imply a Japanese belief that one or two men could not have done the job well. It was an implicit recognition that there are too many men in Japan for any job, but that they must be used and allowed a chance for gainful work of their choice.

With these preliminary observations in mind, it would be well to look briefly at the origins of Japan's modern economy. Like the political system and the Westernized society of Meiji, it had a frantic growth. It evolved, in fact, far more quickly than Japanese political institutions of the Meiji era and there was far less argument about it. Liberals like Itagaki Taisuke and Conservatives like Saigo Takamori could argue or fight a civil war over the objectives of foreign policy, or the advisability of an early constitution. But a steel mill was a steel mill—and all but the most die-hard of the provincial *samurai* agreed that Japan needed steel mills in a hurry.

The Japanese economy began, frankly, as a war industry. As has been suggested earlier, it was not an aggressive war industry, but purely defensive. More realistic than the Chinese of the time, the Japanese in the eighteen sixties knew that the only thing which could ultimately prevent European colonization or semi-colonization in Japan was a strong Japanese army and navy, armed with modern weapons. (Judging by the fate of Africa and other parts of Asia during the same period, they were right.) Modern weapons are the products of modern factories. Therefore, modern factories had to be built.

There were, of course, natural peaceful incentives for building industrial plants—the Meiji reformers were not blind to the benefits of consumer goods and cheap mass production. But heavy industry was the basic consideration. The first arsenal was built 20 years before the first textile plant. The Japanese skipped the long evolution of industry which had taken place in Europe and the United States. Without inching their way through the quieter currents of first small factories and then of larger consumer goods production, they plunged headfirst into the depths of heavy industry. It was not surprising, under the circumstances, that even the most experienced divers would have a case of the economic bends.

In 1868 the young *samurai* of Meiji had already drawn the blueprints of Japan's modern industry: mines, steel mills, arsenals and railroads to connect them. When they looked up from their plans, however, the outlook for tools and construction was discouraging. Japan was not, to be sure, a colonial country with only the most primitive type of economy. But the business and industry of the Tokugawa era was almost as feudal as its politics. The country was above all an agricultural producer. Rice fields were at once the industrial base and the gold reserve. There was considerable home manufacture, but it was all done through the agency of cumbersome craftsmen's associations, like the medieval guilds of Europe.

The one group of people with the organization and the imagination for creating a modern industrial state were the rich merchants of Osaka and, to a lesser extent, the other cities of Japan. Through the two centuries before Meiji these traders had elevated themselves to a key position in the country. As the only men in Japan who dealt in cash, they had become indispensable to the feudal lords and their *samurai*, who were often forced into large cash expenditures by the exactions of the shogun's government. There was hardly a clan leader who had not at one time or another pledged the rice yield of his estates in return for a quick loan. On a smaller scale, the farmers often came into the merchants' debt in the same manner. The concentration of the merchants' wealth in the large cities produced a big consumers' market—and more traders to take care of it. Osaka, the merchants' headquarters, was popularly known as the "Kitchen of Japan." It was plain and workaday, but the country could not get on without it.

It was quite natural that the *samurai* reformers of Meiji call on the proprietors of the Kitchen to cook up some modern financing and industry. The old class barriers be tween the *samurai* and the merchants had ultimately broken down, as their financial interdependence grew. By the eighteen sixties the large families of Osaka were already going through that refining transition period in which merchants become businessmen and usurers become bankers. There was considerable intermarriage and adoption between the *samurai* and the new "businessmen." Many of the lower *samurai* themselves went into trade.

In Europe the Industrial Revolution was a battleground between feudalism and capitalism, a warfare which continued on a guerrilla scale until the rise of Communism made it academic. Nothing like this ever happened in Japan. The merchants wanted to sweep away the trade barriers of the Tokugawa as badly as the feudalists wanted to make Japan a strong modern polity. They made common cause from the beginning—and historically it has ever since been difficult to decide where one class began and the other left off. The alliance joined in 1868 was never broken. The young *samurai* who took over the government, and their friends the merchants who built Japan's new capitalism, always cooperated. Government and business—big business, that is—interlocked. Out of their merger came an economic web society, firmly fixed in the path of the old tradition.

* * * * *

At the very beginning the Osaka businessmen were able to lend the reformers money to overthrow the shogunate. Once this was done, however, they were reluctant to put their money into new and untried economic ventures. They were bankers, rather than promoters or industrial capitalists—and the conservative bankers' mentality continued to dominate Japanese business for decades afterward. The government, therefore, stepped in at the beginning with a large program of industrial development and subsidizing. In other capitalist economies similar activities have been justified as a form of pump-priming. In the Japanese system, with government and business so closely linked together, it resulted inevitably in the government owning a large part of the pump as well.

The new government bureaucrats reserved control of a few basic industries—railroads, the telephone system, the telegraph—on grounds of their strategic value. The other industries, or the beginning of industries, the government initiated and then handed over to the leading groups of big businessmen. The government, for example, took over all the metal and coal mines of Japan immediately after the Meiji Restoration, imported foreign engineers to work and develop them, then turned them over to industry. By 1888 all of them were in private hands. A model government factory for silk spinning was founded in 1872; cotton and woolen factories were set up a few years later. They were duly turned over to private companies at attractive rates. To build up a merchant marine, the government built or purchased ocean-going vessels, then turned them over to the Osaka businessmen at the usual good rates. In some cases they were given away.

This policy of government initiative was wise—probably nothing else would have sufficed if Japan were to have modern industry quickly. But in the shuffle of transfers between the government and the big commercial house, the small free enterprises—so important to the development of Western capitalism—never had a chance to appear. Although small factories and medium-sized businesses later struggled to the surface, they were almost fatally handicapped by the prior existence of well-established big business which could count on firm and almost automatic government support.

The mood of Japanese business for almost a century—and, quite possibly, for many centuries more—was settled by 1880. Government subsidies were expected things, not, as they have been in the United States, a dirty economic word. Big business regarded itself as intimately connected and concerned with national politics—and vice versa. It may have been a shock to some businessmen when the Japanese Army, in the thirties, formally and crudely dedicated Japanese business to the furtherance of political goals. But everything in the evolution of Japanese business to that date had worked to make such a shock easy to take.

This intimate cooperation between government and industry sped the rise of the great commercial houses of Japan. In the hothouse atmosphere provided by the anxious government bureaucrats, the largest and most efficient of the Osaka merchants and bankers increased and multiplied their assets. With their head start they were able to build up structures strong enough to weather depressions which ruined smaller businesses. Feudally organized, they followed the tendency of capitalism to form monopolies. In Japan there was no Sherman Anti-Trust Act or even a like tradition to stop them. Before World War II, there were fifteen combines which controlled 70% of Japan's commerce and industry. The four biggest, the houses of Mitsui, Mitsubishi, Sumitomo and Yasuda, came to be called the *zaibatsu* (literally, "financial clique"), the Japanese equivalent of "the big money."

The House of Mitsui, which before the war controlled 15% of Japanese business, was the greatest of all. It grew great in the classic manner. Sakubei Mitsui, its founder, was a *samurai,* the son of the lord of Echigo. At the beginning of the seventeenth century he started a manufacturing and trading business in sake and soy, at Matsuzaka, on the Ise Peninsula. His youngest son Hachirobei was most successful in carrying on the business. He opened branches in Kyoto, Osaka and Tokyo and was the greatest moneylender of his time. He became the merchant for the government, doing the shogun's business between Osaka and Tokyo. In 1707 the Mitsui were appointed court bankers.

At the time of the Meiji Restoration the House of Mitsui financed the new Emperor's armies and issued notes in the name of the Meiji government. The family got a liberal helping of the mines and industries which the government parcelled out to private enterprise. With this as a start, the Mitsui built up an empire of their own which by 1930 was certainly the largest of its kind in the world. It was still under family ownership—basically the same structure, providing for a cooperative partnership and several branch houses, which Sakubei Mitsui had stipulated in his will in 1694. A holding company, the *Mitsui Gomei Kaisha*, controlled directly or through its direct subsidiaries, or through its subsidiaries' subsidiaries, an incredible variety of industries. They included the Mitsui Bank, the Mitsui Mining Company, the Mitsui Products Company—and through it such enterprises as the Toyo Rayon Co., the Taisho Marine and Fire Insurance Co., the Toyoda Loom Manufacturing Company. There were also the Mitsukoshi Department Stores, the Shibaura Electric Company, the Oji Paper Company, and, through the Oji Paper Company, the Osaka *Mainichi*, Japan's second largest newspaper.

The family ownership system of the large Japanese trusts deeply influenced the Japanese idea of labor relations. Industry was relentlessly paternal. Once Kisei was hired at Yahata, he entered a web of responsibilities and mutual duties almost as strong as the social system of his neighborhood association. On the employer's side of the relationship, there was the obligation to retain his workers in some kind of a job (this did not necessarily include giving them a living wage), to supply them with housing and a certain amount of minimal conveniences. An employee, like a subordinate member of a family, had to be taken care of. Witness the hundreds of surplus workers whom Yamazaki found dutifully being re-engaged at *Asahi* after World War II.

On the other side of the bargain, the employee was tied to his workbench. He was not a free agent; if one firm fired him, or if he quit in protest against bad conditions, it was almost impossible to get on another's payroll. Except for the brief heyday of labor freedom in the early twentieth century, it was generally impossible for employees to strike, demand better wages, or enjoy any of the rights that workers of other countries, by the nineteen thirties, accepted as natural.

There was a crushing sense of helplessness among Japanese workers. A man working in a Mitsui or Mitsubishi factory was as dwarfed as Franz Kafka's hero in *The Castle* by the hierarchy of mysterious personages which governed his life. The small businessman, who wanted to make his way in industry, felt the same way. The only hope was to join one of the colossi, work hard, obey the rules, and ultimately, perhaps, earn a competence as one of the thousands of managerial bureaucrats who ran the faceless operations of Sumitono Goshi Kaisha or the Mitsui Bussan Kaisha.

The only area in Japan where the free enterpriser had a chance was among the welter of small traders, craftsmen and manufacturers who worked for the domestic economy. It was they who turned out the wooden clogs, the straw mats, the parasols, the combs and paper sliding doors, the cheap glassware and pottery that went into the homes of Japan. The individual craftsman has remained in industrial Japan doing the same job that generations of family artisans did before him. But even he had to get his letters of credit at the Mitsui Bank or have his produce transported in Toyoda trucks.

Seen from the surface, Japan of the decade before World War II looked like a well industrialized modern state. The steel ingots from Hideya Kisei's furnace were as strong as most others; Sakaji Sanada's steel looms were of excellent quality, as were the silk products that he wove on them; Fumio Shimizu's 18-inch guns, although gunnery experts of other nations did not know about them at the time, were the finest examples of his craft in the world. The facade of the Mitsui Bank looked as solid and enduring as bank facades anywhere. But the world it represented was in its essence different from the others. Below the surface of the Japanese economy, there was an unparalleled centralized control. There was no distinction between industry and banking—they were done by the same people.

There was no large body of private investors, although often prosperous citizens like farmer Sanada bought bonds when they were officially pressured into it. The Tokyo Stock Market, far from being a bona fide investors' market, was not much more than an exclusive, government-sponsored financial lottery. Most important of all, outside the circle of the *zaibatsu* and those like them, the great majority of the Japanese people, farmers on small plots or craftsmen or mechanics, were completely innocent of any of the economic rights and duties commonly understood by citizens of industrial civilizations.

In the decade of the thirties the centrally run economy of Japan rolled up some imposing statistics. Industry's yearly production rose from six billion yen in 1930 to 30 billions by 1941. In 1930 the Japanese automobile industry turned out 500 cars, trucks and busses. In 1941 it had an output of 48,000. At the beginning of the thirties, coal production was 27,000,000 metric tons per day. By 1940 it was 56,000,000. In the same period ingot steel production was increased from 1.8 million tons to 6.8 million tons.

Japan's export trade boomed. A flood of textiles, machinery and cheap consumer goods poured out of Japanese ports into the world's trading centers. Japan was the world's third largest textile producer, and throughout the thirties, steadily gained ground on all the others. The British and the Dutch clamped desperate restrictions on the import of Japanese cloth goods into their colonies in Asia. In an odd twist of economic justice, Japan's cheap Asiatic products were forcing the European colonizers out of their own neatly hedged markets.

The Japanese people, like many of the world's military intelligence services, were duped by the false sense of economic strength which these statistics gave. They followed their economic leaders into war along with their generals, confident that their growing island industry would be enough to keep the West at bay. It proved inadequate. In the first two years of World War II all the hidden defects of the Japanese economy came explosively to the surface. The industrial war effort was grossly mismanaged, showing not only that generals make poor captains of industry, but that the old interlocking relationship of government and big business in Japan, with all its untraceable subtleties, was not easily adaptable to the needs of a centralized war effort. The Japanese never really understood the concept of industrial mobilization—or understood it too late.*

Japan's supply of skilled workers was not enough to sustain the rush of a desperate war effort. Through a confused war labor policy, skilled workers, like Hideya Kisei, were taken off their jobs and sent to the front. It took Kisei's replacement at Yahata months to learn his old job thoroughly, just as it took the margin of a refresher training course before Kisei became an efficient army signalman in 1941.

The most crushing defect of the economy was the lack of raw materials. The generals had hoped that the conquest of Southeast Asia would remedy this. It did, to a degree. But before the Japanese could bring sizable reserves of oil and metal out of the ground, U.S. navy submarines had begun to shut off Japan's sea lanes. Japan began the war with almost six million tons of ocean-going shipping (i.e., suitable for ocean-going). There was barely 700,000 tons left at the end—despite the fact that shipyards had turned out 4,100,000 tons to replace wartime losses.

Deprived of its only major hope of supply, the island economy of Japan slowly strangled. Although the Japanese doubled their steel production capacity during the war (raising it to 13.6 million metric tons in 1944), for want of raw materials only half of this could be used. By

---

* Japan's effort at economic warfare degenerated into a three-way tug of war between the Army, the Navy and civilian business interests, none of which understood the problems of the other parties involved. The nadir of misdirection was reached when the Army insisted on building its own submarines—for carrying supplies to isolated garrisons in the Pacific.

1945 Japan's industry was nothing but an ironic comment on the importance of communications. There were steel mills without coking coal and ore (most of them producing at about 20% of capacity); there were oil refineries without oil; there were tire factories without rubber. The assembly lines ground to a stop, and most of the factory workers began to drift into the country, in search of food.

* * * * *

When the U.S. occupation army arrived in Japan, the national economy was as low as the national morale. It was not the original intention of the American government to raise it. It was hoped, in Washington, that the Japanese government would prove itself equal to the job of reviving and regulating postwar industry, with only the guidance and certain material helps of the occupation. This expectation was unfounded. The postwar Japanese cabinets were unable and, in most cases, unwilling by themselves to do any real housecleaning among the debris of Japan's smashed and twisted war economy. (It was not until 1949 that Japan had even a capable finance minister.) As a result, General MacArthur's staff, assisted by rotating detachments of economic experts from the United States, was forced to assume this job in addition to its mission of democratizing.

Through the years from 1945 to 1952 the economy of Japan was directed by Americans. The good qualities and the defects of the policies pursued, like those in the political field, were those of the U.S. occupation as a whole: there was the same high purpose and honest idealism; there was the same lack of trained personnel; there was the same disregard of peculiar local problems in the attempt to translate tried and true American theories into Japanese practice. Finally, there was the same irony of international politics. A critical economic experiment was being performed, as well as a social and political one, when the laboratory was suddenly exposed to attack. In the face of Communist aggression, the occupation had to retrench from many of its original economic goals, as well as political, in order to make the Japanese laboratory immediately defensible.

The land reform which the occupation effected was its most successful achievement, and the one least likely to be interfered with by succeeding Japanese governments. The problem of tenant farmers, if not so aggravated in Japan as elsewhere in Asia, was very real. At the end of World War II half of Japan's cultivated land was owned by slightly more than 7% of the farmers. Almost 70% of the farming population were either tenants or part tenants, forced to pay exorbitant rents for the land they hired and virtually unable to purchase land outright— the price of an acre of land in Sakaji Sanada's village (before land reform) was many times the price of an acre of good farmland in many places in the United States.

In December, 1945, General MacArthur directed the Japanese Government to see that "those who till the soil of Japan shall have a more equal opportunity to enjoy the fruits of their labor." Under the terms of a law drawn up by the occupation, all absentee landlords were forced to sell their lands to the government. Resident landlords, besides being limited in the amount of land they could own, were forced to sell all but two and one half acres of tenant-cultivated land. The government arranged to compensate the landlords for the confiscated land, although at prices lower than it was worth.

The law worked. By 1951 there were only 1,670,000 acres of land operated by tenants, as compared with 6,300,000 before the war. Hundreds of thousands of Japanese farm families got a new lease on life. The old tenantry contracts had been loaded in favor of the landlords, who could terminate most renting agreements at will and who had exacted a rent in kind amounting to half the crop. The land reform was a great step towards creating a sound and satisfied farm population. To its credit the occupation remembered that it was discontented farmers' sons from hungry, struggling households who had led the Japanese armies into the Greater East Asia Co-Prosperity Sphere before and during World War II.

In achieving the greater good for the greatest number, the land reform dealt harshly with some honest free enterprisers. Sakaji Sanada was one of them. Before the war he had been one of the largest landowners in Shimoyoshida. Most of his original twelve acres he had bought with his own hard-earned money. He had to give up almost half of it outright (and part of what he has left is held in the name of his dead son Mitsu). The compensation paid was small. It is the one action of the *"America san"* which Sanada recalls with bitterness. Shimoyoshida, in his opinion, has gained nothing by it at all. And the loss of the land has killed his and his wife's hopes of retiring in comfort.

* * * * *

Hideya Kisei thinks differently. He has never regretted leaving his family farm in Kyushu. Like many of the younger generation, he feels there is no future in farming —an attitude which Sanada never ceases to deplore. But since the reform was enacted, he has "shared the joy of the farmers in being able to own their own land." His own family at Kurino were relieved and happy at being released from the bonds of tenantry. "It has changed things radically in the rural areas," he remarked. "It has greatly eased the farmers' problem."

Kisei has, however, one reservation about the land reform law. It is, understandably, the classically American fillip that went along with it—the reordering of the Japanese inheritance laws. All the gentlemen of Japan grew up under a system where land, property and the family name always accrued to the eldest son of a family, with the other children picking up only a few legal crumbs from a father's estate. If it were not for that system, Kisei, who is the third son in his family, might not have left the farm in the first place. The American mind finds something almost morally evil in the law of primogeniture; and it was natural that the Americans should sponsor inheritance laws which distributed property equally among members of a family.

Kisei himself has no quarrel with a system of equal inheritance, but, in the case of Japanese farm households, he thinks it is woefully impractical. Most Japanese farmland is too small to cut up piecemeal—the average farm is less than three acres. If farmers take the new laws literally, Kisei has no doubt of the dire result. Happily, as he concedes himself, in practice the younger children of a family still waive their rights to the land, letting the eldest carry on as before. "I guess," Kisei commented, "it is pretty hard to break down old traditions in any case—but in the case of small farms and a growing population this old tradition is the only way out."

* * * * *

The land reform operated on a limited area of the Japanese economy. It was a gratifyingly concrete operation. There was a specific error, if not an evil, in the system of land tenure. There was a specific solution, which justice and good sense indicated. There was a population in great majority receptive to this solution, which neatly fitted the democratic pattern which the occupation tried to cut out.

The other problems of the Japanese economy were more murky. The entire financial system of Japan needed overhauling, after its ten years in harness with the Japanese war effort. The trade pattern, which had emphasized heavy industry for strategic purposes and relied heavily on colonial markets, had to be shifted. A new labor movement had to be developed. Finally, the control of Japanese industry had to be taken from the *zaibatsu* and their ilk, so that Japanese capitalism would no longer be a synonym for financial feudalism. There was no handy solution for any of these problems, or any way of limiting their scope. They were closely related; the economic health of a trading nation depended utterly on their solution.

Few of the young economists at General MacArthur's headquarters had ever had a chance to run the destinies of a nation. They got off to a galloping start. The new labor unions were organized and assisted. The heads and administrators of the great business houses were "purged" and forbidden any voice in running their concerns. The industrial complexes of the holding companies were broken up into manageable units; plans were made to distribute the ownership of their components as far and as widely as possible. American technical experts began to survey Japanese industry; and SCAP bureaus began casting about for new outlets for Japanese products.

In everything except land reform and, possibly, the rise of labor unions, the gallop soon slowed to a stumbling trot. Although the SCAP economists immediately began breaking up the old Japanese trusts, they did little to stimulate an alternative system of business ownership. The public bought stock in the new companies slowly—there was little incentive to buy it at all. The nation's industry was repeatedly "surveyed," but there was no program for weeding out the uneconomic, subsidized industries that had sprung up as a result of the Japanese war effort. The approach to Japan's trade problem was pedestrian—simply a cautious succession of small bilateral agreements with other countries, a sad contrast to the enlightened schemes for international payments and many-sided trading that were already being worked out by E.C.A. administrators in Europe. Even the growing labor movement was hampered, as Hideya Kisei found out, by American insistence that it could (and must) organize itself on a completely non-political basis (a system of unionization which has succeeded only in the United States). As a result, instead of a frankly political Socialist or semi-Socialist labor party, there was a non-partisan labor movement dangerously infiltrated or dominated by Communists.

There were many able men among the occupation economists. There were able officials in the Japanese finance ministry. There was a great fund of U.S. economic aid. And both Japanese business and labor were malleable clay for almost any economic experiment. The failure of the Japanese economy in the years between 1946 and 1949 was principally a failure of design and of leadership. Economics was never General MacArthur's strong point. The faculty of swift and sure decision which he constantly displayed in other fields was noticeably wanting in this one. There was no strong central direction of SCAP's economic effort, comparable, even, to the leadership of an E.C.A. mission head in Europe. Instead, this economic effort, loosely presided over by one of MacArthur's major generals, was an Occidental bazaar of overlapping authorities and opposed personalities, each hawking his peculiar set of economic panaceas.

In following through the plans which they did turn out, the military economists leaned far too heavily on the Japanese Government. There was a reluctance to interfere with the internal operations of the economy, especially in matters of finance, suggesting the picture of a well-dressed gentleman hesitating to involve himself in the workings of a glue factory. This reluctance was fatal to the plans' success. Until 1949, the Japanese postwar governments displayed a shocking lack of capacity for understanding economic fact. Successive finance ministers operated on the shadiest levels of deficit financing. Somehow an occupation which was forthright enough in giving political orders to the Japanese was shy about dictating some laws of economics. The Japanese economy needed a great deal more occupying than it got.

Washington, presumably preoccupied with European concerns, did little to supply economic direction for the economy of Japan. The question of reparations was left dangling for three critical years. In 1946 the Pauley Commission recommended that Japan should earn its future keep as a mass producer of textiles, with most of its heavy industry shipped as reparations to other Asian countries. Later investigating groups wisely revised this simple suggestion, but no one indicated to the Japanese what factories, or what kind of factories, would be crated and sent away, and what would remain. The future levels of Japanese production were left as matters of debate.

Japanese businessmen understandably did nothing to revive production or improve their plants on a large scale when it was not certain that they would be permitted to keep them. They continued to produce unprofitably, and received government subsidies for doing so. The entire Japanese people lived in a fool's paradise, insulated from the economic facts of life, like their businessmen, by American material and financial help. By 1949 Yamazaki and Shimizu were riding to work in Tokyo in freshly painted railway coaches and busses, past department stores bulging with consumer goods. Sanada was doing well on the farm. In Yahata the Kiseis were able to buy new clothes for their children. Hirohito, through his household officials, had placed the order for his new Cadillac. Three years after the British, facing a similar and less intense problem, had begun a drab regimen of austerity, defeated Japan was enjoying a spurious prosperity which had its origins in the American pocket.

* * * * *

In 1948 the reckoning drew near. William Draper, then Under Secretary of the Army, after in his turn leading a mission to Japan, recommended that the trust-busting in Japanese industry be braked, if not brought to a stop. His reasons were that it critically impaired the efficiency of Japanese business,—unfortunately the trust-busters had not as yet worked up any good substitute for the mechanism they destroyed. And by 1948, in economics as in politics, the pressure of the Cold War with the Communists was forcing the United States to compromise with idealized long-term programs in favor of measures which would show immediate returns in stability, and, by that very fact, in defensibility.

At the same time, the U.S. Government at last officially recognized that it had assumed responsibility for directing the Japanese economy. The idea of reparations in the form of plant and equipment transfers was abandoned (in favor of reparations in money or from current production). In February, 1949, after a preliminary statement of principles from Washington, Joseph M. Dodge, the president of the Detroit Bank, arrived in Japan to make the long deferred overhauling of the Japanese economy.

Dodge expressed his objective bluntly. "The economy," he said, "has traveled the early part of this road in a damaged and unrepaired vehicle, but the vehicle and the passengers have been protected from road shocks by the cushion of U.S. aid. It is time the Japanese began to face up to the unalterable facts of their own life. . . . Wealth must be created before it can be divided."

Dodge's first step was to insist that the Japanese balance their budget.* In 1949 this was done for the first time since 1931. He virtually abolished the system of export subsidies, which he called "an economy on stilts." For the first time in Japanese history, business firms were forced to produce economically, or get out of business. There was no more dipping into the public till to make up for faulty production lines. A drive went on to force manufacturers to export, instead of diverting their products into the home consumer market (often with little pretense at legality), because the returns there were quicker. The taxation system, grossly inefficient, was revised. Another U.S. mission, headed by Dr. Carl Shoup, arrived late in 1949

---

* Balancing the budget means much more to the Japanese economy, than it does to that of the United States, where there is less of a connection between government and business. Only one-sixth of the American national income is accounted for in the budget; two-thirds of the Japanese national income is.

to increase the scale and efficiency of Japanese taxation. (Historically Japanese governments had depended on debentures instead of taxation for most of their financing.)

Austerity at last came to Japan. The new and highly competent Finance Minister, Hayato Ikeda, in a speech to the Diet in April, 1949, said, "We cannot be too serious in consideration of this fact—real political freedom and independence cannot be hoped for where there is no economic independence. If we Japanese prefer to be idly dependent on the help of foreign countries, we would be disgracing both our forefathers and our children."

A balanced budget was the basic lever which slowly swung the Japanese economy into a stable position. It did so by indirection. The Dodge Plan did not attempt to regulate Japanese industry by a complex of economic planning. It resorted to the old-fashioned kind of free-enterprise remedy which Americans, or at least Americans of Joseph Dodge's generation, had learned in their economics textbooks. "Eliminate obvious business and financial malpractices," the theory ran, "set up a few strong credit controls, then let the economy right itself."

The resulting "rationalization of industry" operated on the Japanese economy like a cruel but, in this case, wholesome purgative. With subsidies withdrawn, credit also became tight. A counterpart fund similar to that used in the Marshall Plan was instituted, whereby the Japanese set up a yen fund equal to the dollar amount of U.S. aid. The proceeds of this counterpart fund were used to retire public debt and to give rigidly circumscribed capital loans, under rigidly circumscribed conditions, to firms which had proved their stability. Within a few months inflation was stopped. In the scramble to put their houses in order, businesses which operated uneconomically were squeezed out. The survivors were forced to overhaul operational methods, fire surplus employees and develop as best they could new selling and production techniques to keep in business.

Initially the Dodge Plan produced what seemed like a

sudden depression in Japanese industry, but a depression scarcely as bad as had been expected. Hundreds of small businesses failed, not necessarily because they were uneconomic, but because they had not the capital reserves to keep going. The economists in the labor section of the occupation headquarters tremblingly awaited a vast rise in unemployment, as the surplus workers—against all the old unwritten laws of Japanese industry—were being released from their jobs. But here the old web society of Japan, however weakened, once more turned out to be a friend in disguise to the agencies which had set out to destroy it. No mobs of unemployed rioted in the cities. Few workers, in fact, applied even for unemployment insurance. Just as they had fled to the country during the last of World War II, the discharged workers again went to board with their country cousins. By the old codes of the family system (stronger in the country than in the city), they were unfailingly welcomed. There was no way of showing the change by statistics, but by the thousands the surplus workers of industry straggled off to become, for the time being, surplus workers on their relatives' farms.

By the beginning of 1950 the crisis that many economists had felt must follow the Dodge Plan had not materialized. The surplus workers were filtering back into the cities, finding jobs again, as the "rationalized" businesses began to step up production. There were willing markets for Japanese manufactures in Asia, South America and, to a lesser degree, Europe and the United States. After their bitter medicine, Japanese businesses were able to sell more at lower prices. Trade restrictions against Japanese products loosened. The trade pattern was shifting—away from the planned dependence on textiles and towards additional exports of industrial goods and light machine products. The old mixed bag of exports began to fill up again: cotton goods for Southeast Asia, cameras for the United States, looms for India, bicycles for South America.

In June, 1950, the Japanese economy got an unexpected

boost. With the coming of war to Korea, Japan became the base for the United Nations forces. Fumio Shimizu was by then working as a technical advisor for the reorganized Japan Steel Company, whose executives he had known and done business with before 1945. From their headquarters in Tokyo, Shimizu and his colleagues found themselves running part of a giant ordnance repair program for servicing U. S. military equipment and manufacturing spare parts. In the Tokyo-Yokohama area alone, where Shimizu's company has the bulk of its operations, over 50,000 Japanese mechanics were engaged in this work. Once again he was on the job supervising ordnance research, hiring technicians and debating the types of special steel suitable for armament production.

The furnaces of Yahata poured out their ingots for use in equipment manufacture. Other factories throughout Japan swung into production for the military effort in Korea, as well as for civilian rehabilitation there. During the first year and a half of the Korean war, Japan sold over $567,000,000 worth of supplies to the United Nations' war effort, from telephone poles and railroad ties to parachutes, sleeping bags, locomotives and fire extinguishers.

As war production for Korea expanded, so did peaceful trade with the rest of the world. By mid-1952 Japan was again selling to 76 countries or colonies. The great textile mills of the Kansai district were exporting at 60% of their prewar level. From two million spindles left at the end of World War II, Japan's textile manufacturers had increased their plant to six million, over half of what it was in its heyday of the early thirties. The assembly lines were back in operation at the Toyoda Automobile plant in Nagoya and other rising production centers throughout the country. The Japanese produced 28,000 trucks in 1951. Coal output had gone from 500,000 tons in late 1945, to 3.3 million tons in 1950. Electric power was 60% greater than it ever had been. Japan's industrial index was half again as great as it had been in 1936. This resurrection of Japanese industry surpassed the most optimistic expectations of the SCAP planners in 1945—and certainly proved brighter than the Japanese themselves then thought possible.

The new prosperity was precarious, subject to the twists of the world market and political shifts in the Far East (See Chapter 12). Certainly, the businessmen who counted the Korean war prosperity as a continuing one were deluding themselves as badly as they had in the old days of subsidies. But Japanese business was in relatively good shape for resisting a recession and eager to expand its markets elsewhere, once the Korean windfall was over.

The thick growth of businesses has been severely pruned. What survived had to be hardy. The split-up components of the old *zaibatsu* combines emerged in the best shape—largely because they had inherited not only the prestige of the parent concerns, but some of the best younger managerial talent in Japan. These men, not high enough in their companies to be purged by the postwar economic directives, were forced by exigency into positions of responsibility they would never have held under the old house hierarchies. They grew into an aggressive business leadership, surprisingly young and surprisingly competent. Their firms grew with them—the hard way. Of the 200-odd companies formed out of the wreckage of the Mitsui Products Company (Mitsui Bussan Kaisha) in 1947, after the Mitsui empire was broken up, roughly twenty have survived as stable concerns. The most successful of them, Dai Ichi Bussan, started in 1947 with a capital of $500; by 1952 it had run this up to a half million.

The old ownership of these companies has not returned. Once used to power, the new managers have by and large determined to keep direction and ownership in their hands. (There is, of course, in many of the former *zaibatsu* holdings, a considerable amount of behind-the-scenes direction.) But, facing a crisis time in its history, Japanese businesses have tended to consolidate or even to bank together in new groupings. This is in their tradition. And tradition is a difficult thing to kill when it is reinforced by economic necessity. In 1953, as in 1933, a Japanese cartel can muscle its way into the world market with more resources and more authority than several individually competing Japanese firms.

* * * * *

The spectacular rise in Japanese production did not bring sudden soaring prosperity to the people of Japan. At times it has been more than offset by the shortages of consumer goods—and their consequent high price—in a nation which is producing so strenuously for export. It has given the Japanese a basis for hope. Since 1950 the new direction in the economy has communicated some confidence through the nation. Hirohito, of course, does not have to worry about personal economic matters. The other gentlemen of Japan, however, have all been able to save something each month from what they make. They are immeasurably better off than they were at the close of the war, slightly better off than they were a year or two ago, and almost on a level with their prewar standard of living.

At Yahata, Hideya Kisei has watched his country's economy grow in the most concrete way. The mill is now on a 24-hour day, organized on a three-shift basis. Kisei puts in a great deal of overtime, since on whatever shift it is his responsibility to keep the Number 2 furnace at the Kukioka plant going. New men have come out of the fields around Yahata to work in the furnaces. Those who are there, have had more work than they could handle.

Until 1952 all capital expenditures at Yahata were in the nature of repair and rehabilitation of existing facilities. From early 1952, however, as ore-laden ships crowded in the nearby harbor, the plant started going ahead boldly with new installations. A 1,000-ton furnace, whose construction was stopped in the steel-short days of the war, has recently been finished. Other blast furnaces are planned. There are expansion programs for the rolling mills, the strip mills and the foundry. The Yahata Steel

Products Company, in 1951, had already increased its capitalization from 800,000,000 to 1,600,000,000 yen. Another capital increase has lately followed.

Kisei and his friends are astonishingly well-informed on matters like company capitalization and improvement projects, because, for the first time in the history of Japanese industry, they have an incentive for learning. The new stock ownership of Yahata is scattered. Although banks and insurance companies have acquired a great deal of it, about 30% is owned by individuals, including many of the workers. Kisei has no shares himself, but he hopes to get some. His ambition for Yahata is to see all the shares owned by the workers.* Kisei's take-home pay of 21,000 yen a month, plus his wife's small salary, has pushed their standard of living to its highest point since the war—although Kisei does not do so well as he did in the late thirties, when he was a bachelor working longer hours at a similar production rate. There is enough to eat. "We eat as well," Kisei says, "as any worker in the plant"; but the Kisei diet is hardly luxurious. The breakfast staple is *misoshiru*, a thick salty bean-paste soup which is the oatmeal of Japan; there is also rice, some pickles and, occasionally, an egg. At noon, when Kisei eats at the plant, and for the evening meal, the staples are roughly the same: rice, noodles, fish, vegetables, pickles—cooked in varying ways.

Rice is still rationed. But, although Kisei gets a laborer's

---

* The renovated Japanese stock market opened its doors in Tokyo in the spring of 1949, followed shortly after by the markets in other cities. Under a new set of security regulations there is every incentive for the public to buy stock shares, in the knowledge that they will not be the pawns of the high-class gambling practices that once characterized Japanese stock trading. A strong campaign to enlarge the investing public, after many false starts, showed some results by 1950. There were some initial difficulties in operating the American-style exchanges. Not the least of them was the communications problem—the occupation economists had worked out a system of rules for split-second transactions unthinkingly based on the American, not the Japanese, telephone system.

special heavy ration of rice, he has to buy blackmarket rice each month to supplement his diet. The Kiseis, for the sake of their children, keep a lot of fruit in the house, which is especially plentiful in southern Japan. Once or twice a month, they can afford meat. "At least we are not hungry," Kisei will say, "and that is the main thing."

Probably more than any other people, the Japanese realize that the margin of their present prosperity is very, very thin. The marks of the economy of scarcity are seldom absent. Fumio Shimizu, who has been preaching austerity for the last seven years, is pleased now that his fellow-citizens are approaching their problems realistically, though he is far from satisfied. Yamazaki is most worried about the population problem. He is actively supporting the birth-control movement in Japan. He feels that some Japanese should be allowed to emigrate, pending the ultimate stabilization of the population.

Kisei, who once thought that Yahata's production should be used to alleviate the shortages on the home market, now implicitly believes in the truism "export or die." As he expressed this, "In the broad sense, I am convinced that hard times are ahead. Japan as an independent nation cannot depend on the United States to keep paying her bills. The only way for Japan to stand on her feet again is through export of her products. We must be prepared for a period of great austerity."

Sanada, on the farm, is working diligently. New competition from other looms and small factories has made it more difficult than ever before to sell his silk manufactures at a good profit. Taxes, now enforced as they never were in Japan's past history, have also been hitting him hard. The two newspapers he gets from Tokyo each day, *Yomiuri* and *Nihon Keizai* (the latter, "Japanese Economics," a popularized kind of 'Wall Street *Journal*'), keep him well-informed about new industries, shares and bonds. He is impressed by this industrial growth, but he is cautious and reserves judgment about its success. In his closet, along with the bamboo spear with which the Japanese Army, in 1945, suggested that he fight off the Americans, he still keeps a box of interesting old securities. Their names are lettered in firm, impressive characters: Japan-Manchuria Fertilizer Company, Manchurian Heavy Industry, China Development Company, the Bank of Korea, North Korean Pulp. They constitute an unusually graphic reminder to this citizen of a rising industrial power that stocks and shares are not necessarily worth more than the paper they are printed on.

11

FIVE KINDS OF HOPE

> "To those who only pray for the cherries to bloom
> How I wish to show the spring
> That gleams from a patch of green,
> In the midst of the snow-covered mountain village."
>
> *Fujiwara Iyetaka* (twelfth century)

There are three large smokestacks in Shimoyoshida. They stand out, seen from a distance, like a crude grillwork separating the mountains from the low fields on the edge of town. Two of them are painted a dull black. The third, which belongs to the town power station across the street from Sakaji Sanada's house, is black only at the top. Its lower half is a mottled neutral shade.

Sanada points out the smokestacks to every visitor who arrives. With a half-bitter laugh, he likes to tell their story. During the war the Japanese military authorities, for some reason—probably camouflage—ordered the neighborhood association in Shimoyoshida to paint the stacks black. The townsmen, Sanada among them, finished two of them. They were working on the last one in August, 1945. When the surrender came, they dropped their brushes and never picked them up again. "It is a crazy sight," he warns his guests. "Quite silly in those days, weren't we? That half-finished job is a good reminder of what fools the Japanese have been."

* * * * *

It has been after all less than a decade since Sanada and his neighbors were painting smokestacks obediently and desperately working to fulfill their rice quota, since Hideya Kisei was busy obeying the Emperor's commands in the verdant misery of the Burma jungle, since Hirohito was issuing warlike rescripts to encourage victory. Militarism, defeat, democracy and the Cold War followed one upon the other so fast that their effects and the stimuli they offered are curiously mingled. They separate themselves with difficulty in the Japanese mind. The forties has been an angry decade, whose thin barriers gave no real protection from the streams of puzzling situations, of old ideas and new ones that flooded the islands from every side.

For people so tossed by the undulations of new ideas and situations, the five gentlemen of Japan have preserved a remarkable balance. They totter sometimes. They often misjudge distances and heights. But they have displayed what seems a national ability to right themselves—a puzzling resiliency that is, perhaps, the Oriental equivalent of the English islander's genius for happy compromise. Cynical Japanese and foreigners have compared this to the action of a *daruma*, the rounded red doll that is the toy of Japanese children. Hit it, kick it, drop it in any direction—and it will somehow snap back, tottering crazily but firmly from one side to another on its axis.

The *daruma* comparison is only partly true. The Japanese are resilient; they have rolled with the impact of every major foreign influence in their lives. But they have never, like the *daruma*, snapped back to their original position. Japan after the Chinese importations of the eighth and ninth centuries was a different Japan from what it had been. It never again fitted in its original mold. Japan after the Meiji Restoration was irrevocably changed from what it had been before. Nor is Japan, after the American occupation, the same Japan that it was before. Japan cannot return to the old pattern. If it can be called a *daruma*, it is one that moves in an odd spiraling way, sometimes inclining towards the place it has left, but never quite returning.

The Japanese still perpetuate the externals of the web society. As Tadao Yamazaki has noticed, there is in fact a revival of classic Japanese arts and a study of classic Japanese virtues. It is the ebbing undertow of the strong currents of 1946 and 1947 that brought new dance halls and democracy, bigger baseball leagues and American-style black judicial robes to Japan.

In the late summer of 1950, during a brief weekend in Tokyo, the writer saw from the windows of his Tokyo office an epitome of Japan's "Americanization." A visiting American all-star baseball team was making a triumphal entry into town, riding down the Ginza, Tokyo's main street, in a caravan of open automobiles, each ball player sitting between a pair of Japanese movie starlets. The cavalcade was preceded by the Tokyo Metropolitan Police Band, playing its favorite postwar selection, Souza's "The Stars and Stripes Forever."

It would have been dangerous to conclude, however, from surface observations like these, that the modern Japanese are completely changing the tempo of their existence to harmonize with American march time. The reaction against the surface Americanization was a strong one. The Japanese by no means intend to throw their old manners and customs out the window.

"With defeat," as Yamazaki explained it, "we reverted to a re-examination and restudy of the old good. The most traditional customs and manners, that is to say, the good ones, returned and in a measure emerged above the occupation."

The same *haikara* (literally, "high collar," i.e., upper class) Japanese who most earnestly copied American fashion patterns and placed the first orders for new Fords and

Jeep station wagons, have also in the privacy of their homes spent long hours composing *haiku* or *tanka,* the pithy Japanese poems that smack of the ancient epigrams in the Greek Anthology. They have patronized *judo* and *sumo* matches and bought new editions of the *Tale of Genji* at their book stores, along with Norman Mailer's American best-seller, *The Naked and The Dead* (in translation), which had a great success in Japan. Aside from their natural reverence for the imperial presence, the Japanese showed a great deal of understanding and approval for Hirohito's gesture during one of his early factory inspections. When a worker impulsively put out his hand for the Emperor to shake, Hirohito drew back for a moment, then suggested, "Let's do it the Japanese way," and bowed deeply and politely to the hand shaker.

In 1951 and 1952, this cult of Japanese culture, as well as a form of petulance with Americans, was a natural reaction to the first wave of enthusiasm, when the Japanese adopted the customs of their conquerors on a wholesale level. It will continue and increase; *haiku* and *judo* are Japanese things. They are reviving in greater strength after the MacArthur era, just as they revived after the mass adoption of Western clothes and literature in the Meiji era. But these revivals are natural assertions of the ethos, the certain things about the Japanese that make them Japanese. They do not negate the positive effects of a serious defeat for a set of Japanese institutions, and the determined propaganda in favor of the campaign for democracy. The Japanese on the whole have remained friends of the Americans who came to them. They have been impressed by much of what they have seen. They hope to reproduce it in their own way. The peculiar web society which existed on the 14th of August, 1945, has loosened its hold, but *haiku* and *judo* stay.

The five gentlemen of Japan have been affected deeply by the events of the last ten years, but they have been affected to different purposes. They are as individual in their opinions as they are in matters of personal taste—

though always with the reservation that the heritage of the web society has made them more apt than most individuals to join in a common effort. Sakaji Sanada, the farmer, has kept his old web of personal loyalties relatively intact. In his own mind he has been able to accomplish what more deeply thinking people—and the nation as a whole—have failed to do: a neat adoption of the American-style democracy into his old system. He is a freer person for the change, rid of the regulations and old patriotic codes of which he was never overfond. But he has had no sense of passing through a revolution. The old values and traditions represented on the *kami-dana*, the Shinto "god-shelf" (i.e., the altar in his home), are still in their places. He has merely shifted them about and imperturbably added some new ones.

Tadao Yamazaki feels the revolution far more than most Japanese. He came from an unconventional family, which had already in some ways slipped out of its patterned society. This has made the problem of finding a new way for Japan far less complicated for him than for others. It is a new way that he wants, politically and economically as much as socially. But he is extremely wise about the manner of seeking it. He realizes that any new way, to succeed, must in some manner grow out of the old.

Hideya Kisei is more influenced than Yamazaki by old Japanese tradition. He has not forgotten the *samurai* ethics which were his only heritage from a bankrupt family. Yet he has felt the pull of a revolution in the most concrete way of all, in the noisy meetings of his union at Yahata and the strike demonstrations it staged, without fear of police interference. An independent farmer like Sanada is to some extent insulated from the changes, material and spiritual, in Japanese life. Kisei traffics with them every day.

Fumio Shimizu is a cautionary, but not unfriendly observer of the changes. He has little wish to resume the student curiosity for new theories, which he abandoned for engineering in 1911. He agrees with the definition of

Japanese society in terms of a binding web, acknowledges its defects, but is not optimistic that it can be easily or quickly changed into a better system. He is rather tired.

The Emperor is more akin to Shimizu in his outlook than to any of the others. Like the ex-admiral, he has known the West and felt the gaps in Japanese life. He is less of a pessimist. He would not like officially to favor the term "new Japan," but he is optimistic that a better Japan can be constructed out of the materials at hand. As the honorary president of the builders and contractors involved, he has dedicated himself to the job.

In their views and their acts, these five men show a combination of the old and the new that is not yet a synthesis. They and their fellow countrymen, like other critical Japanese generations before them, are still sorting, still trying to understand, still bending to outside pressures on their nation which cannot be denied or forgotten. Their thoughts, their hopes and their prejudices make up a tentative and sometimes hazy outline of the new Japan. They are its determinants: in the gods they worship, the governments they want and the place they wish to hold in the world around them.

* * * * *

The question of God (or gods) has been the weakest point in the Japanese world. Most Japanese offer the spectacle of a religious people without an expressed religion. The spiritual feeling between man and God, that stands at the roots of morality, is healthiest when it is acknowledged. When it is manipulated, diverted, ignored or explained away, man's soul-hunger is apt to appease itself through devious and often dangerous channels; so modern phenomena like Hegelianism, Nazism and Communism, bear witness, as does a sterile "humanism" or scientific secularism in the United States. In ancient Japan, society, in its way, was naturally religious. In Japan's Middle Ages, the people's religious instincts were absorbed (and overshadowed) by Japanese feudalism. The Meiji planners set out to make a modern state. But, semi-consciously, they melded the religious feelings of the Japanese into a strange union of religion, patriotism and politics. This union was effective for the immediate purposes of the militarists when it could inspire the religious "banzai" charges of World War II. But when it was forcibly abandoned, the Japanese found that the components were far weaker individually, than they had appeared to be in sum. Like the Islamic countries, which have had similar troubles, the Japanese found themselves with fragments of a world that would not fit together again.

Many Japanese are sensitive to this basic religious weakness in their culture. They take it far more seriously than do most Europeans and Americans, who retain at least the tradition of firm moral values, not to speak of strong Christian religious movements within their society. Christianity in Japan can offer much. But its teachings are not widely known. Buddhism and Shinto, for their part, have lost the vitality of an earlier age. Both the warrior monks and, with few exceptions, the philosophers are gone. What is left has been crippled by long association with the state.

Shimizu has given a good deal of thought to Japan's religious defects. He is aware that the lack of any absolute religious or moral yardstick has been the web society's downfall. "The old religions of Japan, Buddhism and Shinto," he has said, "do not teach public moral behavior [i.e., morals outside the contract relationship]. The Japanese do not, at the same time, have faith in these religions, in the sense that the people of the West have faith in Christianity and its teachings. The reason for this, I think, is that the religions have not progressed or adapted themselves to changed circumstances. They have become more or less tradition and custom. The Japanese have had these religions so long that, although their idea of good and evil is based on Buddhist and Shinto morals, they are not today conscious of that fact. This problem of faith is very important. I think myself that Christianity is the answer. Either that or the Buddhists and Shintoists must study and develop their religion to fit the needs of the people."

In 1949 Shimizu's daughter was married. It was a normal Shinto ceremony. The bride and groom sat on chairs facing a small Shinto shrine. A white-robed priest waved a tree branch before the couple to chase away evil spirits, chanting the while. Bride and groom then underwent the *san-san-kudo* (literally, "the three three nine times"), a ceremony in which each takes three ritual sips from each of three ritual sake cups.

As Shimizu listened to the chanted marriage formula, announcing the wedding to the eight million "gods" (*kami*) of Japan, he shook his head. He could not understand it. "How can people have faith in something which they cannot understand," he asked a fellow engineer later that week.

Yamazaki feels much the same. He is absolutely against Shinto, which he feels must be erased from Japanese life. He looks on all other religions, Christianity included, with the eye of a skeptic. But, oddly, he and his wife would like to send their baby to a Christian Sunday School, as soon as he is old enough. He explains this indefinitely and almost shyly: "I think it would be good for his future, if he were to come into contact with something close to Christianity. After he comes of age, he can decide for himself if he wants to pursue his quest for religion further. In view of my own opinions this sounds paradoxical, but it is what I desire." Yamazaki is avowedly not so interested in religious and spiritual problems as Fumio Shimizu, but it would seem that he has rejected Japanese religion and turned towards the absolutes of Christianity for similar reasons.

None of the five men has an intense religious belief. Yamazaki has been impressed by some of the philosophical teachings of the Zen Buddhists, but his interest is strictly academic. He is an agnostic. In his own words: "I'm not attached to any religion which can be expressed in any 'ism.' This does not mean that I have no respect for religion, or disregard it. I know religions exist, and that they are a necessity. It's just that I cannot work myself up to being a religious man.

"I hold in contempt the many stories of Christ [i.e., the miracles]. I understand and realize their existence, what part they have played in the past and will play in the future. The same holds true with the fables of Buddhism and other religions. But I want to be rational and realistic. I do not believe in heaven, hell or the hereafter. I do believe that we are born, that we live and that we die, all on this earth. I do not believe anything beyond that."

Although Fumio Shimizu looks on the gaudy rituals of Shinto with the embarrassed curiosity of an Oxford professor of classics attending a noisy Christian camp meeting, he has a faith of his own. "It may sound strange," he admits, "but I have a faith in an almighty God. It is my own peculiar faith, in that I feel that all things are a manifestation of the Almighty. Even the study of science is a manifestation of that faith." He has created his own set of absolute values, from the contracts of the web society which bore him. He has made good and solid virtues out of fair play and direct dealing, intransitive virtues—to be prized for their own sake—which do not need objects. He did not find these virtues thus stated in the Japanese or Chinese classics. Possibly he grew into them in England, in the days when he was learning the manufacture of aircraft machine guns.

Hideya Kisei's socialism has not interfered with a brand of religion common to millions of his countrymen. He is a follower of the Pure Land sect of Buddhism—*Shinshu*—which continues to teach, as it did in the thirteenth century, that man can only be saved by faith and the mercy of Amida, the Buddha, not by his own good deeds.

Shinshu was the religion of his parents and his ancestors. There was a huge Buddhist altar, as well as a Shinto godshelf in his old home in Kurino. As a child he was taught to bow each morning to the altar, while burning incense to it. His parents, even at times when the family was close to hunger, insisted on giving offerings of newly cooked rice to the Buddha, before each meal.

Kisei knows little and cares less about Buddhist theology. His attitude on religion, although expressed more plainly, is at one with the mind of Western philosophers like the late George Santayana. "I feel that religion is a man-made thing," he explained, sitting in his living room across from the small god-shelf, "but it is vital for peace of mind. I consider it essential for the basic moral education of my children. It is one way of teaching them the difference between good and bad." His wife, like the Spanish women of Santayana's youth, is more religious than her husband. Kiyoko Kisei has insisted that the children should be brought up in the way of the Buddha. She believes.

The Emperor, as the High Priest of Japanese Shinto, is at once disqualified and unable to express his private religious feelings. On stated occasions, he goes dutifully to officiate at major Shinto shrines, guided by his chamberlains through the demands of the ritual. These occasions aside, he has never shown an interest in his native theology.

It is left to Sakaji Sanada to hold up the flickering torch of orthodoxy. About 3,000 yards north of his house stands the Fukugenji Temple, a medium-sized dull black building whose wooden sides have been dignified by 300 years of snow and rain. It faces Mt. Fuji. So does the large gate with the pagoda-like roof, which separates the inner close of Fukugenji from the bumpy dirt street and the tile-roofed houses across the road. Fukugenji is a *Shinshu* temple. Every year at the times of the great Buddhist festivals, Sakaji Sanada and his family go there to say their prayers. They are, even by local standards, religious people.

On the small bulletin board nailed to the left of the temple gate someone has written an old quotation. It is attributed to "Captain Brinkley" [the famous British trader and historian who made his home in Japan]. "See how many foreigners are turning to Buddhism," it reads. "Don't the Japanese people realize that they are fortunate in possessing a religion that teaches peace and enlightenment?" Sanada himself finds some truth in this boast of peace, if not enlightenment. He prays in his house, fingering his large wooden prayer beads as he chants the rosary-like repetitions of the Buddhist *sutras* over and over again. The Buddhist altar—the *butsudan*—in his house is kept neat and well supplied with flowers. His wife, Hie, as part of her community duties, is chairwoman of the temple's women's society, the "Ladies Aid" of Buddhism. She gathers her group together once a month to confer about the temple's upkeep.

The Buddhism of Sakaji Sanada has strengthened his insulation from the events that have gone on around him. He has no deep theological feelings about it; he is not exhorted by Buddhist priests as his Christian counterparts might be. They are not active evangelists. Like many other older Japanese, he has a dim conception of an afterlife and a pantheon of deities who will sanctify the human strivings for good. But the temple below is real, an inheritance from his ancestors and a quality to bequeath to his children. Like the Shinto shrine to which he once repaired in the same manner, the Fukugenji is primarily another strong link in Sakaji Sanada's community with his fellowmen, a horizontal thread which ties him safe within the web.

As a religion, he feels and touches Buddhism, but he does not understand. The Buddhism of Fukugenji, like the snow-deep slopes of Fuji in the wintertime, is a series of barren station markers with no halfway houses between them. It is a religious kingdom with its aristocracy and its masses, but no middle class. Sakaji Sanada rattles his beads and chants the almost meaningless *sutras*. Daisetz Suzuki, the great Zen Buddhist philosopher, at the other end of the scale, explains the theory of *karma* at his home in Kamakura, or writes books about nirvana, or self-annihilation for an audience of philosophers in the West. There is little contact between them.

* * * * *

If Kisei, Yamazaki and the others are currently either weak or wistful about theology, they are strong on civics. The failure of the militarist empire, so long the capstone of the Japanese polity, inspired a distrust in government which Japanese had not before felt. The distrust was complemented by the number one objective of the American occupation—to inject a notion of democratic citizenship and its responsibilities into Japan or, more exactly, to revive the sense of democratic responsibility that grew up with Meiji, before it died in the middle thirties. "The wise man does not hesitate," the liberal leader Itagaki Taisuke said to his constituents in 1882, "the brave man does not fear. Although there are many obstacles on that waste land of liberty which we are anxious to reclaim with your aid, yet staunch toil with hoe and plow will remove them all. . . ."

In the years following the peace, the Japanese have been extraordinarily questioning with their elected leaders. They have not been satisfied with their promises or performance, sometimes justly, sometimes not. To understand their criticisms and their differing views, it is necessary to look shortly at the façade of Japanese politics since 1945—scaffolding for the most part, but in some places surprisingly stoutly built. Its smoothness and seeming continuity, if judged from a distance, has often disguised the violence of the acts and changes within the nation's society. In years which held the potency of revolution, the government has been generally quiet-mannered and conservative. The fact of the occupation made this almost inevitable. The Americans not only eliminated the extreme hunger and want on which violent politics flourish; they also, by insisting rigidly that order must at all costs be kept, made it easy for conservative political groups to impress the voter with this normalcy, and gain power by trading on it.

There was one break in the conservatives' rise to power. The Social Democrats, in 1947, were able to assume the government. For the first time in Japanese history a Socialist, Tetsu Katayama (who is also a Christian), became Premier. Had Katayama's party been dynamic or even sure of itself, with a firm policy and soundly organized support, they could, perhaps, have accomplished something like a real democratic revolution—without bloodletting or revolutionary cabals, in a manner Fabian Socialists dream about. The Japanese people had been stirred by the democratic preaching of the occupation—and on a very broad basis. To factory workers like Hideya Kisei and, less articulately, to millions of other little people in Japan, the thought of a Socialist government, pledged, for the first time in Japanese political history, to the cause of the people, was full of hope.

The Socialists did not fulfill their promise. They took power too early, without the comfort of a large electoral majority. It was, in fact, almost handed to them by the conservative parties, after an election in which no party received an absolute majority. The conservatives reasoned, with shrewdness, that the Socialists, eager for control of the government, would snatch at the chance for a cabinet prematurely, exposing themselves to a risk of total collapse in the future, when they were unable to enact the reforms they supported. This happened. With a Diet majority as precarious as that of almost any French premier, Katayana found that his programs had to be watered down or sometimes forgotten. There was no solid party organization to capitalize on the popular enthusiasm for the Socialists then running through Japan. Bewildered, almost, by power, the Socialists found their approach too academic and unrealistic to use it well. It had come too soon.

Power not only puzzled; it spectacularly corrupted. Some bad graft scandals left the brave new world of the Socialists and other left-of-center groups shattered and singed. The voters were disgusted—and no one was able to explain to them the difference between malfeasance by a

party official and bad principles for the party as a whole.*
Beyond this, the Japanese Socialists, newly and hastily organized from the ruins of their party in the nineteen thirties, were ground between the hammer of Marx's preaching and the anvil of their own good consciences. Like the Socialists on the European continent, they split into extremists and moderates—left wing, right and center. They did not stay in power long this way.

Once the Socialists failed, the reins of power were snatched up again by the conservatives. The Liberal party resumed its seat in power and continued to preside over the trusteeship period in Japanese politics. It was not the best helpmate for an American occupation pledged to democracy. It was a disappointment to the young and the discontented, who wanted dramatic leadership. Its members were a quickly cooked up stew of businessmen, politicians from the old prewar Japanese political parties and conservative rural leaders. They were against the old militarism—for a variety of reasons. They welcomed the occupation's help, although they more or less openly resented its dictation. They were anxious to suture the wounds of the war as quickly as possible, then to reconstruct what was left of the old prewar Japan which they had known, minus the excesses of the militarists. Most of them missed the point about what democracy was, to say nothing of what it should do. They often put up a passive, guerrilla resistance to the reforms which the directives of General MacArthur had ordered.

As Premier and head of the Liberal party, Shigeru Yoshida, a career diplomat of the prewar days, has governed Japan longer than any postwar leader. Locked into his pince-nez and his old-fashioned wing collars, Yoshida looks like the perfect trustee, a man chosen for his vigor and respectability to preside over a bankrupt corporation during the tricky phases of receivership and reconstruction. He is one of the few prominent Japanese states-

---

* Although their theories on the subject are sounder, American voters have had similar difficulties.

men who forthrightly opposed the military and lived to tell about it. He is better equipped than most to deal with Westerners, with a long residence in European countries behind him. He speaks English well, although his efforts to speak it flawlessly in public are very taxing to him.

Yoshida's qualities, however, transcend those of the respectable trustee. He is a stubborn and cantankerous man, scrupulously honest, who expresses himself without fear. In Japanese politics, hedged with the tactful niceties and exasperating circumlocutions of the web society, a blunt man is either quickly eliminated or rises to the top through the sheer surprise and embarrassment of his opponents, if nothing else. Yoshida is a patriotic man; his admiration of long cigars, polite English conversation and Churchillian phrases has not taken away his Japanese tastes and the Japanese code by which he lives. Although he had known the West, he never depreciated Japan. During the occupation period, he set his goal: independence and sovereignty as soon as possible and did not deviate from it.

He alternately resisted the American occupation and gave it his support. He hedged about the broad new guarantees of freedom in the 1946 Constitution, but he went down the line with American economists who wanted to stamp out the inherent waste and corruption in the Japanese tax system. When his own party attacked him, he replied with a simple set of alternatives: "do what I say or I'll get out." The party, until the peace treaty was signed and for a good time thereafter, did exactly as Yoshida said. There was no other man to replace him, no one willing on the one hand to defend what he felt to be Japanese rights against an occupying authority—and to risk the stigma of being called a "foreign puppet" on the other.

Yoshida is not a reactionary in his policies. In action he looks more like a Gladstonian Liberal suddenly parked into a world of violent and un-British social change. "Mr. Yoshida understands what liberalism is," one of his young supporters once admitted, "I do not think he understands what democracy is." Almost all Japanese, when they criticize, feel that another man could have done a better job than Yoshida; but they begin to stammer, when pressed for names.

* * * * *

Although Fumio Shimizu's name was taken off the purge list early in 1952 (along with a large number of other former regular officers in the Army and Navy), he is still habitually shy of talking politics. He has little inclination to criticize the government, even in private, since he holds that any government, by whomever, facing the same problem and the same difficulties of the postwar period would have to handle them in similar ways. He is satisfied, if unenthusiastic about the Yoshida government, although he wishes that Yoshida could be "more flexible." He voted for Yoshida's party in the last election.

Sakaji Sanada, in his periodic trips to Tokyo, has kept up a lively spectator interest in the clashes of the new political parties. During the elections of 1952, he toured the street-corner rallies with his brother, listening to the shouted, closely bunched syllables of Japanese campaign oratory. He is a firm conservative, whose sympathies are divided between the Liberals and the smaller Democratic party, which now professes only hairsplitting doctrinal differences with the Liberals.

But Sanada is not happy with the party leaders. As a hard-working farmer, his interests are more of a vertical class nature than a horizontal grouping according to party or ideals. And he feels that they have been flouted. "Why is it," he complained after the rallies were over, "that none of our Liberal and Democratic politicians speak in behalf of the farmer. They all talk about the peace treaty, rearmament and things like that—but not one word on agriculture or the welfare of the farmer. They must remember that the farmer is the backbone of the nation. Just because the farmer is not the foremost issue today—this is no reason to ignore him. Have we not been used as pawns in times of emergency? Are we not exploited in times of war? Then in times of peace are we not forgotten? It should not be so."

Hideya Kisei speaks for a different kind of interest. He is a Socialist, a capable and a militant party man, who believes in the need and urgency for labor's political action. Like many factory foremen, coal miners and railroad engineers, his hopes leapt high when the Socialists went into office in 1947. He is disappointed that, since its defeat, the party has devoted a valuable part of its energies to internecine brawling between right, left and center factions. This looks to him like a simple dereliction of responsibility on the part of his leaders, who neglect their supporters to involve themselves in "feuds over personalities."

The political ambition of Hideya Kisei is the political ambition of millions like him throughout the industrial world. Japanese labor unions scheduled a general strike for February 1, 1949. Even after the occupation had banned it, in the interests of maintaining order, the thought of the aborted plans made Kisei proud and reflective. He dreamed, as he said, of the "tremendous power which the concerted action of laborers could muster. Why, the entire country could be brought to a standstill. Add to this the cooperation of the farmers and there is nothing that could not be done. This latent power is there for the asking. All it requires is the leadership to arouse and guide it in the right direction. It is most regrettable that the present Socialist leadership does not realize this and take advantage of it."

For all his enthusiasm, Kisei had little resentment against the occupation's strike ban, that is to say, he understood why it might have been necessary. He realizes, and he has seen from his contacts with the Communists, the danger that any powerful workers' movement could be abused by the wrong leadership. Kisei would like some kind of a workers' paradise to materialize, but he dislikes any violent or disorderly effort to attain it. He is a type of a distinctive Japanese phenomenon—the revolutionary who instinctively disapproves of any unorthodox violence. He would be applauded in the British Trades Union Congress; he would probably be denounced as a naive idiot by labor organizations in France.

Kisei dislikes the Yoshida government, which, he rightly feels, is not governing the country for the benefit "of the mass of working people." But he has conceded that the Liberal party, considering the difficult circumstances, has done remarkably well. It deserves to be called a "good" government, by comparison with the prewar cabinets, who were "merely puppets of the militarists." The only prewar statesmen whom he admired was Korehiko Takahashi, an able and courageous finance minister, who was assassinated in 1936 by the militarists for opposing their wild budgetary schemes, and, in general, their entire program for armed conquest. Since the war ended, Kisei, like most of the Japanese people, has yet to find any politician like Takahashi whom he can honestly admire and respect. Laws can be changed more easily than their interpreters. As Kisei acknowledged, "Perhaps the new changes came too fast and my new standards—based on them, may be unreasonably high."

Tadao Yamazaki has taken literally the newspaperman's ideal of the enlightened, objective spectator, who informs the actors in life's play alternately what they are doing well and why they are missing their cues. He is not a member of any political party. "If I were," he often repeats, "I feel that I wouldn't be able to do justice to the job I now hold. I'm afraid I would be biased in handling political reports. I want to be free. I want to give every political party an equal chance. I want to see, hear and write from a cosmopolitan point of view." He has some good historical reasons for this position— It is so easy to fall back into the old Japan or convert ourselves into a little soviet, if we are one-sided in our views."

Hirohito is politically objective for a different reason.

He has not made any political decisions since the August day in 1945, when he told his Cabinet that the war must stop. With all the optimism of an earnest man, he hopes that he will not be called to make any others. He has got along well with Premier Yoshida, a type of Japanese in whom he has had some confidence. But his political opinions he keeps locked inside his study in the palace, known only, perhaps, to the unsmiling busts of Napoleon, Darwin, and Lincoln that perch above his desk.

* * * * *

The Emperor himself is a political opinion. He is a viewpoint in which Sanada, Yamazaki, Shimizu and Kisei differ only in degree. To some Japanese, Hirohito may still stand as the mystic adhesive that binds their web together; to others he has emerged as a clear-cut constitutional monarch; to others he may still be only an indistinct symbol. But he remains. Through war, defeat, occupation and sovereignty he represents the continuity of Japan. His prestige sagged after the war ended; it was to some extent caught in the backwash of disillusionment and distrust of old values. Since then it has climbed. Its nature has changed, as the old imperial symbol stepped out of its niche, came to life, and walked among its people.

Hideya Kisei is wary of the Emperor's potential power. "A powerful emperor system," he says flatly, "should not be allowed." But he adds in the same breath—"Still, I have not changed my idea that the Emperor is our father. He should be left as he is."

Kisei's sentiments on this matter were clarified for him, during the Emperor's tour of Kyushu, when the Imperial party paid a visit to Yahata. Several weeks before Hirohito's arrival, company officials called on Kisei and other union leaders, asking their cooperation in tidying up the plant. For two days, in their spare time, Kisei's "clean-up" committee swept and polished through the Kukioka plant.

Kisei did not do so because he "liked" the Emperor. "I did it," he explained, "because I am essentially a workman and I take pride in my work and the place I work in."

When the Emperor arrived, Kisei and his crew were at work. The Emperor watched them working and did not question anyone. But the effect on the steel workers was no different from the effect which Hirohito's presence had had on farmers, office clerks and coal miners elsewhere during the trip. "I must admit," Kisei says, "that all of us were filled with deep emotion. When we talk about the Emperor, he is just an abstract thing; but when you see him close at hand—it's different, somehow."

Kisei noticed with some amusement that the Communists in the plant, who had protested against his "clean-up" campaign, were just as affected as the others, when the Emperor came. Afterwards they denied it.

Sakaji Sanada no longer stops by the entrance of the Imperial Palace on a visit to Tokyo, to bow respectfully towards the Emperor's Presence. His feelings, he admits, have changed. He thinks of the Emperor now as less of a religious symbol. But he is still the national father. Sanada, unlike the others, is displeased by the Emperor's new role of the peripatetic constitutional monarch. "He has no business going out so much or speaking so much," he objected. Like a good father, who is growing old, Sanada wants Hirohito to go into *inkyo,* the retirement of Japanese elders.

In his more rebellious moments, Sanada expansively talks of the Emperor as an "appendix," a worthy but not essential part of the Japanese political body. "The appendix," he points out, "is part of the body, when the body is born—so it can be left as it is. As long as it behaves, we can leave it alone. Of course, if it becomes troublesome, we can operate." It is hard to say how sincerely Sanada means his figure to be taken. He still feels awed and honored by the Emperor's visit to Shimoyoshida in 1948, when he shook hands with all members of families who had lost anyone in the war. If Sanada were ever called on to assist at such an appendectomy, he would probably make an unreliable and emotional surgeon.

Fumio Shimizu is as dour on the subject of the Emperor as he is on other changing aspects of Japanese life. He retains his own old loyalties in this respect, which were firm but moderate. He is glad that the Emperor has come closer in his actions and utterances to the type of constitutional monarch which Shimizu admired in England. But, concurrently, he wonders seriously whether the new form of the Throne will prove a successful unifying bond among the modern Japanese.

Tadao Yamazaki has nothing against the Emperor. As a realist, he defends the emperor system, solely on the grounds that there is now nothing in Japan to take its place, no "appropriate symbol of democracy" that could be used in Hirohito's stead. To remove the Emperor, or to attempt it, would mean a "political upheaval with the shedding of a great deal of blood." He was impressed by the American policy of retaining the Emperor. "By not insulting the Emperor," he has said, "General MacArthur and General Ridgway permitted the Japanese to save face. Their very action, plus the attitude of the United States, made Japan an ally rather than an enemy. As even the Communists have recognized, the Emperor and the emperor system have an invincible importance in the way of life of the average Japanese."

After making his bow to reality, Yamazaki is quick to explain that as a matter of "philosopher politics," he is unalterably opposed to an emperor system of any sort. It is undemocratic and retards the growth of democracy. He has noticed that conservative Japanese in 1952, just as the militarists in 1937, use the Emperor as a screen and a shibboleth. As he phrases it, "If a man advocates the eventual abolition of the emperor system, he is immediately branded as a Communist. Is this a healthy sign that democracy has taken root here? If a man is employed by a conservative company he may lose his job for expressing an opinion like this." He can say this with impunity, because the newspaper which employs him is one of the few Japanese business organizations with a tradition of free speech among its employees.

Yamazaki is an egalitarian with a vengeance. At the root of his dislike of the emperor system is aversion for the whole class system in Japanese society, which has the Emperor at its head and at its base. The American occupation forbade the use of titles of nobility—except in the case of the Imperial Family; but, as other republican reformers in history have found out, a count remained a count, and a baron a baron, long after the legal right to their titles had been abrogated.*

Japan is a society much like England, where a man can be revealed as a "gentleman" or "not a gentleman," the moment he opens his mouth. The class structure, though far less rigid than England's, has always been accepted. In 1945, it was the same as it had been in the days of Meiji, when Fukuzawa Yukichi experimentally tried addressing passersby, first as a *samurai*, then in the dialect of a local farmer, whose costume he was wearing. He received, depending on the language he used, two wholly different kinds of treatment.

Since the end of the war, the class system has tended to break down, as England's has. Unless this tendency is artificially arrested, the codes and restrictions of Japanese social life will continue to loosen.

* * * * *

Yamazaki does not think that a discussion of "democracy" is philosopher politics. It is too clearly a factor in the "here" and the "now" of Japan. Almost every Japanese

---

* Interestingly, it was the very Americans who banned the titles while working in their official capacities who, at social functions, invariably made a point of addressing ex-barons and ex-viscounts as "baron" and "viscount." A colonel's wife was invariably impressed when a real "baron" came to dinner.

has heard of democracy, and, in varying ways, been affected by it. It has come to some as a revelation of a world rich with promise. Others think of the word only as a synonym for change—or for the obvious physical evidences of the American occupation.

American democracy as such will never come to Japan. The growths of specific national institutions, although one may pretend they are of universal application, are too fragile to transplant. But American democracy has been the agent of a new freedom in Japanese life. The web has sagged and opened under its blows. It may some day harden in a different shape, as dangerous as the old one. It may give way to another system of government worse than the excesses of the web society. But, if this occurs, it will probably be the result of compelling factors from the outside—war or the threat of war.

The five gentlemen of Japan have representatively diverse ideas of what democracy has meant. Yamazaki sees it as the dawn of a new day, while Sanada worries about the bad effect on morals and respect for authority which democracy is having among Japanese youth. Hirohito's ideas on democracy are private ones; it would be pointless to try relating them piecemeal from odd public announcements or scraps of conversation. But the others' are worth recording.

Fumio Shimizu would be the last to say that Japan could learn nothing from foreign countries. He says now what he once told his navy technical colleagues: "There is nothing shameful or humbling in learning advanced techniques or catching up on them." But especially during the occupation period, he has shuddered to watch the wholesale gulping of American customs, largely among the young people. It is a trend which he thinks deplorable. In his view the constant surges towards Americanization, followed by sometimes violent reactions against it and back to old Japanese custom, have given current Japanese life the motions not of a *daruma* doll, but of a cranky pendulum.

Ideally, Shimizu would like to see American democracy

and the American way of life carefully studied and carefully adapted to fit a Japanese setting. He disdains the America of "Hollywood and jazz." This is not the democracy he wants for Japan. But he is intensely admiring of the America of "high technical standards, mass production and democratic procedures and practices." It is this America which he wants studied, the country of "rationalism and good working standards."

Shimizu would probably concede that it would take a supernatural engineer to lay out a blueprint in which democracy and good working standards remained and from which all hints of Hollywood and jazz had been inked out. But he has hit on the genuine problem of Japan's contact with the U.S. occupation. For lack of any standard to measure American culture, many Japanese have tended to accept it or reject it on a wholesale, indiscriminate basis, unable to distinguish between principles and personalities or things.

He is pleased, but frankly surprised that the occupation has gone so well; equally so, that steps towards democracy have been taken. But he is not optimistic about the final outcome. "It is impossible to change a character overnight," he protests, "it must be done gradually." At a crucial point in this gradual process, he finds that its weakest link are the schools. "Democracy," he says, "depends on education. But there are no teachers among the Japanese at present who really understand what true democracy is. How can they teach the young what they themselves are confused about?"

Sanada, for his part, has great trouble abstracting the idea of democracy from its visible works and effects. If democracy means more laws like the land reform, he is against it. If it means more help and kindness from the Americans, he is for it. He is on the whole pleased with the results of the occupation era. The freer political life in Japan is especially welcome to a man who has always enjoyed expressing his opinions loudly and with conviction.

His wife, Hie, even more than Sanada himself, is worried, like Shimizu, about the effect of democracy on the education system. In the old days, when Mitsu and her other children went to school, there was strict discipline. Today, she has heard that even the children of the most conservative families are hard to handle in school. "They don't obey," she murmurs. "Is this democracy?"

This is a real problem. It has decreased in seriousness since the first days of the occupation, when many a sin was committed in democracy's name. But, although Japanese schools are still, by American standards, very strictly run, the standards of discipline are still uncertain, uncertain in direct relation to the uncertainty of ethics among parents and teachers. Even at the Peers School in Tokyo, where Hirohito's son, Akihito got his secondary education, the atmosphere is far less controlled than it was before the war. The problem of where discipline stops and where democracy begins is nationwide and knows no barriers. Every Japanese has met it in one way or another, in politics, in the unions, and at home. The thin line that separates liberty from license is the most complicated lesson which they have struggled to learn.

Kisei has recognized a sharper change in his way of thinking than any of the others. He remembers the first occupation directives encouraging trade unionism and "freeing" labor as "a tremendous eye opener." Before this, he had accepted everything at its face value. "Now," he says with a pause, "I want to think about it. I want to draw my own conclusions, then impart them to others for further cogitation."

In some respects his view of democracy is not far from that of Sanada or Shimizu. As he explains, "The United States brought democracy in and dumped it on the Japanese. According to the Americans themselves, democracy is something which grows and must be built up by the people themselves. I think the idea should have been brought in more gradually. I hear that, in many schools, the teachers are unable to control their pupils because they fear to to be branded as undemocratic. That is foolish. Discipline is discipline. Authority is authority. As long as there is no abuse, then irresponsibility should be disciplined."

Like Shimizu, Kisei is worried about education, which he feels is the necessary premise of any democratic society. Although his own life in the web society has been an interlocking chain of group loyalties and responsibilities, he has sensed that this very collectiveness of the web society is its greatest defect. "Education of individual responsibility is vital," he says. "Without it, real democracy will not be realized here."

Left to himself, on a farm or in a small business, Kisei would probably now be voting for the Liberal party, with as foggy an idea of democracy as farmer Sanada. All he knows of democracy—and it is not inconsiderable—he absorbed from his work in the union, grappling with the concrete problems of one important segment of democratic society. If, by an odd turn of fate, new militarists, either Communist or Fascist, attempted to take over the country tomorrow, many Japanese, still confused, would acquiesce or temporize with them. But Kisei and many of his fellow-workers at Yahata would probably fight to keep their rights.

Yamazaki feels equally as strong about this idea of individual responsibility. He defines democracy as "freedom of the individual and respect for human rights." He thinks of American democracy as the "perfect example" of individualism, a fact which makes it an essential object of study. But he feels with the others that American democcracy in all its manifestations can no more succeed in Japan than American farming methods designed for the broad fields of Iowa can be profitably applied to the tiny checkerboards of farmland on the Kanto plain. "We couldn't very well start as the Americans did, when they founded their republic," he argues. "We're going to have to pattern our democracy by incorporating our experience, our history and the character and nature of our people. We simply can't cram democracy down everyone's throat and say 'This is democracy,' as it is possible to do with Communism."

* * * * *

Kisei and Yamazaki have bridged in their lives the gap between an old order and a new one. They are young and cautiously confident of the future. Each of them sees a frontier ahead. The three older men play their parts in the changes less energetically. They feel perhaps, that it is too late in life to look for a new tradition, while patiently unlearning the old. Two of them, Hirohito and Shimizu, are passing on their hopes to a second generation.

Akihito, the Crown Prince of Japan, is now nineteen, and in his first year at the Peers' University. His education has gone far beyond that of his father, in the direction of democracy and Westernization. At the express wish of Hirohito, the Imperial Household found him an excellent American tutor, Mrs. Elizabeth Gray Vining, a Philadelphia Quaker, who deeply influenced the Prince's ideas on the world and his position in it, before her departure from Japan in 1951. Where Hirohito was given a book of stern Confucian precepts by General Nogi, Mrs. Vining was prone to give Akihito works like Genevieve Foster's *George Washington's World*. What the ultimate effect of his mixed education will be, no one can safely predict. But it has imparted a rarely comprehensive education in democracy to the future high priest of Shinto.

Toyotaro Shimizu is making a success of himself in the engineering business. In 1952, he went to Nagoya to help supervise the construction of the new plant being built there by the Tomakomai Paper Company. He is pleased with his work and more optimistic than his father about the success of the changes in Japan. His father's ideas seem "old-fashioned" to him, although they are very good friends. In some respects, however, he is very like his father. In college he derided people who "meddled" in politics, as it seemed. Engineering students, he is proud to say, belong to a profession which is "conservative and dislikes radical change. It is solid, based on concrete facts, governed by steady laws."

There is a touch of the cloister about the way he says this, reminiscent of the elder Shimizu, a man of good head and good will, who quietly stuck to his assigned job, without interfering or caring about the death struggles of the weak Meiji democracy and the rise of the militarists in the thirties. It is to be hoped that Toyotaro will not end up as his father did, making 18-inch guns or rockets for some badly used battleships.

* * * * *

Sakaji Sanada has no hope at all. He has only, at last, the belated confirmation that his son Mitsu lived honorably before he died.

In the fall of 1949, the editor of the Tokyo *Asahi* received an odd letter. It was sent by Benigno del Rio, a Spanish Filipino businessman in Manila, in an effort to trace the whereabouts of a young Japanese sergeant named Mitsu Sanada, who had once befriended him. The letter was published in the newspaper; Sakaji Sanada saw it, and replied. The correspondence that followed told him much about Mitsu that he had believed, but not known.

In 1942, at the request of the Spanish Ambassador in Manila, the Japanese occupation forces arrested del Rio, a well-known shipping owner of loudly anti-Franco sympathies. He and his father were detained for two months. Their prison, Villamor Hall, was run by the Japanese gendarmerie, the *Kempeitai*, a part of the Japanese Army notorious for their cruelty and ruthless methods. Among the *Kempeitai* jailors, there was one exception to this rule, a quiet farm boy named Mitsu Sanada, who treated his prisoners kindly. He liked to visit and pass the time of day with them.

After the del Rios were released, Sanada became a frequent visitor to their Manila home, a comfortable mansion with a priceless 7,000-volume collection of Spanish classics in its library. Always without warning, while the neighbors, expecting a *Kempeitai* raid, waited in terror, the tall, grinning Japanese with the three sergeant's pips on his uniform would lumber up to del Rio's porch to spend a quiet afternoon or evening. Del Rio taught him to play chess, a game that Sanada grew very fond of. As they played, far into the hot Manila afternoon, Sanada often talked softly about his father's cool farm near Mt. Fuji. Occasionally they discussed politics. Del Rio assured him flatly that Japan would lose the war. Sanada would only smile and reply that the Japanese Army could never be beaten.

Mitsu brought food and other gifts to the del Rios and their friends. When he returned from a trip to Taiwan, he presented his host with a pair of Japanese wooden clogs. The del Rios were nervous about having a Japanese visit them, but Sanada never tired of coming. Occasionally he brought a few friends, who also wanted del Rio to teach them chess.

At two A.M. on December 23, 1944, del Rio was arrested and taken to Fort Santiago, one of 300 Filipinos who were killed, tortured or beaten in an orgy of reprisals conducted by the *Kempeitai*, a forerunner of the brutal Japanese sack and pillage of Manila. Eight hours later Mitsu came to the house for a farewell visit, before heading north with the Army. When Señora del Rio told him that her husband had been taken away, the kindly sergeant was shocked. He bowed nervously, stammered his regrets and went away.

Del Rio survived, although he had been badly tortured. Months later, while he was recovering from his injuries, some of his friends from Baguio, the cool mountain city in the north, made their way back to Manila. American troops had entered the city on February 5th, but Baguio was still then in the hands of the Japanese, who were drawing their armies northward.

The Baguio people had seen Sanada, shortly after he left Manila. He had been reassigned to combat duty. When he heard that they were hungry, he had nodded sympathetically and gone away. A day later he returned in a truck with some sacks of flour and rice, and several large slabs of caribao meat.

Late that spring, he visited them again, and left a chest of his belongings with them. He asked that they send it to his family in Japan, if he were killed. Shortly afterwards their house, with all the contents, was bombed and destroyed. They never heard of Sanada again.

Del Rio never forgot the kindness of his one Japanese friend, for all his own bitterness towards the Japanese. In 1949, noticing an article about the newspaper *Asahi* in *Time* magazine, he wrote to the editor, telling Sanada's story. When he heard from Sakaji Sanada, Makoto Takano, the editor of *Asahi*, promptly wrote del Rio, informing him that his friend had been killed.

Del Rio replied promptly. He sent five dollars to Mitsu's family, to buy some flowers, for All Souls' Day, to put on the kindly sergeant's tombstone. "This happens always," he wrote, in English, "good people die and the meanest are alive. He hated war . . . Good Sanada! Gentleman Sanada! It was a pity that Japan did not have one hundred thousand Sanadas during the war. Probably we the Filipinos had not then hated the Japanese and they have not looted, pillaged, murdered and destroyed the Philippines. Probably Japan have not been defeated. . . . Yes, I will always remember El Caballero Sanada, the Jap."

Sakaji Sanada sent del Rio a letter thanking him for the remembrance. "My heart was filled with gratitude," he wrote, "at your kind and sympathetic words. . . . I shall plant a cherry tree in front of Mitsu's tomb as a remembrance of your good will, which has nothing to do with national borderlines."

On his next visit to Tokyo, Sakaji Sanada stopped in at the Dai Ichi Bank, to convert Benigno del Rio's pesos into yen. It took him almost an hour to fill out all the complicated forms required. When he came back to Shimoyoshida, he did his best to honor del Rio's request. The autumn frosts, however, prevented him from planting the tree immediately. Even in the spring he had difficulty, for the soil around Fukugenji Temple is hard lava rock, where plants do not easily grow. After much effort, Sanada managed to transplant three mountain cherry trees, one in back of the vault that contains a memorial to Mitsu, and two in front.

The cherry trees somehow found roots in the unfriendly earth and Sanada thinks that they will not die. He tends them carefully on his visits to the temple. They are all that is left of the Japanese caballero Mitsu Sanada, one of the few products of the old web society who made morality more than a family contract and carried his trust and *shinyo* with him in his dealings with all men. The new Japan will miss him.

12

THE PROSPECT OF JAPAN

"Alas, in what a world do I find myself. War here—war there—no man's life secure—no man's property worthy of being called his own. . . ."

The priest Shosei (A.D. 1469)*

In the fading evening hours of September 15, 1950, two commanders of small units stood on the bridge of an LST which lay beached, bows open and ramp down, on the sandy northern slope of Wolmi Island, across from the port of Inchon, Korea. Captain C. B. McKinstrey of the United States Marine Corps and Captain Matao Konishi, of the Japanese Merchant Marine, had hardly expected to enjoy the pleasure of cooperation so soon. Captain McKinstrey had been captured by the Japanese after the siege of Wake Island; he had spent 44 months during World War II in Japanese prison camps. Captain Konishi, after skippering several ships under Japanese Navy charter during the war, had had *Amaho Maru*, his last, torpedoed from under him by an American submarine off Hokkaido on April 17, 1945.

Captain Konishi and his crew of 50 Japanese merchant seamen had finished a trip in convoy with the U.S. Navy

* Shosei, who later left his monastery and took the name of Nakamura Yasuke, was the great-grandfather of Toyotomi Hideyoshi, the regent who unified Japan in the sixteenth century.

task force of warships and transports that supported the invasion of Inchon. Just a few hours after the infantrymen of the 5th Marines had secured Wolmi Island, his LST was unloading the guns and heavy gear of Captain McKinstrey's unit, a part of the 12th Marine Regiment, the artillery arm of the First Marine Division. Some of the guns, landed from other LSTs were already in position, about to finish the ruin of smoke and fire that covered the city, now half captured, after 18 hours of gun fire and rocket bombardment.

Captain McKinstrey and Captain Konishi got along very well together. Konishi repeatedly apologized for his frayed dark-blue uniform—all his others had been torpedoed during the last war. McKinstrey was remarkably philosophical about some unpleasant experiences he had had as a Japanese prisoner. The two men were not formal allies. Captain Konishi's ship was unarmed and his men had no direct connection with the United Nations war effort in Korea. They worked their ship on a contract with the U.S. Government. They were in no way impressed into their jobs, just volunteers who liked the sea, excitement and the offer of extra pay and bonuses. But their presence at Inchon, and the presence of other crews like them, showed in the extreme how far Japan had been committed internationally, a full year before the peace treaty and the establishment of an independent Japanese government.

Japan helped loyally and to great effect in the prosecution of the Korean war. Japan was the original tactical base for the military effort. After the Korean front was stabilized, Japan remained the strategic base for this effort. Its factories produced supplies for the U.N. forces, which ranged in worth from valuable to essential. Its people demonstrated a sincere support of the U.N. troops— as good a proof of this as any was the long lines of Japanese donors waiting to give blood at the blood banks for the troops, established throughout the country. At one point in the Korean fighting, every major American tactical unit had left Japan for Korea—the occupation forces left in Japan could not have mustered a regiment. Yet there was no disturbance among the Japanese, nor any attempts at sabotage either at U.N. bases or in the factories which produced for U.N. war effort.

The popular support of the Korean war was, at its particular point in time, the sign of Japan's alignment with the United States and with its allies in the struggle against Communism. This alignment was sealed and formalized at San Francisco in September, 1951, when Premier Shigeru Yoshida told the treaty conference:

"Unfortunately, the sinister forces of totalitarian oppression and tyranny operate still throughout the globe. These forces are sweeping over half the Asiatic continent, sowing seeds of dissension, spreading unrest and confusion and breaking out into open aggression here and there—indeed, at the very door of Japan. Being unarmed as we are, we must, in order to ward off the danger of war, seek help from a country that can and will help us. That is why we shall conclude a security pact with the United States, under which American troops will be retained in Japan temporarily until the danger is past, or international peace and security will have been assured under the United Nations auspices, or a collective security agreement be made.

"Japan was exposed once to the menace of Tsarist imperialism from the north. Today it is the Communist menace that threatens her from the same direction . . . It is imperative for the sake of our very existence that we take adequate security measures . . ."

Shortly after the treaty the security pact with the United States was signed. The Advancing Garrison Army vacated its headquarters in downtown Tokyo and moved to the less conspicuous site of the old Japanese War Ministry on Kudan hill, with many of its headquarters units vacating the city entirely; but its presence remained a deciding factor in Japanese policy. It was now the army of a powerful ally, in Japan for the same reasons and on much the same terms as the American bomber bases in eastern England and the U.S. naval headquarters at Grosvenor Square in London. American officers were busy training the National Police Reserve, the security force which is the nucleus of a Japanese army. American money continued to make up the deficits (happily decreasing) in Japan's international balance of payments. On its face the new alliance was far more binding than either the long-standing Anglo-Japanese alliance of the early twentieth century, or the hedging Japanese involvement in the Axis Tripartite Pact of 1940—more binding, in fact, than any alliance in Japanese history.

The pact was sincere, but its support was conditional. With the fuzziness common to most efforts at international communication, both the Japanese people and the American people, as the parties of the second part most directly concerned, had some misconceptions about its nature and extent. American support did not mean, as some Americans hoped, that, overnight, a Japanese army, miraculously dedicated to democracy instead of to the Greater East Asia Co-Prosperity Sphere, would appear to right the balance of power in Asia and reconquer Manchuria on behalf of the United Nations. Japanese support did not mean, as many Japanese hoped, a token commitment, capable of being abandoned as an expensive luxury, if necessity or opportunity dictated a deal of some sort with Japan's Communist neighbors. It is the purpose of this chapter to look at the gentlemen of Japan in the light of their international position: how far do their wishes and intentions correspond to the facts of politics and economies.

* * * * *

The bulk of the Japanese people, to begin with, have manifested a friendliness towards the United States which is, barring the case of the Philippines, without parallel in Asia. This is not to say that they are, simply, "pro-American"; unfortunately foreigners never seem able to love Americans the way Americans feel they should be loved. It is not to minimize the petulant reaction (already noted) after six years of docile submission to an American occupation. It is not to minimize the ill-feeling caused by the minority of G.I.s in Japan who have not behaved well. As Sakaji Sanada has said, "Occasionally there are bad ones. And it is the bad ones which always leave a bitter, lingering taste." It is not to minimize the perverse but natural human resentment of the poor recipient towards the rich donor, generally expressed, as it is in Europe, by oblique attacks on American culture, or the lack thereof. Since the occupation's controls on the press were lifted, Japanese highbrow periodicals like *Bungei Shinju* can publish learned articles berating Americans as "obtuse and materialistic," taking a leaf from the tattered book of European periodicals like the British *New Statesman and Nation*.

But these are relative pin pricks. Despite them—and the occasional outbreak of well-planned but highly localized Communist demonstrations (Japanese Communists are not nearly strong enough to organize opposition on a national scale), the Japanese have remained well disposed towards the United States. The five gentlemen of Japan display various degrees of friendliness, but it is in all cases friendliness—and this extends on a broad level throughout Japan's population. America has convinced the Japanese of its good intentions by the force of example.

Hideya Kisei has the most reservations about the United States. Suspicious of any capitalist economy, he by no means wishes to appear a wholehearted, uncritical friend of the Americans. But he has already expressed his thanks for the lessons learned from them. "And at least," he concedes, "the Americans have paralleled their words with deeds, while the Russians have advanced only words." Scraped to the bottom, this is the margin of the pro-American feeling in Japan. It is a considerable one.

Only Sakaji Sanada has a complete, uncritical acceptance of American help and a dependence on American policy. He hopes that the Americans will stay in Japan long after 1953. "There is nothing to do but rely on *America san*," he has said. "My life is in *America san's* hands and I am satisfied as long as *America san* remains." He relies on the United States, in a very personal sense, to protect him from the eventuality of World War III; he is prepared to accept whatever responsibilities this reliance involves.

This feeling does not hold with the others, nor, probably, with the majority of Japan's people. There is pride and relief that Japan is now an independent nation, that Japan, after a period of relative isolation, has for the second time in history made its appearance as a sovereign participant in international politics. "Japan is an independent nation," Hideya Kisei says. "She must now get along under her own power, without interference by outside nations. It is said that the United States is fighting Communism throughout the world. I feel strongly that Japan should not follow the lead of the United States in this blindly. The Japanese should think carefully to decide whether this is for the good of the people. If so, good. If not, we should decline."

In the same breath, however, Kisei admits that present circumstances have forced Japan into line with U.S. policy. While he feels that the United States has a great responsibility for the future of Japan, he agrees, that, since the Americans are offering to protect Japan, "the Japanese people have a great responsibility in their relations towards the United States." To state an absolute ideal of independence, with complete freedom of choice on the one hand, then admit being bound, in a sense, to American policy, on the other, may seem like a strange kind of double talk. It is, however, part of the distinction which the Japanese have always been quick to make between ideals and actualities.

Making their second debut in world politics, the Japanese sensibly are acting with the caution of a man walking a delicate tightrope. There is no net beneath them, if they fall. Though distance gives Americans the luxury of making mistakes in Asia and living to tell the tale, there is no such cheer for Japan: one misstep and out. This narrowness of their survival margin has made the Japanese hold many second thoughts about tying themselves to American foreign policy.

On an operational level, the Japanese have noticed and noted the wavering course of United States relations with Asia, at least before the commitment was made in Korea. Like Europeans in the NATO countries, the Japanese criticize the fits and starts of Washington's diplomatic machine with increasing concern as these movements increasingly affect their own ultimate security. They do not criticize blindly, although their knowledge of life in America has its appalling gaps. They are served by a press and radio network which blankets the country and which avails itself of the reports of American press services, as well as the correspondence of its own reporters overseas. Here again, the Japanese present the aspect of a relatively sophisticated public. If a congressman in Washington introduces an immigration bill with restrictions aimed at the Japanese, he need not think that the news of his activities is a purely domestic matter. Tadao Yamazaki, at the *Asahi* news desk in Tokyo, will be receiving a cabled report of the bill a few hours after it is introduced. He and the other men at *Asahi* will edit, editorialize and condense. The next day Sanada's neighbors in Shimoyoshida will be reading all about it. (Sanada, who does not take *Asahi*, will read all about it in the rival *Yomiuri*.)

It is not surprising, then, that Hideya Kisei is well aware that the United States has expended its major postwar effort in Europe. He does not derive comfort from the fact that he has evidently been considered less protectible and, by implication, more expendable, than workers at Essen or Le Creusot. He has reacted sharply: "I think that the United States must expend as much effort in Asia as it has in Europe. Asia is now perfectly ripe for Communism. If America does not act fast and wisely, she will lose out."

Fumio Shimizu has had for a long time a more detailed criticism to make. He now feels free to give it: "American policy in the Far East is still vague. I get the impression that U.S. policy is based on food. 'Go along with us and you eat; go along with Russia and you don't eat' might be a good way to express it. This may sound a bit extreme, but, when boiled down to essentials, food is the basic consideration.

"At the risk of being thought ungrateful, I say that up to a certain point, this policy is excellent. But sooner or later a stage is reached where food is not enough. Japan, I feel, has reached this stage. Unlike an animal who is satisfied with a full belly, man must have other nourishment. I think that this point should be considered more seriously—otherwise the goodwill built up in Japan and elsewhere through the magnanimous acts of the Americans will all turn sour."

The Japanese by no means see eye to eye with the United States on the subject of China, India and Southeast Asia. The revolution which animates Asia in 1952 was, after all, started by the Japanese ten years before. It was the Japanese who discovered the magic slogan "Asia for the Asiatics," swept down with it through Indo-China, Malaya, Indonesia and rolled their tide to the borders of India. Though the Japanese mismanaged the colonial territories which they "liberated" far more grossly than had the former proprietors, they shattered for all time the notion that the white man of the West was invincible in the East. Something in the chemistry of Asia changed on the day Malays, Indians and Burmese watched dumpy Japanese guards herding their former *Herrenvolk* into prison camps.

The Japanese are essentially sympathetic to any fight of Asians to gain their liberty from the West. They have a horror of being maneuvered into any position where they stand before the bar of Asia, accused as the hireling and accomplice of something called "the West." Everything in the Japanese heritage makes them sympathetic towards the efforts of Indo-Chinese to liberate themselves from Frenchmen or Malays to liberate themselves from the British, quite before they have even begun to consider the overlay of political complexities involved. To overstate the case a bit, Japan was the Tom Paine of the revolution in Asia; however much the home kingdom may have changed in the meantime, there is a reluctance to come out in the open as the converted accomplice of Lord North or George III.

Thus, Yamazaki, when he thinks of Asia, thinks of a liberation movement first and a mosaic of Communist and anti-Communist only incidentally. He expresses it well, although some of his observations on the Communist situation are certainly questionable:

"I am sure that anyone will agree that Asia is rapidly becoming a free world. There are many troubled spots in Asia, but the forces there are fighting for freedom. These efforts for freedom are being assisted by socialism, western democracy, and, of course [sic], Communism. A great deal of it is an ardent desire to be free at any cost. And until freedom comes, the Asiatics will side with those forces which are their allies. In many instances the Asiatic peoples want to solve their own problems by themselves. The best and outstanding example is Iran.

"As for Communism in the Far East, we must admit that it is now a deadly powerful thing which is being used to advantage in all backward countries, trying to liberate themselves from foreign colonization and the supremacy of the white man. The best example of this is Red China, where, whether we like it or not, the country is unified as it never was before, where land reform has been effected [sic] and thus far proved successful, where a rotten, corrupt government has been abolished.

"India is another example, although Communism is not the major factor responsible for India's independence. The intelligence and efforts of Mahatma Gandhi and Pandit Nehru are the nucleus of India's advance in a troubled world. Today, India is the guiding light for Asia. Right or wrong, India is trying to bring about world peace."

The Korean war disabused many Japanese of an early optimism about Communist China. But, like Yamazaki, they are not wholly prepared to write China off as an implacable enemy, to be placed under quarantine. They recognize a danger there, but one cannot help suspecting that the Japanese, as "old China hands," feel themselves capable of dealing with Red China to their own advantage, where the Western nations have failed. They may be proved right. Or they may sharply discover that the new Communist China represents a quality rudely outside of their old experience.*

* * * * *

The attitude of the Japanese towards Russian Communism has none of the wishful thinking noticeable in their references towards Mao Tse Tung. Here, in the tactical warfare of politics, they have come closest to the attitude of the United States. The ties between Japanese Communists and the Russian Communists have been publicized. Every Japanese newspaper reader is familar, also, with the Russian conquest of Eastern Europe, the Berlin blockade and Russian obstructionism in the United Nations. There is continuing resentment in Japan about some 300,000 Japanese from Manchuria, Sakhalin and the Kuriles who are either dead or still held prisoner by the Russians. Aside from a few trade overtures and the conciliatory tone of Stalin's New Year's Message of 1952 to the Japanese

---

* Although the Japanese have made a treaty of sorts with Nationalist China, most of them have a low opinion of Chiang Kai Shek's capacity, and of the degree of popular support he is capable of mustering. They have followed the lead of the United States in dealing with the Formosa regime as an equal. Japanese governments will continue to do so, only insofar as it is to their advantage.

people, the Russians have done nothing concrete to dispel the distrust and hatred felt for them by the Japanese. The Japanese have been traditional territorial enemies of the Russians for over a century; since 1945 the reservoir of their old enmity has been lavishly fed by the Russians themselves.

Sanada has the same horror of the Russians that he has of native Japanese Communists—nothing that *America san* could say or do to the Russians would be too severe. Fumio Shimizu soberly assessed the extent of the Russian menace—and arrived at the same conclusions about it as Dean Acheson or Douglas MacArthur. He is only surprised that the Soviets' saber-rattling has not led to war already. "The only thing I can say," he adds, "is that, if Japan were in America's place, war would already be raging. The Japanese are short-tempered and rash. I heartily support the American policy of armed preparedness. Without this, I feel that Communism would gradually swallow up the world bit by bit."

What Kisei and Yamazaki have to say about the Russian Communists is said more sadly and wistfully. They have carried their disillusionment with Japan's domestic Communists, however, into the field of international politics. Kisei, for example, was not impressed by the soft words of Stalin's New Year's message to Japan, in 1952. "The only impression I got," he remarked, "was that the Soviets, through Stalin, were trying to butter up the Japanese, so that they would side with them in the struggle against the United States. It might be different, if there had been some Russian action before this time. So far we have had only words—no facts or deeds. I see nothing good in the message."

With an oddly practical naïvete, he has continued his evaluation of Communism by what it produces. "I have no quarrel," he repeats, "with the Communist idea. It is the methods that I object to. The professed objective is to build up a workers' paradise. From what I have heard, Russia is certainly no workers' paradise."

Yamazaki has studied the U.S.S.R. as best he could, and found it wanting. "The foreign policy of the Soviets today smacks of Machiavellianism," is his conclusion, "It is far from Lenin's ideology on foreign relations. As contemporary history shows, the Soviets, to further their own interests, shrewdly concluded a military alliance with Nazi Germany during the early part of World War II, then, a bit later, the neutrality pact with Japan. When both alliances became detrimental to Russian interests, they were broken.

"The Soviet attempt to Communize the world is another example of Machiavellianism. And it looks as if the Russians won't stop at anything to realize their ambition. This Machiavellian Communism is a far cry from the Communism laid down by Karl Marx."

Like all good liberals, however, Yamazaki is anxious to stress that he "loves and respects" the Russian people, whom he expects to solve their own problems. "They must make every endeavor to break away from this Machiavellianism, indeed from Leninism and Stalinism," he declares, "If they don't, they are heading for their own destruction."

* * * * *

The mention of the word "destruction" and the hints, never far below the surface in Japan, of the possibility of a third world war, bring the Japanese face to face with the strategic dilemma in which they find themselves. This goes far deeper than the "tactical" questions of whether or to what extent they approve of American foreign policy in the Orient. The strategic alternatives are set clearly: either hold to the ideal of perfect neutrality which General MacArthur outlined for Japan at the start of his stewardship and insist that this utter unarmed neutrality be maintained; or face the fact of changing world conditions and rearm—at the very least, participate in a collective security scheme involving limited Japanese rearmament, against an obvious threat of attack. The first course invites ultimate Communist conquest. The second courts war. Although Japan has moved far in the direction of the second alternative, the issue remains a topic of great debate.

The horror of the Japanese at the prospect of a third world war cannot be overstated. The atom bombs left deep scars. It was not a Chamber of Commerce gesture, when the people of Hiroshima staged celebrations of their new Peace City. The wreck of the World War II bombings is still evident in many parts of Japan. The memory of Japan's slow strangulation by blockade and the annihilation of thousands of soldiers in unavailing "banzai" charges on Pacific islands has not left the Japanese.

It is by all accounts a tragedy that Japan should be considering the extent of its rearmament so soon after it was dedicated, as a reformed international law-breaker, to a policy of unending peace. It is in fact the exteme dramatization of the changes in the world since the spent goodfellowship of the victorious Allies in 1945. The Japanese recognize this very well. The gentlemen of Japan, with their countrymen, are aware of the dangers in rearmament, not only of the provocation it might give on the outside, but of the unhappy heritage of Japanese militarism, which it might confirm again. The very mention of the word is political dynamite. Japanese politicians, conspicuously the Socialists and other opposition parties in the current political spectrum, are against rearmament as a matter of principle. They deplore it in the automatic way that they deplore corruption and high taxes. It is also a fashionable target for the wrath of intellectuals. It is not a pleasant topic of conversation.

Yamazaki, Sanada and Kisei think similarly on the rearmament question. They discuss it with some reluctance, because on the whole they have a good appreciation of all that rearmament means. It signifies the end of the brave, postwar dreams of a Switzerland of the Pacific, the end of the insulation provided by the American occupation against the cross draughts of world politics. It is the beginning of Japan's recommitment to the world of power politics, a commitment which cannot be revoked. After years of reading about the Cold War, then the Korean War in their daily newspapers, the Japanese have understood that they must, inevitably, make a commitment of this sort, given the prevailing state of the world. Until 1952, they were able to harbor this understanding without totally giving up their illusions about perpetual peace. The naked collision between ideals and reality is a painful one, even for the Japanese to concede.

Yamazaki has given long periods of soul-searching to this subject. His ideals have not changed. As stated, they are uncompromising: "I think politicians the world over today are overstressing rearmament to combat Communism . . . Japan, instead of talking rearmament, should be trying to get the world to disarm. If we have abandoned war, then, to keep in harmony, we must not advocate rearmament. To do so would cast suspicion and distrust upon us. If we rearm, so will others.

"I am absolutely opposed to rearmament. I don't think it is possible for the world to talk peace and rearm. It is like waving a flag of peace in one hand, while the other hand, holding a pistol, is hidden behind your back. The rearmament race between the Soviets and the Western democracies is the prelude to war. . . ."

After these uncompromising words, Yamazaki then makes his hesitant bow to realities. "In actuality," he said, "if we must rearm, then we must think twice—to decide whether it will be in the interests of peace, whether it will be in the interests of Japan and of the rest of the world."

Kisei owns himself puzzled about the rearmament question. "Basically," as he explains, "I'm against it. It is unproductive. But, under the circumstances of today, there seems no getting out of this. What I am afraid of is that these conditions will lead Japan back to its former path of armed aggression. There is always the danger of becoming involved in war because we are armed. On the other hand, we cannot remain naked in the present situation. I admit I am bewildered and sad about this entire question."

Sanada is in favor of rearming for the same realistic reasons; he is similarly cautious about the consequences. He wants to rearm only to the point where Japan can defend itself—absolutely no further. "We need so much rain for our rice paddies," he explains, "to do the rice some good. The same goes for armaments. We've got to be careful and see that we don't get too much—otherwise it will be like getting too much rain. You know what happens when you get too much rain. It begins to flood your paddies and overflow into others. . . ."

None of these men, in the European or the Indian sense, could be called a political "neutralist." If a label could be attached to their common attitude, they might best be called "reluctant realists." The index of their realism rose sharply in the years 1951 and 1952. In April, 1951, Kisei was adamantly opposed to any form of rearmament, without conditions. So was Yamazaki. It was his view that, in the event of a war, Japan should at all costs remain neutral and, perhaps, "mediate" the differences between the Communists and the Western democracies.

They have not totally abandoned these hopes. The thought of Japan profitably arbitrating a shooting war between the Russians, Chinese and Americans has made a particularly attractive daydream for many Japanese statesmen. But, in the face of facts, most Japanese, like Kisei and Yamazaki, have compromised with their ideals or speculations. Involvement in a war is not a happy prospect. But they have recognized that it is a possibility.

They have turned to meet this possibility with the same practical soberness with which they met the impact of World War II and the greater shock of the defeat. A National Police Reserve of 75,000 men was established in 1950 and trained by American army officers. Many former Japanese officers and enlisted veterans quickly enlisted in it. The original quota for recruits was greatly oversubscribed. This force has been increased, and there is acceptance of the fact that it is the beginnings of another Japanese army. In August, 1952, Prime Minister Yoshida called it just that.

It is not startling that ex-Admiral Shimizu has done more concrete thinking about the problem of a Japanese security force than any of the others. He was quicker than the others to realize that "world circumstances dictate that Japan be prepared to defend herself." Convinced that this premise is sound, he has worried more about the technics of the defense than the question of its advisability.

Shimizu shakes his head at the lack of any "patriotism" in modern Japan. "I see nothing wrong," he argues with liberals of his son's generation, "in being patriotic to one's country. As a result of their defeat, the Japanese seem to have picked up the mistaken idea that militarism and patriotism are synonymous. The pressing need today is to find some central theme to revive a strong and healthy patriotism. Soldiering is a profession, like any other. But, unlike others, good soldiering does not come from money considerations, or profit or personal gain. It comes from pride in one's country and a strong cause.

"In the past Japanese soldiers fought and died gladly for their emperor and their country. In postwar Japan, what would a soldier die for? There is nothing." This may be overstating the case, but Shimizu has certainly hit at a weak point in the polity of the new Japan. Active patriotism needs some definite directions to follow. In a country just restored to sovereignty, such directions are slow in coming.

If a focus for morals can be determined, Shimizu has more specific suggestions about a new army. He is actively dedicated to a policy of using the knowledge and experience of the old military men in this connection. With his engineer's eye view of human relations, he believes that the survivors of the old military caste can be used in an advisory capacity, while denied a chance to participate "actively" in the direction and control of any new fighting force. "Intrigues and behind-the-scenes activities" of the old military men should be suppressed.

He is hopeful that a new Japanese army, if one appears, will be organized "after the American system," with civilians having the ultimate control. He likes to recall that the military were in fact subordinate to the civilian arm of the government in Japan at least until the close of the Russo-Japanese War. "In the future," he adds, "I feel that Japan will again have this sort of armed force, with civilians deciding its policy and its movements."

Shimizu is cautious, as are the others, about the possibility of a Japanese army playing Frankenstein for a second time to its embarrassed civilian creators. He thinks the lessons of the last war will act as a check on Japanese militarism for the next 20 years. "After that," he observes, "the future depends on the education Japan has got in the meantime. It is here that the aid of the United States is essential. Otherwise, I fear that existing conditions—that is to say, small space and an ever growing population—will again force Japan into the wrong path of either aggression or of Communism."

The problems posed for Japan by "existing conditions" in the Far East have transcended the dilemma of small space and ever growing population. The most obvious is the factor which makes some kind of Japanese rearmament necessary: in a strategic sense, Japan, as the announced ally of the United States, is already under attack by the very fact of Chinese and Russian Communist armies beyond her sea borders. Of themselves, the Japanese are defenseless as they have never been before. They are vulnerable to air attack. They have no air force or navy to resist the progress of an enemy invasion. They have scarcely any armed forces to hold off invading troops, if they should land.

This is peculiar weakness where there was once peculiar strength. The Japanese historically represent a military phenomenon: the combination of a sea and a land power. In the original days of their isolation the Japanese were land-fighting soldiers. A populous country produced large and efficient armies. The force of 195,000 well-disciplined troops which Hideyoshi sent to invade Korea, was far beyond the size of any army which a European country could put into the field.* His invasions of Korea, although checked by Chinese intervention on land, failed primarily because the Korean navy interfered with his sea lines of communication. The defeat of Hideyoshi's ships at the hands of Admiral Yi Sun Sin must have made an impression on the Japanese. The next time they came out of isolation, they relied on a strong navy themselves.

From the Sino-Japanese War of 1895 to the beginning of World War II, Japan was a sea power and a land power as well. The exposed position of the islands made sea power necessary; and a large population enabled the Japanese to combine the classic functions of the great land power and the great sea power which Germany and Britain had divided in European politics.

Air power made life uncomfortable for island sea powers. The Japan of 1953 shares the disability of the England of 1953. It is, outside of Britain, potentially the world's juiciest concentrated target. The thought of waves of Soviet bombers droning over the rising blast furnaces of Yahata and the reconstructed wood and paper residences of Tokyo is enough to make any Japanese fiercely neutralist. If looked at long enough from one side, the bombers and the huge armies of the Communist powers on the mainland, by their very existence, make any Japanese commitment to the United States a prelude to suicide.

But there are cards on the other side of the table. The Japanese Communist may argue that his country is militarily forced to come to terms with the Communists in any crisis between the Soviet Union and the United States. All five gentlemen of Japan, however, have poignant

---

* Compare the 54,000 troops, both ashore and aboard ships, which had been collected by the greatest military power in Europe, for the subjection of England, at the time of the Spanish Armada, a contemporary invasion effort.

memories of the last time that Japan challenged the power of the United States in armor. Soviet air power may be great, but the Japanese have positive evidence only of the destructiveness of American air power—which is enough to last them for many lifetimes. The Japanese are very conscious of the fact that they were beaten, not by the Soviets, but by the United States. And in six years of intimate contact with Americans, they have realistically measured the efficiency and the industrial output which can drive the American military machine. Most Japanese now share Admiral Shimizu's realization that Japan is hopelessly vulnerable to a superior sea power. Life behind a sea blockade is not pleasant. It is no great consolation to be allied to the world's greatest land power, if the world's greatest sea power can keep iron ore away from the foundries and rice away from the homes.

The presence of American military bases in Japan has provided a practical insurance against actual invasion by the Communists on the Asiatic mainland, if such a step were ever contemplated. It is not a satisfactory assurance, because the very fact of foreign troops assuming the sole responsibility for defending Japanese soil is a source of irritation to many Japanese, constant fodder for the people who are anxious to make capital out of spurious charges of "Western imperialism." It is hardly a perfect scheme of things for the Americans, who are forced to take on the burdens of a grave and demanding military commitment.

If the Japanese gradually assume some of the burdens of their own defense, the token army represented by the National Police Reserve is hardly more than a beginning. At the best, if increased and improved in quality, it can preserve Japan from internal troubles agitated by the Communists and, stretching things a bit, deal with any sneak raid on Japan from the north until sufficient American force can be brought to bear against it.

Carrying the argument further, even a large army in Japan can do nothing but offer a target for Communist propaganda from the mainland—and it can be conceded that the Chinese Communists have a historically honest suspicion of Japan's aggressive instincts. A Japanese army in Japan can do no more than hinder or check an invading army—a far different thing from hindering an attacking enemy. For if ever actual land warfare comes to the Japanese islands, Japan is already beaten. The Japanese islanders live or die by the control of the sea and the air. An army is necessary for Japanese attack, but the basis of Japanese defense rests on a navy and an air force.

It is hardly the purpose of this book to argue for the immediate establishment of a strong Japanese navy and air force. But, logically, if Japan is ever to rearm, a navy and an air force should be the first concern. In 1953, the American Navy and the American Air Force are the ultimate guarantors of Japan's safety. The Japanese, however, have never felt secure while riding on someone else's coattails—which is exactly what that situation means. If they ever begin to approach military self-support, it will be first in their basic role of a sea and an air power, a power which possesses, at the least, enough fast surface craft to keep its sea lanes relatively clear of enemy submarines and enough fighters to provide an interceptor network around the four vulnerable islands. It was these two deficiencies which insured the defeat of Japan in World War II.

* * * * *

The discussion of Japanese rearmament is pure fancy if it is not based on the more fundamental question: how shall Japan live? The Japanese are right in complaining that their present trade balances, barely breaking even despite the windfall of Korean war industries, cannot begin to support a rearmament effort. In the last analysis, how much Japan rearms and for what and for whom Japan rearms will depend on the success of Japan's trading. The old financial fetters of trade are operating most vengefully on the great trading nations. They are complicated by dangerous political balances and the appearance of a centralized economic effort, directed from Moscow, which added to the retaliatory gestures by the United States, has made a mockery of free trading in much of the world. As an independent nation, Japan has had many of the restrictions on its trading removed. The United States can be counted on, it is hoped, to help in dissolving more of them. With all these new complications, however, the one great industrial producer of Asia now will essentially have her future determined by the prices of products, the speed with which they can reach their markets and the shrewdness of the man with the tattered sample case who again must make his rounds about the world, trying to find the markets in the first place.

The 9,500,000 industrial workers of Japan make their country totally different in its outlook, its aspirations and its usefulness from all the other nations of Asia. Notwithstanding the sizable industry in India and the skilled precision workers that can be found in Malaya or Pakistan, the great problem of Asiatic nations, shared by all except Japan, is to get wealth out of the ground, teach their peoples to utilize it, and so distribute new riches among unskilled and poverty-stricken populations. Japan does not have this problem. Japan's predicament is the predicament of Western Europe—in particular, of Britain and Germany. Like that of Western Europe, the Japanese problem can be illustrated by a circle: how to produce enough to pay for enough raw materials without which it is impossible to produce. As with Western Europe, there is another circle. This involves the existence of a standard of living far higher than that enjoyed by non-manufacturing countries, which must be maintained as high as possible (largely by trading with non-manufacturing countries) to guard against the vulnerability of well-fed and relatively sophisticated populations to revolutionary propaganda, if the standard of living drops.

The old trade pattern of Asia has shifted. There was a day when the Japanese, for example, could export great quantities of basic textile goods to India. Now India's own textile industry, which has grown fast, is a rising competitor of Japan's for the trade of less developed areas. Japan, in great measure, must set its sights at a higher level to provide a good share of India's imports, in the direction of looms for Indian textile factories, consumer goods for Indian workers. The old trading pattern was the simple one of finished-goods producers selling and buying with producers of raw materials. Now the younger nations of Asia are desperately trying to build finished-goods industries of their own. As this new competition reaches the level of primary industries, like textile production, the Japanese must lean more heavily on more advanced levels: heavy machinery, precision instruments, machine tools. The spiral of competition runs upwards.

Japan has responded well to the shift in trade patterns. Heavy industry is making a desperate effort to produce bulk goods like generators and turbines at competitive prices. The precision industry has already had considerable competitive success. Since the war, to cite one instance, the Japanese have been turning out a 35 millimeter camera with a lens which is at least the equal of the classic German models—at far below the German price. Goods like this have slowly been finding a new market in the United States, where the old attitude towards Japanese machine products was, to say the least, deprecating. But all Japanese industry is handicapped by old plants, equipment that has been used beyond the point of economic return, and the long lack of contact with technical advances elsewhere in the world between 1937 and 1945—or, more accurately, 1948. There is also a vast difficulty in getting raw materials readily and cheaply enough to produce.

The problem of where to trade and how to trade is, in Japan's case, more fundamental than the question of what to trade. Before World War II Japanese industry fattened on its trade with the hinterland of China and Korea and the areas adjacent to them. Trade with Southeast Asia was sizable. There was a considerable traffic, mainly in silk and luxury goods, with the United States and Europe. But it was the $435,000,000 of exports to China which made up over one-third of the nation's total exports.

After World War II, unsettled conditions inside China and, later, the anti-Communist Far Eastern policy of the United States kept Japan from recovering its old China trade. The areas of trading, by force of circumstances, shifted southward. In 1951 Japan's export trade with Southeast Asia, India and Pakistan totalled $779,000,000 —even allowing for inflated postwar currencies, a big increase over the $337,000,000 of exports to those areas in 1937. Imports from Asia-minus-China to Japan were worth $664,000,000 in 1951, as against $420,000,000 in 1937. Trade with Europe, in 1951, was slightly larger than the 1937 figure ($145,000,000 in exports against $101,000,000; $162,000,000 in imports against $134,000,000). These increases went part of the way towards balancing, on fairly even terms, the loss of the trade with China. But the real weakness of Japan's plight showed in the trade figures with the United States—in return for $190,000,000 in Japanese exports, the American economy provided $667,000,000 in goods and services for Japan—payable in dollars.

* * * * *

Faced with their precarious trade situation, the people of Japan instinctively leapt on the possibility of trade with China. This is the great concrete disagreement which Kisei and Yamazaki, at least, have with American policy vis-à-vis the Orient. Yamazaki is convinced that the economic advantages of China trade would far outweigh both the consequent break in the economic front of the democracies and the danger that Japan, through trade, might be sucked into the Communist orbit. "Here is a vast nation with 400,000,000 people," he has objected. "We traded with them until 1945 and they traded with us. Now that market is gone. Who are we going to trade with to fill in the gap that has been left? We need China and China needs us. I don't think ideological differences need enter into the picture."

Kisei is more realistic, but wistful about the loss. He feels sad about China. "China trade," he echoes, "is the solution for Japan's future ills. China can sell cheap materials and buy a tremendous amount of Japanese manufactures. Without China trade, the prospect is very dim. Even with China trade we would have to go through a period of hard times. Without China trade, I feel that the severe austerity period will last as much as ten to fifteen years. Whether Japan can weather such a long period, I cannot say. But it would appear that she must. I feel that Japan's future trade with Red China will depend on American foreign policy in the Far East. Under the present circumstances, I think that trade relations would be difficult."

The opinion of Kisei and Yamazaki has found fuller voice in Japanese big business circles. The big manufacturers from Osaka for several years have demanded some sort of renewed trade relations with China. Are they and so many of the Japanese people correct in regarding resumption of China trade relations as a cure-all for Japan's economic troubles?

It is doubtful if they are. They would seem to overstate their case badly and, thereby, deceive no one so much as themselves. Trade with Red China in 1953 is not trade with weakened Nationalist China in 1937. In that year Manchuria, Korea and Formosa, which accounted for a large part of what was known as the "China" trade, were Japanese colonies. As such, they were the spoils of Japanese businessmen, at once the storehouse for Japanese raw materials and the dumping yard for Japanese manufactures. China itself was little better. There was a large Japanese navy in Chinese waters and Japanese army divisions flexing their trigger fingers on various portions of Chinese soil to insure, among other things, that the Japanese trader could trade on his own terms. In Japan's imperial thirties, the man with the sample case did business under optimum conditions.

With such a fertile field for business operations, the Japanese preferred China trade to any other. This is not to say that, under any circumstances, Japanese manufactures and Chinese raw materials do not make an excellent trading partnership. But the halcyon days of old are gone forever—or at least for the foreseeable future. The Communist Chinese have demonstrated their reluctance to trade on any terms but their own. A limited exchange of goods has taken place between China and Japan; certainly more can take place without any harm befalling the Japanese. But there can be no returning to the old days. China, too, has been industrializing itself, wants to manufacture its own raw materials, and dislikes the prospect of enriching Japan. The Japanese fleet is no more. And the trigger fingers this time are Chinese.

Failing a resumption of the prewar milk and honey trade in China, Japan must balance its trading ledgers in another way. Present trade must be further expanded—and, if anything, new outlets for Japanese goods and new sources for Japanese manufacturing must be found. At the same time, the problem continues in its circle—the raw materials must be imported cheaply enough to permit the Japanese to sell at attractive prices, thereby earning the money to pay for them. All in all, a big order.

The first requisite for successful Japanese trading is a revived Japanese merchant marine. Freightage is a large part of a product's costs. The dislocation of Japan's trading patterns since World War II has often provided the Japanese with extreme and unpleasant illustrations of this fact. In 1951, for example, the Japanese were importing coking coal and anthracite from the United States. A ton of coal delivered in the United States cost about $12; by the time the coal was transported to Japan, the price had risen to $30. Accessibility to the nearby source of supply (and, of course, demand) in China was the great reason for China's popularity in Japan as a trading partner. Chinese coking coal, even after postwar dislocation of the industry, was quoted at prices at least $10 less per ton than the American figure. If Japan is expected to build a viable economy on its trade, there must be enough Japanese shipping to enable raw materials to be secured at minimum costs.

Before World War II the Japanese merchant marine was the world's second largest. The Japanese sail ships well —the economy of their operating costs is impressive, when compared with those of almost any other maritime country. In the thirties Japanese freighters, heavily subsidized by the government, undercut their international competition to an astonishing degree. In the last two years, the resurgence of the Japanese merchant marine has been equally astonishing—by 1952 the old Japanese shipping lines were once more flying their flags in New York harbor. But throughout the fifties the shipbuilding program in Japan must be further speeded—and surplus ships bought or borrowed from the United States, as some already have been, with the aim of putting a great percentage of Japanese trade in Japanese bottoms. This is a basic condition, under the circumstances, for a sound Japanese economy.

It is almost equally basic to increase the internal efficiency of Japanese factories. The dragging handicap of old methods and machines, added to the combination of far-off trading sources and shipping deficiencies, in 1952 had been pricing Japanese finished goods out of the world market. Japan has reached the point where current profits must be sacrificed ruthlessly for capital plant improvement, a fact very keenly realized by Japan's industrialists.

The final problem is where to get the raw materials from and where to direct the finished goods. This is hardly something which can be worked out with a slide rule. Trade patterns in the world at present have the fluctuations of a kaleidoscope. Japan's unexpected windfall, that came from the Korean war, has already been mentioned. To cite a similar example—in 1949, at the height of ill feeling between India and Pakistan, Pakistan boycotted the textile plants in India and diverted its raw cotton exports to Japan at reasonable prices, receiving Japanese finished goods in return.

On the debit side, the loss of China to the Communists of course overshadows everything else. In dealing with the south of Asia, however, there have also been numerous times when old political prejudices against Japan or the fear of postwar Japanese expansion inhibited natural trading instincts. There is hardly a nation in the world which has not been bitten with the urge to industrialize itself. If the new leaders in Southeast Asia have discovered that steel mills do not rise out of rice paddies at the sweep of a blueprint, they have not abandoned hope that they can gradually produce more finished goods themselves, reducing their dependence on outside sources.

There is room for Japanese trade to expand further in Southeast Asia and with India and Pakistan. There is a large market for Japanese cheap consumer goods throughout the Asiatic continent, in the bazaars of Baghdad as well as those of Singapore. There is trading opportunity in Africa, where postwar Japanese goods have already begun to make their inroads. There is a rich opportunity for more trade with Indonesia, which desperately needs Japanese manufactures and which can supply much of the rubber, tin and oil which Japan once went to war to get. The Japanese have already reinstalled a flourishing trade with Formosa, the island rich in rice, tea, and sugar, which like the legendary schmoo in Al Capp's comic strip, continues to give smilingly of its riches, no matter how many people come to exploit it. Whether or not Chiang Kai Shek's Nationalist Chinese soldiers remain in Formosa, the island probably will return to Japanese economic domination at least.

These Asian countries, engaged in a mutually profitable trade with Japan, could greatly reduce, and, in time, end Japan's present economic dependence on the United States. To a great extent this already has been done (Japan is no longer the beneficiary of the formal American aid program that it received for so long under the occupation).

But such traffic, already large, could become a broad stream of north-south trade which in time would compensate the Japanese for the loss of their old landed estates in China, Manchuria and Korea. It would do more than this: it could give Asia the industry and the consumer goods to raise its standards of living, in itself the stabilizing factor that would go farthest to check the susceptability of the Asiatic populations to Communism.

Although only Fumio Shimizu has completely accepted the impossibility of trading with Communist China, the other gentlemen of Japan, along with their countrymen, know very well the realistic problems of Japan's trade, as well as its potentialities. Hideya Kisei states the problem: "Japan as an independent nation cannot depend on the United States to go on paying its bills. The only way for Japan to stand on its feet again will be through export of its products." Tadao Yamazaki appreciates the possibilities: "It cannot be denied that Japan is the most industrialized nation in Asia. People talk about Japan becoming the 'Factory of the Far East.' That should be so, for it means the survival of Asia, if the Asiatic countries can secure Japanese products which are just as good as those of the United States, for example, and certainly within the reach of the average Asian's household budget and pocketbook." Although he feels that Japan should specialize in light industries, not heavy manufactures, he, like his countrymen, will be only too happy to sell everything and anything they can.

* * * * *

Because the foregoing estimate of Japan's new trading possibilities is couched in terms of "could" and "would," it need not be Utopian. But there are some definite conditions, difficult to fulfill, on which its realization depends. The first demands free trade and a minimum of unfair competition. It was in part satisfied, when the peace treaty, over British protests, was signed without any clauses restricting Japanese trade. But the fact remains that Japan is a puissant competitor of Britain, especially in the field of textiles, in the markets of Asia and Africa. This is a basic trade rivalry which no amount of political fence-mending can disguise.

The Japanese, since the end of World War II, have begun to recapture some of their old markets in Asia—with new ones besides. The British have been hard put to meet this competition; in the long run they cannot meet it— the Japanese can produce more cheaply and they are nearer the markets both in geography and in sentiment. Americans have often held a suspicion that the British have advocated the idea of Japanese diplomatic relations with Communist China partly for commercial reasons—China trading would take the Japanese merchants away from the old British colonial markets in southern Asia and Africa. Be this as it may, Japan and Britain are competitors in this area—and there is a constant temptation for a politically stronger nation to restrict the economic competition of a nation, at the moment, politically weaker.

The Japanese are aware that the international bad habits of their prewar days—the "dumping" of products at prices far below the going rate, the poor quality of many manufactured goods, and the constant undercutting of international price levels by government-subsidized Japanese manufacturers—have given Japan a doubtful commercial reputation. These devices need no longer be countenanced. Thus far the Japanese have given signs that they will not resort to them. On the other hand, it is imperative that the countries of the non-Communist world allow Japan the elbow-room of free competition, if only from the considerations of their own ultimate self-interest. The Japanese are a tragic and a dangerous people, if crowded.

The second condition involves a problem of currency. Japan has been selling extensively to countries that are in the sterling bloc—India, Pakistan and the British African colonies, for example. Japan's big trade deficit is in dollars. Through the years of the occupation, Japan's foreign exchange was based on dollars and on the dollar area. Since the sterling countries were unwilling and unable to watch more of their gold shift itself to Fort Knox, trade between Japan and the sterling countries was very carefully worked out, so that exports would balance imports as nearly as possible. This inhibited Japanese selling. There is no doubt that far more in consumer goods could have been sold to some of these countries, if the old financial fetters had not held down the balances.

Japan still has a sterling surplus and a dollar deficit—the same tragic plus and minus that explains so many of the troubles of Europe. Unless the Japanese can devise new and spectacular ways of pushing their exports to dollar areas (which include South America, formerly a good trading ground for the Japanese), or unless they can find sterling sources for raw materials and essential manufactured goods to replace the present dollar sources, this fiscal tragedy will hang like a millstone on the neck of the Japanese economy. In Europe the International Payments Union and a system of "off-shore purchases" have eased this problem among European countries. Something of the kind must be done by Japan—or the dollar deficits will have to continue as virtual gifts to Japan from the United States.

The fulfillment of the second condition leads directly into the third: Japan cannot recover without the cooperation of other countries, especially and specifically the continued help of the United States. American aid in one form or another must continue to go into Japan, but it would be wasteful to the Americans and not very stimulating to the Japanese if the bulk aid of the occupation years had been continued. Help is most needed to modernize the Japanese industrial plant and increase the already fertile sources of hydroelectric power, to provide as before a limited amount of necessary raw materials for Japanese industry.

The obvious answer is a method which was openly suggested by the United States occupation authorities in Japan in 1951, although it should have been suggested and implemented by action several years before that time. General William F. Marquat, the former head of SCAP's Economic and Scientific Section, drafted a formal statement of intention, after a three weeks' conference in Washington, offering Japan all available help from the United States for its re-entry into the world market. He proposed that Japan's industrial potential be used in a broad plan to increase the productivity and prosperity of underdeveloped areas now suffering from a bad shortage of capital as well as consumer goods—specifically, Southeast Asia.

There is no reason why the sketch he then outlined and the first tentative gestures later made towards its activation cannot grow into a great economic counter-offensive by the democracies in Asia. Japan must be integrated into the hardly realized Point Four program of the United States, as well as the Colombo Plan for sharing the development of the sterling-area countries in Asia. Japan, as Yamazaki and his fellow-Japanese know and as some American planners have mentioned, is the Factory, the Workshop of Asia. Japanese goods can begin to build a bloodless Greater East Asia Co-Prosperity Sphere that would be a co-prosperity sphere in fact as well as name. A stream of manufactures flowing southward and then westward to all the non-Communist countries of Asia can create an economic situation of strength throughout those countries—machines for the new industries, clothing and consumer goods for restless and awakening populations, trucks for new roads, drugs for new hospitals. All this the industry of Japan can do. In return the Japanese people can secure their rice and raw materials and, in time, increase the domestic production of consumer goods to the level it once held.

Such a co-prosperity sphere need not stop with goods. Japanese technicians who eat rice and are of a common stock with most Asians are well equipped for the job of instructing them in how to use machines and how to till their fields scientifically. They are better equipped than Americans, who eat bread, meat and all that is expensive in Asia, demand large salaries, often out-do the Old World British with their brash desire for clubs and compounds and rarely have a sincere interest in Asia in the first place—they do not live there. Some Japanese technicians have gone in this way to India, successfully. They could go almost anywhere. They are at least as close to the Asiatics with whom they would cooperate as the average Englishman in America.

What is suggested is that the United States and Britain regard Japan as a working partner in what must become a large and unified scheme for the peaceful development of Asia. East Asia, at least, must be encouraged to develop the same degree of cooperation in its economy as Western Europe. This can be done in East Asia with far greater prospect. The industrialized nations of Western Europe, possibly excepting France, share the problem of finding markets for their manufactured goods and getting food for their people from the sale of goods. They compete against one another, with an attendant waste that can no longer be afforded. Western Europe in the latter half of the twentieth century, for all its industry, and all its mines, is dangerously close to becoming a have-not area. Not so with Asia. East Asia's only problem is to get the resources out of the ground and work them. Without the industry of Japan, they cannot be tapped quickly. With the industry of Japan, this wealth will begin to flow.

Yamazaki is right in assessing the suitability of Japanese products for Asiatic markets. Japan is Asia's producer by geography, by tradition and by price. It will be objected that to run the Asia development program through the factories of Japan will mean competing with American factories and with British factories. The new Japanese merchant marine will mean dangerous competition for American and British ships. The answer to this line of reasoning is plain and short: prejudice cannot interfere with facts. East Asiatic trade amounts to a tiny sliver of American industrial output, and if we subtract the large trade with Australia and New Zealand, hardly a great percentage of Britain's. There is little future for it; American products generally cost too much for Asian pocketbooks and are not designed for Asiatic problems. Asiatic trade takes up over 50% of Japanese output and has taken more: it is Japan's life. It is conducted, furthermore, in an area where the Japanese have proved they can outsell British and Americans alike, unless artificial barriers to free competition are put in their way It can be argued that the United States is making competition for itself when it leases a Liberty ship to the Japanese. To a very limited extent this is true—the same charge was leveled against the Marshall Plan in Europe. It is worth considering, however, that a few U.S. shipping firms inconvenienced by Japanese competition may be preferable to a half-democratic Japan rapidly driven to Communism, because its people cannot live within the framework of the free world's economy.

There are other handicaps involved in bringing the Workshop of Asia to full production. The other Asiatic countries are reluctant to continue as raw material producers alone. The memory of how Japan once exploited them is green. If the Japanese recognize the ward spiral of industrial development, they will produc · goods which are beyond the capacity of the other Asiatic countries to produce now, or in the next generation. Admittedly in their relations with their old neighbors, the Japanese will have to do a political, as well as an economic, selling job.

The most pertinent way in which the Japanese can convince the Asiatic nations of their good intentions is in the matter of reparations, which in some cases have already been agreed upon. This puts an added burden on the Japanese, and automatically lengthens the austerity period. Considering the political facts of the moment, this is regrettable. Considering the wanton destruction caused by the Japanese armies throughout East Asia, it is, by any moral standards, right and necessary.

Granted the cooperation of Japan, the other Asian countries and the United States in a large trading network, the danger involved of Japanese trade with Communist China diminishes. Originally, the fear lay in Japan's making itself critically dependent on trade with a country which, like its Communist siblings, unabashedly uses trade as another weapon of political power. Once involved in a working trade relationship with "Asia-minus-China," Japan could trade with China itself in the assurance that if Communist political pressure suddenly cut off the trade currents, the loss would not be a vital one.

* * * * *

The partnership between the United States and Japan after the occupation cannot be left to economics. Admiral Shimizu's advice is to the point on the dangers of an "eat with us; go hungry with the Communists" policy. The groundwork has been laid for a long and lasting American-Japanese association. Concretely, several things can be done to improve it. The most obvious is enactment of something approximating a fair immigration quota for the Japanese, a people who have already furnished some of the republic's most loyal and useful citizens.* To further communications, there should be an extended program of college and school scholarships for Japanese in the United States (and American exchange students in Japan). It is hoped that resources can be found to support more technical missions like those which came from Japan to the United States during the occupation days. One visit is worth a hundred newspaper reports. As Admiral Shimizu puts it:

"I do feel that more and more young Japanese should be sent to the United States for study of the real American way of life, which is, in essence, democracy. The Japanese Government has a great responsibility here, also. I don't mean only the sending of scholars and students, but also

---

* The McCarran Act of 1952 raised the Japanese quota from zero to 100. This was at best a niggardly gesture, part of a mean-spirited law reflecting the prejudices of its author.

young technicians, mechanics, doctors, lawyers and clerks. Japan, through the peace treaty, is now on the side of the West. To progress in the future, she must have full cooperation of the United States. She will not get it if her people do not understand the real United States."

Japan is one of the rare places in Asia where such ambitious radio and newspaper propaganda programs, envisaged by organizations like Radio Free Asia and the Voice of America, might accomplish results. There are nine million radios in Japan. Its newspaper network is one of the most extensive in the world.

It has often been suggested, in the course of this book, that Japan presents a striking parallel to Britain, not only in geographical location but in the character of the people and their relation to the peoples of their continents. The Japanese, even more sharply than the British, now find themselves at the frontier of a land mass whose vast northern bulk is in the hands of an enemy. Like the British, the Japanese are inventive, forthright and courageous; but modern invention has played a cruel trick on the island bulwarks. This is true in more respects than that of military geography. The splits and sags in the old Japanese web system are far more critical to the ethos than the changing social philosophy which is gradually laying low the British social order of centuries past.

But, in common, the changes in each island reflect revolutionary waves from continents, which no Canute could prevent from broaching the island bastions. From past history, it is safe to predict that the Japanese, like the British, can harness these waves to their own purpose.

It is even more difficult for the Japanese than for the British to maintain their bastion militarily, in its position aflank the enemy fortress. Almost all the country around Japan's immediate water borders is hostile. Help sometimes seems very far away. As Japan was the site of a great American experiment, it is now the American responsibility to see Japan through this tense period, insuring the safety no longer of an apprentice, but of a respected equal with great potency for good. The Japanese give much promise of justifying such a trust.

The Japanese have within them the means of becoming something far greater than allies of the democracies in their struggle. On May 6, 1952, the sixth anniversary of the new Japanese Constitution, Hirohito suggested this function himself, when he mentioned the future of Japan as a "bridge" nation between East and West. This thought has existed in the minds of many Japanese. There is every reason for thinking that such an ideal may become a fact.

The new Asian statesmen who now "speak" for all the other Asians, do so in suspiciously general terms. Pandit Nehru is an Aryan, a British-educated idealist whose Western Socialism sits like the uppermost ingredients of a pousse-café on the lower layers of his purely Indian sympathies; he can no more speak for the Chinese or the Japanese or the Indonesians than his ancient Indian brand of Buddhism could survive in Japan and China without the sweeping and radical changes that made it virtually another faith. But Japan is one Asian country that can logically and validly aspire to mediate between West and East. The Japanese took up Western civilization not as colonials, but on their own terms. Of all the great cities of the Orient—Calcutta, Djakarta, Manila, Shanghai—only Tokyo has what might be called native modern buildings. By and large, the Japanese built their new cities in their own way, with their own money and from their own adapted designs. No other Asian country can say this.

The ferment which now agitates all of Asia was known in Japan almost a century ago. Japan had its collisions with Western culture early. If the Japanese have not digested all of this culture, they have been able to adjust themselves to its oddities of taste. No nation since imperial Byzantium has even attempted such a fusion of East and West.

It is forty years since Oswald Spengler suggested that "today we think in continents." In 1913 this was more a prophecy than a statement of fact. Today, at last, it is a widely recognized truism. For the first time since the rise of Islam and the Mongol invasions, the peoples of the European tradition have realized, with awe and wondering, that the continents outside them are animate forces to be reckoned with, to be listened to, to be registered as friend or enemy.

They realize this as yet very imperfectly. The United States, to placate its European relationship with the French, for example, can still flout justice at the bar of the United Nations by refusing to hear the complaint of Tunisians, because they are Africans whose interests happen to conflict with those of Europeans. This it did in 1952. The comparatively strong reaction of Americans to this offers evidence that the mass of people realize the implications of the new continental world better than their diplomats.

* * * * *

In a bygone day the West could refer with contempt, pity or indulgence to the "masses" of Asia. "Masses" was a term of opprobrium, referring to a factor which need not be thoroughly investigated so long as it could be disciplined with the ease of scientific weapons and the confidence of technology. In its indulgent moments, the nineteenth century set out to bring "light" to Asia, the light of Christianity and Western civilization. It did the job badly and with only half a heart. It is perhaps a rigid justice that Asia now threatens the West, not with its old faiths or the old faiths of the West so much as with a half-learned importation from the West, a Marxism which the nineteenth century engendered.

In the twentieth century the West fears Asia. The masses have multiplied themselves by the acquisition of the very weapons with which the West once disciplined them. The result is a spectacle of a drowsy giant putting on his armor. The Western tank commander shudders to find that the barbarians have not only men but anti-tank guns—the

Greek meets the Scythian, and finds to his horror that the rascal is well-armed.

Oddly, at the same time that armed conflict impends, the intellectual of the West cocks an ear to the Orient to discover what he can of value there—the Hellenists look towards the desert, because the philosophers of Athens and Alexandria no longer charm with their old logic. Sturdier spirits in the West find this indiscriminate searching negative, and the act of despair. But they, too, are in a sense open to suggestion from the East. The assurance of their intrinsic Western superiority is not strong. In the world of ideas they are more humble. Some of them have even become Christian again.

The West has not bent the knee. The ancient seats of its learning and power have moved to a new hemisphere, to settle in a polity which today dominates the world. This United States is confident in many things, but uneasy about its new international role. Its people are particularly puzzled as they look across the Pacific. A bridge is sought, which can somehow make communication between the old and new powers of the West and the rising and undetermined forces in the East, before the gauge is finally cast down. Does such a bridge exist?

The other four gentlemen of Japan would agree with what Hirohito has already said in answer. Their country, by its location, by its culture, by its very ethnology, has produced a "bridge" people. With their culture tangent to both East and West, the gentlemen of Japan may conceivably become the mediators between the continents, capable, perhaps, of helping to avert the potential conflict that dwarfs in its implications even the present assault on both East and West by the fierce totemism of the Communists.

EPILOGUE

Spring and fall are the seasons of Japan. The Japanese have made a cult of them, deeper than the natural fascinatio which other peoples feel for the times of change. There is no tradition in Japan to match New England winters or summers in the Lake Country. The static seasons do not encroach on the reign of the changeful ones. In April and May the millions go out, as if driven, to watch the white of the opening cherry blossoms creep northward along their hills. It is *hanami*—the flower-seeing time. In October the maple leaves are a brighter crimson than anywhere else in the world. The Japanese have a name also for this experience—*momijigari*—the maple-viewing season. They are awesomely touched.

The change and movement of nature meets empathy in the Japanese soul. They are a restless people, impatient, changeful and subject to change. They live on fragile islands, crowded, treacherous and beautiful. The earth shakes beneath them and coughs through their mountains; the seas smash without end on their chipped coast; the winds tear the leaves from their bent trees. Their life is mortgaged to the uncertainties of nature and crimped by the smallness of nature's goods. Their roots are uncertain, transplanted from the solidness of others. Climate and geography have left them little that abides. Theirs is no brotherhood to feel among the nations. Their strength is in their community and the fearful, prideful impulses that drive it as one.

It is not hyperbole to call the Japanese a dynamic people. They do not sit as the great peoples of the continent—Russians, Chinese, or Americans, fortified in their confidence by the breadth of their land. They move. It is their destiny to move, not sweepingly but in starts, not smoothly but with tremors and convulsions.

Struggle is in their bones and hard work is the condition of their life. Perhaps that is why their small children are so pampered and indulged—the parents pity the stress that is to come. They do not shirk struggle—and its rigors have made them hard but not brittle, pliant but never dissolving. It has not yet made them weary. It has never bowed them for long. It has not lessened the extent of their art and their capacity to feel. It has left their culture narrow but deep. The Japanese artist scorns the mountain and dotes on the small flower at its base. The flower he is sure of—and he knows. The mountain is uncertain and may be hostile. He is disturbed, if he looks at it too long.

The Japanese have been dangerous and may be dangerous again; in the intensity of their feelings, in the power and violence of their acts, in the cramped complexity inside their heads. A bold trepanning has been attempted on them, not without trauma, not without worry and confusion among those who carried it through. For the moment, it has relieved the pressure. With artificial helps, the subject has lived well and hopefully through a trying period in his life.

The helps are withdrawn. The Japanese faces the

world of nature again, to live in it by his own resource. His course is begun well, but he has no knowledge where it will lead him. He has no certainty but the power of his own deeds, and the poor rock of his four fragile islands. The deeds must be his granary. Dynamism and wits must do for the broad fields, the deep mines and the sweeping frontiers which he does not have.

He feels his insecurity. He hopes it will not betray him, as once it did. His goal is not fixed, but need and spirit drive him on, and the challenge of the time has come to him. Struggle, pride, fear—march. The 85 millions of Japan seek their fate.

Other TUT BOOKS available:

BACHELOR'S HAWAII *by Boye de Mente*

BACHELOR'S JAPAN *by Boye de Mente*

BACHELOR'S MEXICO *by Boye de Mente*

A BOOK OF NEW ENGLAND LEGENDS AND FOLK LORE *by Samuel Adams Drake*

THE BUDDHA TREE *by Fumio Niwa; translated by Kenneth Strong*

CALABASHES AND KINGS: An Introduction to Hawaii *by Stanley D. Porteus*

CHINA COLLECTING IN AMERICA *by Alice Morse Earle*

CHINESE COOKING MADE EASY *by Rosy Tseng*

CHOI OI!: The Lighter Side of Vietnam *by Tony Zidek*

THE COUNTERFEITER and Other Stories *by Yasushi Inoue; translated by Leon Picon*

CURIOUS PUNISHMENTS OF BYGONE DAYS *by Alice Morse Earle*

CUSTOMS AND FASHIONS IN OLD NEW ENGLAND *by Alice Morse Earle*

DINING IN SPAIN *by Gerrie Beene and Lourdes Miranda King*

EXOTICS AND RETROSPECTIVES *by Lafcadio Hearn*

FIRST YOU TAKE A LEEK: A Guide to Elegant Eating Spiced with Culinary Capers *by Maxine J. Saltonstall*

FIVE WOMEN WHO LOVED LOVE *by Saikaku Ihara; translated by William Theodore de Bary*

A FLOWER DOES NOT TALK: Zen Essays *by Abbot Zenkei Shibayama of the Nanzenji*

FOLK LEGENDS OF JAPAN *by Richard M. Dorson*

GLEANINGS IN BUDDHA-FIELDS: Studies of Hand and Soul in the Far East *by Lafcadio Hearn*

GOING NATIVE IN HAWAII: A Poor Man's Guide to Paradise *by Timothy Head*

HAIKU IN ENGLISH *by Harold G. Henderson*

HARP OF BURMA *by Michio Takeyama; translated by Howard Hibbett*

HAWAII: End of the Rainbow *by Kazuo Miyamoto*

THE HAWAIIAN GUIDE BOOK for Travelers *by Henry M. Whitney*

HAWAIIAN PHRASE BOOK

HISTORIC MANSIONS AND HIGHWAYS AROUND BOSTON *by Samuel Adams Drake*

HISTORICAL AND GEOGRAPHICAL DICTIONARY OF JAPAN *by E. Papinot*

A HISTORY OF JAPANESE LITERATURE *by W. G. Aston*

HOMEMADE ICE CREAM AND SHERBERT by *Sheila MacNiven Cameron*

HOW TO READ CHARACTER: A New Illustrated Handbook of Phrenology and Physiognomy, for Students and Examiners by *Samuel R. Wells*

IN GHOSTLY JAPAN by *Lafcadio Hearn*

INDIAN RIBALDRY by *Randor Guy*

JAPAN: An Attempt at Interpretation by *Lafcadio Hearn*

THE JAPANESE ABACUS by *Takashi Kojima*

THE JAPANESE ARE LIKE THAT by *Ichiro Kawasaki*

JAPANESE ETIQUETTE: An Introduction by *the World Fellowship Committee of the Tokyo Y.W.C.A.*

THE JAPANESE FAIRY BOOK compiled by *Yei Theodora Ozaki*

JAPANESE FOLK-PLAYS: The Ink-Smeared Lady and Other Kyogen translated by *Shio Sakanishi*

JAPANESE FOOD AND COOKING by *Stuart Griffin*

JAPANESE HOMES AND THIER SURROUNDINGS by *Edward S. Morse*

A JAPANESE MISCELLANY by *Lafcadio Hearn*

JAPANESE RECIPES by *Tatsuji Tada*

JAPANESE TALES OF MYSTERY & IMAGINATION by *Edogawa Rampo;* translated by *James B. Harris*

JAPANESE THINGS: Being Notes on Various Subjects Connected with Japan by *Basil Hall Chamberlain*

THE JOKE'S ON JUDO *by Donn Draeger and Ken Tremayne*

THE KABUKI HANDBOOK *by Aubrey S. Halford and Giovanna M. Halford*

KAPPA *by Ryūnosuke Akutagawa; translated by Geoffrey Bownas*

KOKORO: Hints and Echoes of Japanese Inner Life *by Lafcadio Hearn*

KOREAN FOLK TALES *by Im Bang and Yi Ryuk; translated by James S. Gale*

KOTTŌ: Being Japanese Curios, with Sundry Cobwebs *by Lafcadio Hearn*

KWAIDAN: Stories and Studies of Strange Things *by Lafcadio Hearn*

LET'S STUDY JAPANESE *by Jun Maeda*

THE LIFE OF BUDDHA *by A. Ferdinand Herold*

MODERN JAPANESE PRINTS: A Contemporary Selection *edited by Yuji Abe*

NIHONGI: Chronicles of Japan from the Earliest Times to A.D. 697 *by W. G. Aston*

OLD LANDMARKS AND HISTORIC PERSONAGES OF BOSTON *by Samuel Adams Drake*

ORIENTAL FORTUNE TELLING *by Jimmei Shimano; translated by Togo Taguchi*

PHYSICAL FITNESS: A Practical Program *by Clark Hatch*

READ JAPANESE TODAY *by Len Walsh*

SELF DEFENSE SIMPLIFIED IN PICTURES *by Don Hepler*

SHADOWINGS *by Lafcadio Hearn*

A SHORT SYNOPSIS OF THE MOST ESSENTIAL POINTS IN HAWAIIAN GRAMMAR *by W. D. Alexander*

THE STORY BAG: A Collection of Korean Folk Tales *by Kim So-un; translated by Setsu Higashi*

SUMI-E: An Introduction to Ink Painting *by Nanae Momiyama*

SUN-DIALS AND ROSES OF YESTERDAY *by Alice Morse Earle*

THE TEN FOOT SQUARE HUT AND TALES OF THE HEIKE: Being Two Thirteenth-century Japanese classics, the "Hojoki" and selections from the "Heike Monogatari" *translated by A. L. Sadler*

THIS SCORCHING EARTH *by Donald Richie*

TIMES-SQUARE SAMURAI or the Improbable Japanese Occupation of New York *by Robert B. Johnson and Billie Niles Chadbourne*

TO LIVE IN JAPAN *by Mary Lee O'Neal and Virginia Woodruff*

THE TOURIST AND THE REAL JAPAN *by Boye de Mente*

TOURS OF OKINAWA: A Souvenir Guide to Places of Interest *compiled by Gasei Higa, Isamu Fuchaku, and Zenkichi Toyama*

TWO CENTURIES OF COSTUME IN AMERICA *by Alice Morse Earle*

TYPHOON! TYPHOON! An Illustrated Haiku Sequence *by Lucile M. Bogue*

UNBEATEN TRACKS IN JAPAN: An Account of Travels in the Interior Including Visits to the Aborigines of Yezo and the Shrine of Nikko *by Isabella L. Bird*

ZILCH! The Marine Corps' Most Guarded Secret *by Roy Delgado*

Please order from your bookstore or write directly to:

CHARLES E. TUTTLE CO., INC.
Suido 1-chome, 2–6, Bunkyo-ku, Tokyo 112

or:

CHARLES E. TUTTLE CO., INC.
Rutland, Vermont 05701 U.S.A.